Setting Standards for Financial Reporting

Setting Standards for Financial Reporting

FASB AND THE STRUGGLE FOR CONTROL OF A CRITICAL PROCESS

Robert Van Riper
III

Q

QUORUM BOOKS
Westport, Connecticut
London

*HF5681
.B2
V28
1994*

Library of Congress Cataloging-in-Publication Data

Van Riper, Robert.
    Setting standards for financial reporting : FASB and the struggle
for control of a critical process / Robert Van Riper.
        p. cm.
    Includes bibliographical references and index.
    ISBN 0–89930–907–0 (alk. paper)
    1. Financial statements—Standards—United States. 2. Accounting—
Standards—United States. I. Title.
HF5681.B2V28   1994
657'.021873—dc20   94–2987

British Library Cataloguing in Publication Data is available.

Library of Congress Catalog Card Number: 94–2987
ISBN: 0–89930–907–0

First published in 1994

Quorum Books, 88 Post Road West, Westport, CT 06881
An imprint of Greenwood Publishing Group, Inc.

Printed in the United States of America

The paper used in this book complies with the
Permanent Paper Standard issued by the National
Information Standards Organization (Z39.48–1984).

10 9 8 7 6 5 4 3 2

Contents

1 A "Last Chance" for Self-Regulation 1

2 A Goldfish in a Pool of Sharks? 13

3 A Baptism of Fire 39

4 An Encounter with "No-Cost" Accounting 55

5 Agent of Change in a Conservative Environment 73

6 What's Sauce for the Goose . . . 85

7 A Kaleidoscope of Complaints 97

8 The Business Roundtable Steps Up to Bat 117

9 Another Waltz 'Round the Table 133

10 The Trustees Go Into a "Prevent Defense" 157

11 Accounting "Truth"—or Consequences? 173

12 "The Public Interest"—or Public Intent? 187

Epilogue 197

For Further Reading   199

Index   201

Setting Standards for Financial Reporting

Chapter One

A "Last Chance" for Self-Regulation

Just as it is dishonest to put down what is not owed, so it is dishonest not to put down what you do owe. For his accounts are just as much condemned who omits to make an entry of the truth, as his who puts down what is false.

Marcus Tullius Cicero[1]

When caught, white-collar criminals who falsify the financial reports of publicly owned corporations invariably make headlines on the business pages—and sometimes even on page one. Though widely publicized when they occur, instances of outright fraud in financial reporting are rare aberrations.[2] Of much greater significance is a continuing confrontation between people and organizations committed to objective measurement and full disclosure of corporate results, on the one hand, and those within the corporations who, though honest by conventional definitions of the term, march to a different drummer, on the other. The results of this confrontation, much more than fraud, are what the users of financial information need to be concerned about.

Contention is intense, and its outcomes have ramifications that extend throughout our economy and society, but the subject of it is information resulting from a process, or discipline, whose mere mention is likely to evoke among the uninitiated reactions ranging from yawns to deprecating jokes.

Unfortunately, accounting "truth" comes in many shades. And its ultimate consequences are impossible to predict. The uncertainties on both sides of this equation provide a field for debate to which those engaged in financial accounting and reporting are well accustomed—and in which the stakes keep getting higher.

The need for rules of conduct for accountants and for standards of financial reporting has been recognized, at least by some, for more than three-quarters of a century. Rules of conduct generally are regarded as belonging within the self-disciplinary purview of professional associations, but talk of rules or standards for financial reporting often gives rise to concern that because such rules affect something loosely called "the public interest," their formulation should not be entrusted to the private sector. Partisans of the private sector, however, fear the rigidity of governmental agencies and—ironically, as we shall see—their susceptibility to political influence and manipulation.

The cost of applying standards for financial reporting has long been a concern of the corporate preparers of financial information, a concern that traditionally has been expressed in demands that those who promulgate standards pay closer attention to the "cost-benefit ratio." More recently, spokespersons for the corporate community have extended those demands to include a plea that possible economic, or even social, consequences should be taken into account before standards are promulgated.

In 1990, the chairman of the Financial Accounting Standards Board (FASB), Dennis R. Beresford, told an international conclave at the Stern School of Business Administration at New York University that

the underlying cost of an accounting standard from a reporting entity's perspective is loss of control over information; that is, loss of ability to decide whether, when, or how to present information. It is loss of management flexibility and, to a significant degree, loss of the advantage of insider information. The counterpart of the reporting entity's loss is the using entity's gain—access to information with analytic power, the power to make better investment decisions.[3]

Though Cicero enunciated, in a courtroom oration on behalf of one Quintius Roscius in the first century B.C., what many still accept as the essence of accounting, the vocation generally attributes its origin to the work of Luca Pacioli, renowned Italian Renaissance mathematician, friend of Leonardo da Vinci, and contemporary of Christopher Columbus. Two years after the noted voyage of discovery by his countryman, Pacioli described in his monumental *Summa de Arithmetica Geometria Proportioni e Proportionalita*, and thereby preserved for posterity, the double-entry method of bookkeeping then favored by the more progressive Venetian merchants.[4]

Accountants have been able to agree on few eternal verities, or even general principles, in the half a millenium since. As they never tire of explaining, theirs is an art, not a science. Laypeople who lack the advantage of having taken at least Accounting 101 in college are likely to assume that the art is basically arithmetical. In fact, it depends heavily on words whose meanings are not always understood in the same way by those who use them, and on concepts constructed with those words. The resulting lack of precision is reflected in the standard wording of the final paragraph of the independent auditors' report, or "auditors' letter," that accompanies published financial statements when they are found to merit a "clean opinion":

In our opinion, the financial statements referred to above present fairly, in all material respects, the financial position of [reporting entity] at [dates of year end and previous year end], and the results of its operations and its cash flows for the years then ended in conformity with generally accepted accounting principles.[5]

Accounting has been characterized over the centuries, and particularly in the present one, by myriad schools of thought and infinite shades of opinion on mostly esoteric issues. But awareness has grown in the last few decades that publicly reported accounting information has the power to influence behavior and therefore may have an impact on stock prices, management decisions, executive compensation, and other outcomes of importance in the business community.

It should not be surprising, then, that controversy has so sorely vexed those who presume to establish standards, or principles, for financial accounting and reporting—or even to engage in the much more modest enterprise of merely identifying and cataloging "accepted" practices. Pacioli could not have imagined the extent to which politicization of the seemingly neutral and straightforward art of bookkeeping would occur five centuries later.

Controversy has heightened, shifted ground, and taken on sharper edges over the past half a century. Its ever-increasing intensity can be traced in the life spans of the three bodies successively charged with trying to bring order out of a jumble of often freewheeling financial reporting practices: the Committee on Accounting Procedure (CAP) of the American Institute of Accountants (now the American Institute of Certified Public Accountants, or AICPA), which operated from 1938 until 1959; the Accounting Principles Board (APB), also a senior committee of the AICPA, which lasted from 1959 until 1973; and the independent Financial Accounting Standards Board, which succeeded the APB in 1973 and still is in existence at this writing.

The FASB's predecessors perished in waves of widespread dissatisfaction with their performance, both in general and with regard to particular issues. Though it was built on a strong multidimensional foundation designed to broaden participation in the standard-setting process, and therefore increase acceptance, the present Board in its two decades of operation has seen an increase in rather than the expected diminution of criticism and contention that its carefully conceived structure was intended to bring about. The reason appears to be that after five centuries of disputation over countless relatively small issues, accounting practitioners and their clients and employers began in the 1960s to sort themselves out into two broadly based camps, articulating at first tentatively and then with increasing vehemence fundamentally opposed views about the essential nature of the accounting discipline and therefore about how standards for financial accounting and reporting should be established.

Although the issue had been raised often in specific circumstances before the FASB came into being, that Board's actions and declared policies have served to focus the argument and sharpen the contentiousness of it. Most participants do not yet acknowledge that a fundamental philosophical debate is under way: The arguments still tend to be couched in practical terms. Indeed, *pragmatism* is one of the most frequently heard buzzwords. But all are aware, at least intuitively, that a provocative, potent, and broad-based ideological argument has come into play in the ongoing debate over what financial information the public needs—and how it should be reported.

The central issue is whether financial accounting and reporting should be a scrupulously neutral exercise, self-disciplined to measure and report economic activity as objectively as possible in order to provide information that can be used with confidence as a basis for making economic decisions. Or should it be directed instead by concern for the economic health of individual enterprises, entire industries, or even society at large? In other words, should the primary concerns of accountants and accounting stand-ard setters be the reliability and objectivity of reported information, or should they focus first on the possible economic and social consequences of the information? That question, of course, raises others regarding the nature and uses of information in general.

To the uninitiated, there are few activities drier than financial accounting and reporting, but the information reported is relied on by investors, credit grantors, vendors, labor unions, taxing authorities, and others as at least the starting point for analyses on which decisions are based that have, in the aggregate, profound effects on the lives of all Americans. Financial reporting also reveals to the educated eye how managers think about the prospects of their companies and industries and how they perceive oppor-tunities and risks. And it is the slate on which corporate managers mark their own grades and strive for personal advantages, including various forms of compensation. Small wonder, then, that we have experienced more than a half a century of tension between corporate management and those who establish rules or guidelines for financial reporting.

The first crude attempt at setting such guidelines was a bulletin publish-ed by the Federal Reserve Board (FRB) in 1917 under the austere title "Uniform Accounting." The Fed was concerned because many corpora-tions customarily discounted their commercial paper at member banks, but its notion of uniformity still is anathema (and a rallying cry) for many issuers of financial information whose bywords are "flexibility" and "judgment."

There were occasional outcries in books and magazine articles in the 1920s and early 1930s about unreliable financial reporting and "hoodwinking of shareholders," but hardly anyone paid them any heed. It was a time of economic exuberance that the historian Samuel Eliot Morison called "the greatest orgy of speculation and over-optimism since the South Sea Bubble."[6] Critics of financial reporting practices, as well as the corporal's guard of clear-eyed observers who predicted the bubble would burst, were dismissed, not very politely, as doomsayers, dangerous to the nation's prosperity. But after the companies whose shares made up the Dow Jones Industrial Average lost nearly 90 percent of their value in less than three years, and some industrial giants were even harder hit, there was a reckoning.

In 1932, the American Management Association called for "the leading professional societies" to establish a joint committee on accounting standards. Indirectly as a result of that initiative, dialogue began on an informal basis between committees of the American Institute of Accountants (AIA) and the New York Stock Exchange. At first the accountants were reluctant to acknowledge that promulgation of accounting standards was either practical or desirable. They insisted on trying to identify and define only those practices about which corporations and their public accountants were in general agreement.[7] This, of course, was before there was a legal requirement that the financial statements of large public corporations be audited by independent public accountants, and the accountants' position in the financial reporting mix was much less secure than it became a short time later. Meanwhile, the Stock Exchange itself decided to require that companies applying for listing have their financial statements audited by independent public accountants.

In January 1933, the Senate Committee on Banking and Currency, upstaged to a large extent by its dynamic general counsel, Ferdinand Pecora, conducted hearings on the operations of the securities markets. Among many other things, members of the Committee pointed to the lack of uniform standards for preparation of financial reports as a contributing cause of unwarranted speculation in stocks during the 1920s—and thus of the 1929 market crash that was the dramatic overture to the Great Depression.

It was not until a year later that agreement between committees of the Stock Exchange and the American Institute of Accountants was reached on five very general guidelines for financial reporting.[8] Franklin D. Roosevelt and his "New Deal" already had been swept into Washington on a tidal wave of popular discontent over performance of the economic system.

One of the landmark pieces of legislation in the New Deal's "first hundred days" was the "Truth in Securities Law," now known by its formal name as the Securities Act of 1933, that emerged from the Senate Banking and Currency Committee hearings. That Act, with its stated purpose "to provide full and fair disclosure of the character of securities . . . and to prevent fraud in the sale thereof," stipulated, among other things, that the financial statements of most publicly traded companies must be audited by independent public accountants. (Though this was not its intent, the 1933 Act thereby ensured the extraordinary prosperity and independence vis à vis their clients of major public accounting firms for the next half a century.)

Four decades later, the founders of an ambitious new standard-setting body, the FASB, described the purpose of financial reporting in more elegant terms than the Securities Acts had. They said that decisions regarding allocation of financial resources, which, in the economists' definition, are always "scarce," depend on the quality of information on which judgments are based. Later still, the standard setters themselves went further in formulating their statement of mission. They equated the usefulness of financial reporting with "the primary characteristics of relevance and reliability and . . . the qualities of comparability and consistency."[9]

For a brief time, the requirements of the 1933 Act were administered by the Federal Trade Commission (FTC), but the Securities Exchange Act of 1934 transferred that authority to a new Securities and Exchange Commission (SEC) that it created. The 1934 Act directed the SEC to prescribe the form and content of financial statements issued by those publicly held companies large enough to be required to register with the Commission. Then, even more than now, government interference in business and the professions was anathema, but the political tide was running strongly against the private sector.

In the area of financial reporting, the significance of the 1934 Act took several years to manifest itself fully, but the legislation ultimately created an arena for lively contention among issuers, auditors, and users of financial information. Now there was mandatory auditing of publicly traded companies, plus a mandate to the SEC to prescribe rules for financial reporting. Remaining to be answered as the Commission began its work was the question of how, by what specific method and mechanism, those rules were to be formulated.

The early 1930s, after Roosevelt's accession to power, was a time of great self-confidence in Washington—and rapid proliferation of new regulatory and administrative agencies, popularly known individually by their initials and collectively as "alphabet soup." The SEC's first chairman was the feisty Joseph P. Kennedy, Wall Street speculator par excellence and father of a future president. Of Kennedy's appointment, Roosevelt is reported to have said: "It takes one to catch one."

The Commission and its staff were stocked with high-caliber talent, and over the six decades since, the SEC has consistently been regarded in both the private and public sectors, and by historians, as one of the most effective and exemplary regulatory agencies. But given a topic as arcane and elusive as financial accounting standards, the regulators were at a loss as to what to do. For almost four years a debate simmered within the Commission and its staff between those who recognized the impracticability of erecting a highly specialized and technical standard-setting apparatus within the Commission and those who regarded any delegation of authority to the private sector as a cop-out.

Finally, three of the five commissioners voted in 1938 to rely on the public accounting profession to lead in developing standards in the private sector while the SEC retained an oversight function and final authority. This set the stage for a long-running drama of self-regulation that still is being played out. The fact that the private sector was granted the privilege of developing standards—a privilege that it valued highly then and still does—by a narrow 3–2 Commission vote took on a keen irony more than a half a century later.

The private sector body the Commission had in mind in 1938 was the American Institute of [Certified Public] Accountants, which promptly reorganized and upgraded its Committee on Accounting Procedure. However, the reconstituted Committee was charged not with establishing rules or standards but merely with identifying "acceptable" accounting practices, including alternative practices in many circumstances.[10] This was consistent with the conventional wisdom of accountants at the time, and the SEC lacked sufficient professional expertise in the accounting area to recognize the implications. In that charge to the CAP were planted the seeds of the notion of "generally accepted accounting principles," referred to by the cognoscenti to this day as "GAAP" (pronounced "gap"). Thus, the accounting profession drew a distinction, in which the SEC acquiesced for more than two decades, between enforceable rules and general guidelines. That distinction, though partially eliminated later by actions of both the SEC and the renamed AICPA, lives on in the minds of accountants and particularly of business executives. It continues to muddy discussions of accounting concepts and standards today. More than four decades after the SEC acquiesced in it, Donald J. Kirk, as chairman of the FASB, would call GAAP and the notion of general acceptance "false labeling."[11]

Discomfort with the lack of specificity in its work led to the disbanding of CAP in 1959 and its replacement by another senior committee of the AICPA, the Accounting Principles Board. In its early years, the APB was expected to concentrate on development of accounting theory, but it soon was caught up in specific problems arising from newly invented kinds of business transactions and newly developed accounting practices. These were the "go-go" years of the 1960s, and as that decade drew to a close, a litany had grown, made up of the names of once-famous, or at least high-flying, companies that had surprised and brought grief to investors by less-than-candid financial reporting. The names included W. T. Grant, a memory from the main street of nearly everybody's hometown; Penn Central, a diluted evocation of the glory days of the Pennsylvania and New York Central Railroads; Talley Industries; Stirling Homex; National Student Marketing; and Leasco's acquisition of the Reliance National Life Insurance Company.

Their sins included keeping significant liabilities off their balance sheets by concealing the true obligations they had assumed in the form of leases; "front-end loading" of revenue at the time sales contracts were executed but sometimes years before the corresponding payments could be expected to be received; and abuse of "pooling-of-interests" accounting to conceal the true cost of acquiring other companies.

As the decade wore on, criticism of the APB mounted. In a phrase that was popular at the time, it was seen to concentrate on "firefighting" and to ignore "fundamentals." Somewhat contradictorily, the APB also was faulted for its inability, as a part-time, volunteer body, to act quickly enough to keep up with developments in the marketplace. A more telling criticism was that a Board made up almost entirely of public accountants whose partners and clients were alleged to exert self-interested pressures was not equipped to perform a "public interest" standard-setting function. Under-representation of issuers of financial statements, who viewed themselves as being most directly affected by the Opinions of the Board, was a serious, and probably decisive, point of contention.

The volume of criticism reached a level that impelled Marshall S. Armstrong, then the elected president (a title later changed to chairman) of the AICPA, to convene a conference in Washington early in 1971 of three dozen leaders in the public accounting profession to consider possible ways out of this morass. (The exact venue of the conference was rarely mentioned in subsequent years because of nervousness about the connotations that developed around it: It was held at the Watergate, but about a year before that hostelry's name became a virtual synonym for wrongdoing.) Decisions were taken there to launch parallel studies of the objectives of financial statements and of the structure for establishing accounting principles.

The two Study Groups became known by the names of their respective chairmen. The study on objectives was headed by the late Robert M. Trueblood, managing partner of Touche Ross & Co. The study on establishment of accounting principles was led by Francis M. Wheat, an attorney specializing in securities law and a former commissioner of the SEC. The "Wheat Committee," though appointed by the president of the AICPA, was notable at the time because its seven members included only three practicing public accountants. Besides Frank Wheat, the other non–certified public accountant (CPA) members included an investment banker, a university professor, and Roger B. Smith, vice president–finance of the General Motors Corporation, who later became chairman of GM and a persistent, activist critic of the FASB's approach to standard setting.

After 12 months of intensive activity, including a two-day public hearing, the Wheat Committee published its report at the end of March 1972.[12] It dealt first with what it called "the threshold question"—whether standard setting should remain a responsibility of the private sector or whether it should be taken over by a governmental body. The Study Group cited several reasons for retaining the function in the private sector: the susceptibility of government agencies to political pressures, the tendency of such agencies toward inflexibility and lack of responsiveness, and the likelihood that the private sector's highest levels of technical expertise and experience would be less available to the standard setters. Focusing on the SEC as the most likely governmental standard setter, the Group also observed that accounting standards apply to a far larger universe of enterprises than the approximately 10,000 companies required by law to register with the Commission.

The report went on to recommend a radically new, independent structure for standard setting. There would be a Financial Accounting Foundation (FAF), separate from all existing professional organizations; a Financial Accounting Standards Board with seven members, all salaried and serving full-time for five-year terms with possible reappointment for a second term;[13] and a Financial Accounting Standards Advisory Council (FASAC) whose members would be broadly representative of the various segments of the standard-setting body's constituency. The trustees of the Foundation, drawn from five sponsoring organizations, would be responsible for appointing the members of both Standards Board and Advisory Council, funding their operations, and exercising general oversight, except with regard to technical decisions of the Standards Board.

This is the structure for private sector standard setting that, with relatively minor modifications, remains in place at this writing. (In 1984, the Foundation trustees established a Governmental Accounting Standards Board [GASB] to set standards for state and local governmental entities, and three trustees nominated by national associations of governmental officials were added. The GASB takes a similar form and stands in the same relationship to the Foundation as the FASB.)

Despite some pockets of resistance among public accountants, the urgency felt by most parties concerned with standard setting in the spring of 1972 was reflected in the remarkable speed with which the Wheat Committee's proposals were accepted and put into effect. The Governing Council of the AICPA, which was being asked to give up a by-then traditional and highly valued function of the public accounting profession, approved in May. The Financial Accounting Foundation was incorporated in June. The first chairman of the FASB, the same Marshall Armstrong who had initiated the Trueblood and Wheat Study Groups, was appointed in November. A temporary office was opened in Stamford, Connecticut, on the first business day of 1973, and the FASB officially succeeded the APB as standard setter on July 1 of that year.

Just 12 months after the Wheat Study Group's report was published, the seven members of the new Financial Accounting Standards Board were introduced to the world at a banquet in the grand ballroom of the Waldorf-Astoria Hotel in New York. The featured speaker was Reginald H. Jones, widely respected chairman of the General Electric (GE) Company. He spoke of the economic ills confronting the nation in 1973, some of which were strikingly similar to those we face two decades later. He stressed the need to generate new investment capital and linked that problem to a need for improving the credibility of financial reporting. He then urged the corporate executives in his audience to stand behind the FASB. "The buck has to stop with corporate management," he said. "I am sure I don't have to emphasize to my associates in general management that this new venture is especially important to us, not just to the accountants; for we share with them the responsibility for using realistic and workable ground rules for financial reporting."

Jones then uttered the words that supporters of the FASB still like to quote. "We must recognize," he said, "that the new Board will not be a cure-all for every ailment. We must recognize that with its first decision the new Board is going to gore somebody's ox—and that will be the time for us to pull together—not to splinter apart."[14]

He closed by quoting a *Wall Street Journal* editorial that had been published a few days earlier. "The fate of the FASB," the *Journal* observed, "will not only tell us what kind of accounting we will have but, by measuring whether the business community can force itself to take the long view, also tell us more than a little about how well that community can meet many of the other challenges it faces."[15]

It has not worked out the way Reg Jones and the *Wall Street Journal* editorial writer hoped. Nor has the downside of *Business Week's* grim warning yet been realized. That magazine called the FASB "the last chance to avoid government control of accounting."[16]

Elevation of the economic and social consequences argument from a mere debating ploy for use in specific circumstances to a full-fledged ideological position was perceived by only a few of the accounting world's most astute observers. However, the thunderclouds it would generate already were gathering as Reg Jones spoke.

The observations made by Jones, the *Wall Street Journal*, and *Business Week* on the occasion of the FASB's launching grew out of the history of contention over previous attempts to establish any degree of uniformity of accounting practices. The members of the new Board were well aware that their fledgling organization must try to hold together a divided constituency whose principal segments argued strenuously for interests and objectives that most often were in conflict. As the Board's third chairman, Dennis R. Beresford, was to remark a decade and a half later:

In general, the issuers [of financial reports] want few standards, or only very broad standards, with plenty of room for the exercise of judgment in their application; auditors are inclined to want more standards, and more specific ones, that will defuse differences of opinion with clients; and users want a maximum of reliable, relevant information.

He also observed that "it is not uncommon among banks to find the chief financial officer or controller [issuers] opposed to a particular proposal, while a lending officer [user] from the same bank supports it."[17]

In such an environment, the concept of self-regulation, though eminently desirable to the private sector when a threat of formal government supervision of a business or profession exists, faces many formidable obstacles as we shall see—including the reluctance of private interests to submit to any kind of regulation at all. As well conceived as it was by its originators and founders in 1972, the present structure for standard setting is no exception, although there are certain steps that can be taken to ensure its continuation—if those now responsible for it are able to muster the wisdom and will.

NOTES

1. "Speech for Quintius Roscius the Actor," in *The Orations of Marcus Tullius Cicero*, trans. Charles Duke Yonge (London: Henry G. Bohn, 1856).

2. See *Report of the National Commission on Fraudulent Financial Reporting* (Washington, D.C.: October 1987), 26.

3. Dennis R. Beresford, "Financial Reporting: Comparability and Competition" (address at the Stern School of Business Administration, New York University, New York, October 1990).

4. Luca Pacioli, *Summa de Arithmetica Geometria Proportioni e Proportionalita* (Venice, 1494). Believed to be one of the first books printed from movable type, according to John B. Geijsbeek, *Ancient Double-Entry Bookkeeping*, (Houston: Scholars Book Co., 1974), 8.

5. As prescribed in the American Institute of Certified Public Accountants Auditing Standards Board *Statement on Auditing Standards No. 69* (New York: AICPA, 1992), 1.

6. Samuel Eliot Morison, *The Oxford History of the American People* (New York: Oxford University Press, 1965), 936.

7. John L. Carey, *The Rise of the Accounting Profession: From Technician to Professional 1896–1936* (New York: American Institute of Certified Public Accountants, 1969), 169.

8. In paraphrase from the AIA committee report "Audits of Corporate Financial Reports" (New York: American Institute of Accountants, 1934), the guidelines were: (1) revenue should not be recognized until a sale is made, and current period expenses should not be deferred in anticipation of sales; (2) expenses should be

deducted from income in measuring earnings, not charged to capital surplus; (3) after an acquisition, dividends paid by a subsidiary to its new parent out of prior earnings are a return of capital, not income to the parent; (4) dividends on treasury stock should not be treated as income; and (5) receivables from officers and employees should not be included with trade receivables.

9. FASB, *The Mission of the Financial Accounting Standards Board* (Stamford, Conn, 1983).

10. John L. Carey, *The Rise of the Accounting Profession to Responsibility and Authority* (New York: American Institute of Certified Public Accountants, 1970), 13.

11. Paper delivered by Donald J. Kirk at the annual meeting of the American Accounting Association in August 1980 (Boston), and published under the heading of "Statements in Quotes" in the *Journal of Accountancy*, April 1981, 85.

12. American Institute of Certified Public Accountants, *Establishing Financial Accounting Standards* (New York: AICPA, March, 1972).

13. Under the bylaws of the Financial Accounting Foundation initially published in 1973, terms of the original members of the FASB were staggered so as to ensure that no more than two would expire at the end of any year. Short terms of the original members were not included in the total time they would be permitted to serve. Hence, Donald J. Kirk served for 14 years and Robert T. Sprouse for 13.

14. Reginald H. Jones, "The Challenge of Capital Attraction" (address to the Financial Accounting Foundation, Financial Accounting Standards Board, and guests, New York, March 28, 1973).

15. "More Than Accounting," *Wall Street Journal*, March 7, 1973.

16. "The Accountants' Last Chance," *Business Week*, March 31, 1973.

17. Dennis R. Beresford, "The Economic and Social Consequences of Financial Accounting Standards" (address to the Financial Executives Institute conference on current financial reporting issues, New York, November 1, 1988).

Chapter Two

A Goldfish in a Pool of Sharks?

Change is not made without some inconvenience, even from worse to better.
                    Richard Hooker, noted sixteenth-century theologian[1]

Despite skepticism in some quarters, and wariness in others, including the Board's own offices in a campuslike setting in Stamford, Connecticut (deliberately chosen to put distance between the FASB and the pressures of New York and Washington), the new organization was launched amid general optimism and enthusiasm. It was literally unique in almost every respect, most notably in the fact that it was a rule-making body financed and operated entirely in the private sector but whose decisions would be backed by federal law and a powerful federal regulatory agency. A "bold experiment in self-regulation," some called it, carefully conceived and soundly financed.

Ever since the Interstate Commerce Commission (ICC) was called into being by Act of Congress in 1887 as America's first attempt to impose government regulation of a private industry (then only railroads), Corporate America has argued against regulation of any kind on philosophical grounds and then, when in danger of losing that argument, has often offered a somewhat nebulous and as yet, after these many decades, ill-defined concept of self-regulation as an alternative to the governmental kind.

Nobody has formulated, let alone gained consensus on, a definition of *self-regulation*—or any general principles regarding it. Its forms are so diverse that it is impossible to generalize about them.[2] It is a concept to which a great deal of lip service has been paid but very little hard thought has been given. Nor has self-regulation always been designed to serve constructive purposes. Over the years, its outward trappings have been used to camouflage price fixing; to restrict entry into industries, trades, and professions; and to establish product or performance standards designed to limit competition. And then, as is the case with regulation by government, there is a historic tendency for those subject to regulation of any kind to try to gain control over the agencies designated to regulate them—a temptation that some of the ostensible supporters of private sector standard setting have been unable to resist.

A working definition for a meaningful kind of self-regulation might be: the establishment, dissemination, and enforcement by agreed-upon nongovernmental agencies of rules to protect the public in areas not specifically covered by law.

Seen in this light, self-regulation is, in a somewhat imprecise but nevertheless real sense, an extension of the legislature's intent. It follows from this premise that in order to be successful, self-regulation must have substance. It must, in fact, *be* regulation—within the private sector, to be sure, but in response to public expectations.

A. Clarence Sampson, when he was chief accountant of the SEC, put the case succinctly. His advice to the private sector was: "Make it unnecessary for Congress to act."

If one is to place one's faith in self-regulation, the structure and process for setting financial reporting standards constitute the paradigm. The founders went to extraordinary lengths to devise a structure that would combine the elements of expertise, public responsibility, and independence from special interests. Within the constraints of professional pride and politics, which under the circumstances prevailing in 1972 were not severe, the new institution indeed was soundly conceived—but, as became apparent later, its structure may not prove strong enough to withstand forever the ire of those who object to its decisions.

The Foundation that was to raise funds and appoint the members of the new Board drew its financial support from the members of five sponsoring organizations, each of which would nominate one or more trustees of the Foundation. They were the American Accounting Association (AAA), the professional organization of accounting educators; the AICPA; the Financial Analysts Federation (FAF) (now the Association for Investment Management and Research, or AIMR); the Financial Executives Institute (FEI); and the National Association of Accountants (NAA) (now the Institute of Management Accountants, or IMA). This lineup was joined in 1976 by the Securities Industry Association (SIA).

In the beginning, the AICPA was granted five seats on the nine-member board of trustees and a nominal (though not effective) veto power over the nominees of the other four organizations. These were clear concessions to professional pride and politics. However, the total number of trustees was increased several times over the years, and the AICPA soon lost both its predominance in numbers and its theoretical power of veto over trustee nominees. In 1993, there were 16 trustees, including 3 from state and local governmental organizations but still only 5 practicing CPAs.

The financing came forward with remarkable alacrity: $200,000 per year was pledged for five years by each of the (then) "Big Eight" public accounting firms, and there were additional commitments from other firms of all sizes. The corporate community responded, mainly through the FEI, not with multiyear pledges but with annual contributions that, in total, would surpass those of the public accounting profession in a few years. The fund-raising target for the first year, $3.5 million, was exceeded by more than $250,000, and the amount raised was more than a $1.5 million greater than expenses. From a standing start, net revenue from sales of publications grew steadily until it exceeded contributions by the end of the first decade, and it continues to do so by a substantial margin. Meanwhile, the annual cost of operating the FASB rose to $15 million by 1993.

While the Foundation's finances remained in good shape for almost a decade and a half, the operational side of the structure began to run into some life-threatening problems much earlier. These will be described in subsequent chapters. Significantly, however, those problems, which, as we shall see, originated mainly in the private sector, did not diminish the flow of contributions from the private sector: That flow merely increased less rapidly than income from other sources.

The excess of revenues over expenses narrowed gradually over the years but did not reverse itself until 1988 when extraordinary expenses of an elaborate "five-year review" of both the FASB and the GASB, coupled with the move of their offices from Stamford to new quarters in nearby Norwalk, Connecticut, pushed the Foundation into its first deficit. (Since the GASB came into being in 1984, the funds of the two Boards have been strictly segregated.) The red ink persisted in 1989 and 1990, due in part to the slowing of publication sales brought about by the dual trends of mergers among accounting firms and increasing use of electronic media to disseminate needed technical information within the firms. In 1992, the Foundation was in the black and seemed to be back on course.

In the 1970s and for most of the 1980s the trustees fretted about the need to formalize their financing arrangements, but fund-raising was not then a major concern. One concrete step, however, a reserve fund for the FASB that was built up in those years and was severely criticized by the AICPA and others, averted a financial crisis at the beginning of the 1990s.

The Foundation's original Board of Trustees was made up of the heads of three large national public accounting firms, two regional firms, a prominent investment banker, a distinguished professor of accounting, the chairman of Caterpillar Tractor Co., and Thomas A. Murphy, vice chairman (soon to become chairman) of General Motors and later, in his gentlemanly way, a critic of the approach to standard setting that evolved at the FASB. For him, W. A. Paton and A. C. Littleton's 1940 monograph *An Introduction to Corporate Accounting Standards* was le dernier cri.[3] By and large, his successors at GM are still of the same mind—and this has been the source of some of the most serious attacks on the modern private sector standard-setting structure.

The president was Ralph E. Kent, the senior partner of Arthur Young & Company (now part of Ernst & Young) who had been one of the key leaders in the movement to get the Foundation and the FASB organized. Trustees are elected for three-year terms and are eligible for reelection to one additional term.

The Wheat Report and the original bylaws of the Foundation called for the FASB to be made up of four persons whose primary experience had been as CPAs in public practice, again a concession to professional pride and politics, plus three from other relevant disciplines, "who, in the judgment of the trustees, are well versed in problems of financial reporting."[4] Aside from the requirement of four practicing CPAs, which was dropped in 1977, the trustees have never stipulated a hard and fast formula for the makeup of the Board, but they did spell out in 1985 what they considered to be the ideal "mix" of professional backgrounds—and carefully noted that it would not be attainable under all circumstances.

Among its four practicing CPAs, the original Board included Marshall Armstrong, of course, as chairman. He had been managing partner of Geo. S. Olive & Co., a prominent regional firm based in Indianapolis, and, as noted previously, the elected president of the AICPA. He also had been a member of the APB. The vice chairman was the late John W. Queenan, longtime managing partner of Haskins & Sells (now a part of Deloitte & Touche) and the only person to serve on all three private sector standard-setting bodies, the CAP, the APB, and the FASB. Already retired from his firm, he had been a member of President Richard Nixon's Price Commission and, like Armstrong, was a former president of the AICPA.

The two other CPAs on the Board were 40–year-old dark horses. Donald J. Kirk was a Price Waterhouse partner in New York and had been a Navy jet pilot in the Korean War. His public accounting experience was precocious for a person of his age. Walter P. Schuetze, a Texan, had served as a Russian-language specialist in the Air Force. He began his accounting career in a local firm in San Antonio that was merged soon afterward with what was then Peat, Marwick, Mitchell & Co. He also had unusually impressive credentials for an accounting firm partner of his age. Both prodigies would be heard from later, and not much later at that: Kirk as successor to Marshall Armstrong as chairman of the FASB in 1978, and Schuetze, after he resigned from the Board and returned to Peat, Marwick in 1976, as a principal spokesman for the AICPA on accounting standards issues and active contributor to the Board's process. In 1992, approaching his firm's mandatory retirement age, he accepted appointment as chief accountant of the SEC.

The other three members were Arthur L. Litke, who had been chief of the Office of Accounting and Finance of the Federal Power Commission; the late Robert E. Mays, controller of Exxon Corporation; and Robert T. Sprouse, professor of accounting in the Stanford University Graduate School of Business and coauthor, with Maurice Moonitz, of a research report commissioned by the APB on basic concepts that was well regarded by many but was not accepted by the APB because it was considered to be too advanced for its time.[5]

Under the Foundation's bylaws, members of the Standards Board were required to sever all connections with prior employers and to divest themselves of all investments or other financial arrangements that might be, or appear to be, conflicts of interest.

The third essential element was, and still is, the Financial Accounting Standards Advisory Council. It was envisioned by the Wheat Committee as having about 20 members, but it began life with 27, plus Marshall Armstrong, who served somewhat incongruously as chairman. (That arrangement was changed in 1977 when Paul Kolton, former chairman of the American Stock Exchange, became permanent chairman of the Council.)

FASAC was not designed to be a polite cheering section or support group for the FASB, and it has never become one. In fact, its membership has included more than a few highly articulate critics of standards and proposed standards—and of each other's viewpoints. On retiring as chairman in 1992, Kolton remarked: "Over the years, the members of FASAC have raised contention, honest contention, to a new kind of art form." The Council is charged with "consulting with the FASB as to major technical issues, the . . . agenda of projects and the priorities of the projects, matters likely to require the attention of the FASB, the selection and organization of FASB task forces, and such other matters as may be requested by the FASB or its chairman."[6] In 1973, FASAC had among its members Frank Wheat, plus another former SEC commissioner, a former chief accountant of the SEC, a former chairman of the Federal Reserve Board, the comptroller general of the United States, and a representative array of experts from the fields of finance, accounting, industry, education, banking, and the legal profession. In general, that kind of mix has been maintained ever since, although a recommendation by a committee of the Foundation trustees in 1977 resulted in its becoming more precise. The chief accountant of the SEC regularly attends the quarterly meetings (which also are attended by all members of the FASB) as an observer but with the privilege of the floor.

FASAC was the basic instrument for creating meaningful dialogue with those most interested in the development of financial accounting standards, but it was only the beginning of a reaching-out process to obtain counsel from all segments of the constituency that has accelerated and expanded over the years.

This is the "structure" that was created, in the words of the Foundation's Certificate of Incorporation in 1972, to

issue Statements of Financial Accounting Standards designed to establish or improve standards of financial accounting and reporting for the guidance and education of the public, investors, creditors, preparers and suppliers of financial information, reporting entities, and certified public accountants."

That language later was simplified, but the meaning remains the same.[7]

The Rules of Procedure also specified, and continue to specify, an elaborate set of safeguards, generally referred to as "due process," to ensure the thoroughness and objectivity of the Board's research and deliberations and to provide appropriate opportunities for the public to consider and comment on the issues. Despite its claim of "openness," however, in its first five years the Board conducted its deliberations in private and declined to reveal its "inclinations" on the issues until a draft Statement, or *exposure draft*, was issued for public comment. That also changed in 1978.

Within the first few months after the FASB became fully operational, Lee J. Seidler, sometime accounting professor, sometime investment banker, and full-time gadfly, published an article about the new Board titled "A Goldfish in a Pool of Sharks." His thesis was that the new Board was unlikely to succeed because, being an independent body, it lacked a powerful built-in constituency to defend it against Corporate America, such as its predecessors had had as senior committees of the AICPA.[8] For a dozen years or more, it appeared that Seidler's thesis was wrong. Contrary to his prediction, a loose coalition of issuers, auditors, and users of financial information, and others having an interest in financial reporting, held together quite consistently on the central question of standard setting in the private sector, despite disagreements over specific standard-setting decisions. By the mid-1980s, however, the coalition was beginning to weaken— and some of the pillars of the public accounting profession were part of the problem.

At about the same time Seidler's article appeared, a well-known academic gadfly published a piece in which he said the new Board would not succeed because only one of its members was an academician and collectively the members had contributed very little in the way of articles in the learned journals. While it is easy, in retrospect, to regard the author as irrelevant, he was taken seriously on Capitol Hill, as we shall see later.

So, even before it had time to make any decisions, save those regarding its technical agenda, the FASB was hearing the rumblings of distant thunder on the Left. The Right was yet to be heard from, but it didn't take long.

Corporate America kept its powder dry until it had specific targets, in the form of proposed standards, to shoot at.

The FASB did its best to provide those targets as quickly as it could, although the process seemed painfully slow to many of its supporters. The first step was to decide on an agenda of technical projects. In the future, as we shall see, agenda decisions would become increasingly contentious as Corporate America made ever-more determined efforts to limit the scope of standard setting. The initial agenda decisions were made after consultation with the FASAC and the sponsoring organizations that, all told, suggested more than 30 topics that they considered pressing. Of these, 7 were selected—one for each member of the Board who would function as project director and chairman of an advisory task force. The task force would assist in assessing research needs, identifying alternative approaches to a standard, and developing a detailed neutral document called a *discussion memorandum* that would be the basis for written comments from the public and for a public hearing.

The topics chosen reflected major concerns of the entire financial reporting community—issuers (also frequently called preparers), auditors, and users of financial information—at the time. They were:

- Foreign currency translation, suddenly brought to the fore by international agreement to allow rates of exchange to "float" after many years of being pegged.
- Reporting by diversified companies, made urgent by the rush to conglomeration in the 1960s.
- Criteria for determining materiality, perhaps the most elusive of all accounting issues.
- Accounting for leases, a response to the trend toward minimizing debt by leasing rather than purchasing assets.
- Accruing for future losses, an examination of the use of accounting "reserves" to cushion such losses and, in some cases, to "smooth" earnings.
- Accounting for research and development costs, an area in which practice varied widely. (It was noted at the time that research and development leading to Boeing's 747, Lockheed's L1011, and the McDonnell Douglas DC10 was accounted for in three quite different ways.)
- Broad qualitative standards for financial reporting, an umbrella term under which the Board would grope for a handle on, and an approach to, a conceptual framework to guide its standard-setting efforts.

Of these, all but criteria for determining materiality culminated in one or more significant FASB pronouncements. Broad qualitative standards soon became known as the conceptual framework project, which gave rise to six Statements of Financial Accounting Concepts. The second of those devoted 10 of its 170 paragraphs to materiality, but no Statement of Standards ever was issued. Unlike Statements of Financial Accounting Standards, Concepts Statements are not enforceable rules and do not require changes in accounting practices but are intended to provide a common basis of theory for the Board's consideration of specific accounting issues—and a common language in which the issues may be understood and discussed by all interested parties.

A few months after establishing its initial technical agenda, the Board issued a call for public comment on the possible need for interpretation, amendment, or replacement of pronouncements issued by its predecessors. (Under the FASB's charter, Accounting Research Bulletins issued by the CAP and Opinions of the APB would remain in effect until and unless amended or superseded by FASB pronouncements.) In November 1973, with more than 100 lengthy comment letters in hand, the Board added a project on accounting for business combinations and related intangibles. The intent was to amend two of the APB's most controversial Opinions, Nos. 16 and 17, on those subjects, but after a discussion memorandum was published in 1976, further action was deferred, first until a public hearing was held on the elements of financial statements, part of the conceptual framework project, and then until a Statement could be issued on that subject. The Statement eventually was issued in 1980, but business combinations was not brought back to life.

After 479 years of known accounting history, it was difficult for laypersons to understand why, as the FASB began operations in 1973, accountants had not yet agreed on the objectives of financial reporting—or even on definitions of such seemingly basic terms as *assets* and *liabilities*.

The project on "broad qualitative characteristics" would bring objectives to center stage early in the drama, but definitions of the elements of financial statements, including those seemingly commonplace notions of assets and liabilities, would have to wait a few years.

Qualitative characteristics, by now known as the conceptual framework project, had its first tangible manifestation in a discussion memorandum in mid-1974 that, in effect, was merely a reprint of the report of the Trueblood Study Group on Objectives that had been published the previous year. It set forth 12 possible objectives for financial statements, the first of which was "to provide information useful for making economic decisions." Despite the fact that the thrust of the Securities Acts of 1933 and 1934 was in the direction of investor protection and adequate provision of information needed by investors for making "economic decisions," only 37 percent of those who submitted written comments on the discussion memorandum on objectives 40 years later could agree that the objective of providing information for economic decision making should be adopted. (Sixty-one percent of the commentators were corporate preparers of financial statements or industry associations representing them.)

The problem was a cultural, or generational, warp. For many genera-
tions, preparers and auditors of financial reports, particularly the
preparers, had been trained to believe that the main purpose of financial
reporting was to let the present owners of the business (shareholders) know
how well their hired managers had looked after, and preserved, their
invested assets. The notion that outsiders, including those who might have
an interest in investing in the enterprise for perhaps a shorter-term gain
than had been contemplated by the original investors, might have a different set of information needs was not taken seriously. The old way of looking
at financial reporting focused on the notion of "stewardship"—in other
words, how those nice people we hire to run the business for us have taken
care of our money. However, a new breed of investor, in the ascendancy
most of the time since Joe Kennedy's pre-SEC days, and certainly in the
1960s, was looking for financial information that would be more useful in
picking and choosing the most promising among many investment oppor-
tunities. He, or she, wanted that information to be reliable and objective—
and his, or her, need for reliable, objective information was a principal focus
of the Securities Acts.

This collision of viewpoints was brought into focus by the debate over
objectives of financial reporting and soon became evident in comment
letters and in testimony at the Board's subsequent public hearing on the
discussion memorandum. A third leg of the argument was that management's own need for financial information should take precedence over all
other considerations in financial reporting, regardless of the Securities Acts.
For example, one of the world's greatest utility companies took umbrage
over the fact that in the first proposed objective, management was not
specifically included in the definition of users of financial information and
noted that the company's system of financial reporting had been designed
primarily to serve management's own needs. Users, or investors and
creditors, were invited to understand the enterprise in terms of the same
basic reporting structure as used by management in operating the business.
A large national hotel chain echoed this view but went further, suggesting
that financial analysts, investors, "speculators," government regulators,
and other public representatives should be required to make their own
interpretations from the basic financial statements that are prepared for
management's use. The letter pointed out that the objectives of management would be different from those of "the security speculator," social
activist, and government regulator.

The vice president–controller of one of the world's largest oil companies
said, at the public hearing, that the primary purpose of financial statements
is simply for management to tell what the results have been under its "game
plan," not to help users of financial information to make investment
decisions. Later, under questioning by the Board, he distinguished between
a "broad" description of that game plan, which would be implicit under

the stewardship concept of financial reporting, and a more detailed one that he was afraid might yield useful information for competitors.

The Financial Executives Institute also offered testimony to the effect that "the overriding purpose of financial statements is for management to report to shareholders on what has happened in the past. . . . We feel that the main audience . . . is present shareholders." In its written submission, the Institute had maintained that the FASB would have to recognize that the reporting system must permit management to determine what information external users should have.

As might be expected, the (then) Financial Analysts Federation supported adoption of the proposed objectives with only minor modifications and noted that accounting controversies often start with disagreement about who the principal users of financial information are. The FAF also observed that preparers of financial reports frequently fail to understand the economics of the investment process to which accounting should be responsive. The analysts predicted that adoption of the proposed objectives would provide a common approach to the solution of accounting problems and therefore would diminish or eliminate future controversies.

The objectives eventually were adopted in essentially the form that the FAF supported, but they neither diminished nor eliminated the controversies that would follow.

Responses to the discussion memorandum on objectives also afforded the Board its first significant opportunity to listen to arguments regarding the nascent philosophical question of neutrality versus economic and social consequences.

From the earliest adoption of accounting guidelines, issuers of financial statements have complained about the costs of implementation versus expected benefits. They have tended to believe that a major share of the benefits should accrue to themselves rather than to a broader public of external users of financial information and have considered the costs accordingly. In 1968, Maurice Moonitz warned that corporate management's stake in the consequences of accounting rules is too great for "nonprofessionals" to accept the decisions of a disinterested body of technical experts voluntarily, "no matter how eminent those experts or how persuasive the research support for their findings."[9] A decade later, Stephen A. Zeff observed that "the increasing involvement of 'nonprofessionals' in the standard-setting process, and the economic (and social) consequences of the accounting standards themselves are inextricably related."[10]

Zeff went on to point out that although the accounting literature did not acknowledge economic consequences as an acceptable argument in discussions of proposed accounting standards until the early 1970s, it had at least been implicit in such landmark debates as those over replacement cost versus historical cost depreciation in the late 1940s and the investment tax credit in the early 1960s. Dialogue regarding the setting of standards, however, continued to be conducted mainly in terms of theory, reason, research, the presumed neutrality of the resulting financial information—and traditional cost-benefit concerns.

In 1973, in the months immediately after the FASB officially succeeded the APB as standard setter, the argument broke out into the open. In July of that year, Dale L. Gerboth, until that time a member of the research staff of the AICPA, published an article in the *Accounting Review* titled "Research, Intuition, and Politics in Accounting Inquiry" in which he undertook to demonstrate that the critical issues in standard setting are not essentially technical in nature but actually are political. "Politicization of accounting rule-making," he wrote, "was not only inevitable, but just. In a society committed to democratic legitimization of authority, only politically responsive institutions have the right to command others to obey their rules."[11] Gerboth already had been hired as a member of the FASB staff when his article appeared, and he stayed long enough to play a significant role in developing Statement No. 13, *Accounting for Leases*, the Board's most elaborate venture in the universally unpopular "cookbook" approach to standard setting that politicization of the process tends to encourage. Seven Amendments, 6 Interpretations, and 11 Technical Bulletins were issued subsequently to clarify application of the standard.

A few months later, David M. Hawkins of the Harvard Business School delivered a guest lecture at Baruch College of the City University of New York in which he advocated harnessing the FASB to national economic goals and the government's programs to achieve those goals.

The determination of what constitutes approved corporate reporting standards is a political process involving the interests of many parties, with the government as the dominant interested party. Those who make decisions on corporate reporting standards must be responsive to the political considerations. At this level of responsibilities accounting becomes a branch of political economics.[12]

In one of his early speeches as chairman of the FASB in the spring of 1973, Marshall Armstrong stated the opposing view unequivocally but without benefit of being able to see how the economic and social consequences argument would be broadened before that year was out.

The rule-makers for financial accounting and reporting cannot, should not, and as far as the FASB is concerned, will not try to steer investors away from one alternative use of their capital toward another. Nor will we involve ourselves in attempts to "heat up" or "cool down" the economy. Our role is to establish standards for financial information that portray economic reality—and therefore provide a reasonable basis for other peoples' decisions on capital allocation.[13]

He added that he and his fellow Board members were "determined to maintain the intellectual independence and objectivity that were designed into the FASB's structure and rules of procedure, because we believe that only in this way can we discharge our responsibilities to the public."

Armstrong's successors as chairman, Donald J. Kirk from 1978 through 1986 and Dennis R. Beresford from 1987 to the present, reiterated those themes many times. For example, Kirk told the Business Council in 1979 that

if the FASB is to succeed, it must avoid being, or even appearing to be, an advocate of any particular viewpoint or set of interests. . . . If information is designed to indicate that investing in a particular enterprise involves less risk than it actually does, or designed to encourage investment in a particular segment of the economy, financial reporting will suffer an irreparable loss of credibility.[14]

He elaborated on this theme throughout his chairmanship, declaring on one occasion, "The Board's primary concern must be relevance and reliability of the information that results, not the effect that the new rule might have on a particular interest."[15] On another, he said:

Standards could be set in other ways. Standard setting could be a process of negotiation, horsetrading, logrolling—it could be a process dominated by those appointed to represent particular interests. Every standard could be developed in the same way as tax bills are created in Congress. The results could be determined by lobbying. If you lobby hard enough, you get your way.[16]

Discussing neutrality in a 1990 speech at New York University, Kirk's successor, Dennis R. Beresford, emphasized that

Neutral information is unbiased information; it does not intentionally favor one party over another; it is not colored for the purpose of influencing behavior in any particular direction. Like reports on consumer prices, the GNP, or the census, financial statements are meant to serve evenhandedly all users who need that kind of information.[17]

In arguing against David Hawkins's position in a *Journal of Accountancy* article in 1978, David Solomons, of the Wharton School at the University of Pennsylvania and a member of the Wheat Committee, wrote that the end product of accounting is a system of measurement. Therefore, the position advocated by Hawkins would "threaten the integrity of financial reporting and deprive it of whatever credibility it now has." The essential nature of accounting, he said, is

financial mapmaking. The better the map, the more completely it represents the complex phenomena that are being mapped. We do not judge a map by the behavioral effects it produces. The distribution of natural wealth or rainfall shown on a map may lead to population shifts or changes in industrial location, which the government may like or dislike. That should be no concern of the cartographer. We judge his map by how well it represents the facts. People can then react to it as they will.[18]

By the time Solomons wrote those words, however, the genie was out of the bottle. Commentators on the discussion memorandum on objectives in 1974 had a new instrument of argumentation with which to expand the old question of costs versus benefits of accounting standards. Since it was new and still quite unfamiliar, they used it tentatively, even somewhat contradictorily. For example, in its comment letter the American Accounting Association acknowledged that usefulness is a necessary characteristic of financial reports but proposed explicit recognition of social costs and benefits in weighing alternative financial accounting solutions. At the public hearing, however, the Association's spokesman allowed that "present complexities and inadequacies in social welfare measurement would not allow an operational set of financial statement objectives to be logically derived from the asserted social welfare objectives."

Similarly, the FEI wrote that in considering the objectives of financial statements and implementation standards, the FASB should recognize the potential economic, social, and even political consequences of its decisions. However, the Institute's representative at the public hearing testified, "FEI is concerned with the cost of preparing information. . . . Objectives of financial statements should help resolve real problems in financial reporting. They should not be designed to achieve somebody's idea of social, political, or economic goals."

One very large corporation wrote that the FASB should be careful to ensure that financial reporting reflects favorably on the free enterprise system and is in no way harmful to it. Another echoed that thought and added parenthetically a prediction that a large portion of the Board's constituency would suspect that the whole effort to determine objectives was designed to be as useful to economic planners and socialists as to business management.

Still another complained that it was becoming increasingly difficult for management, which was said to be the primary user of financial statements, to keep up with accelerating changes that were threatening to overturn all of previous accounting history. At the time, the FASB had issued one Statement of Financial Accounting Standards, a brief and simple one on disclosure of information about foreign currency translation. More than 100 would follow in the next two decades, and many of those would be lengthy and complex.

Crucial to the FASB's hopes for success would be establishing and nurturing open lines of communication and a sound working relationship

with the SEC and particularly with the Commission's chief accountant and
his staff. Doing so was high on Marshall Armstrong's list of priorities from
the outset. He faced formidable obstacles, not because of any lack of
goodwill on either side but because of a combination of events both inside
and outside the Commission that demanded the attention of its chief
accountant.

The SEC had supported establishment of the FASB and intended to
continue its well-established policy of relying on the private sector for
leadership in developing standards for financial reporting, but something
like a vacuum had been created by the decision of the AICPA in May 1972
to cede the standard-setting function to an independent body—14 months
before the FASB would become fully operational. The APB continued to
work on some projects and even issued seven Opinions in that period as
projects long under way finally came to fruition, but it removed several
topics from its agenda and added no new ones.

Meanwhile, the SEC's longtime chief accountant, Andrew Barr, had
retired and been succeeded by John C. ("Sandy") Burton, a young, ener-
getic, and aggressive regulator. Within a period of two years there were
three different chairmen of the Commission and an almost complete turnover of Commissioners. What Sandy Burton saw when he took office in
July 1972 was a rapid accumulation of new accounting issues and a partial
hiatus in the private sector's standard-setting activity. An unprecedented
volume of Accounting Series Releases and Staff Accounting Bulletins soon
began to issue from the Commission, giving rise to fears at Stamford and
elsewhere in the private sector that the SEC might preempt major portions
of the standard-setting function before the FASB was fairly under way.
Marshall Armstrong and his followers had further cause for concern in
statements by Burton to the effect that setting disclosure requirements
should be the SEC's responsibility while the FASB concerned itself with
establishing measurement rules. Armstrong and his fellow Board members
believed strongly that the two were inseparable from a rule-making standpoint.

Another Burton initiative that caused consternation at the FASB was the
issuance of disclosure requirements explicitly aimed at the information
needs of "professional analysts" rather than the average investor. Not only
was this a departure from prevailing practice, but it also was seen as
threatening preemption of the Board's conceptual framework project, including its efforts to define "users" of financial information and to establish
objectives for financial reporting. There was further concern about an SEC
initiative regarding line-of-business reporting in which Burton, in effect,
was dealing with a narrow part of a broad problem on which the FASB
already was hard at work.

Nevertheless, Burton continued to express his support for the FASB and
promised that the relationship between the two organizations would be

one of "mutual non-surprise,"[19] thus acknowledging the desirability of open lines of communication. In *Accounting Series Release 145* (ASR 145), the SEC declared a moratorium on adoption of catastrophe reserves by insurance companies until the FASB could issue a Statement on accounting for contingencies. In 1974, ASR 163 established a moratorium on capitalization of interest by other than certain utilities and two specific industries, indicating that the Commission would reconsider this release in light of any FASB pronouncement on the subject.

On December 20, 1973, the SEC issued its historic *Accounting Series Release 150* (later codified as *Financial Reporting Release No. 1, Section 101*) that stated that "principles, standards, and practices promulgated by the FASB in its Statements and Interpretations will be considered by the Commission as having substantial authoritative support, and those contrary to such FASB promulgations will be considered to have no such support."[20] In that language and elsewhere in ASR 150, the SEC was careful to make it clear that while the Commission would look to the FASB "to provide leadership in establishing and improving accounting principles," it was not abdicating its own responsibilities under the Securities Acts.

Seven months before ASR 150, the AICPA had amended its Rules of Conduct to require Institute members to certify that a client's financial statements are prepared in accordance with GAAP only if they comply with all applicable FASB pronouncements.[21] Meanwhile, the state boards of accountancy, which have licensing authority over public accountants, had begun to change their regulations to identify FASB as the authoritative source of GAAP. Thus, for practical purposes, all issuers of audited financial statements, whether publicly owned or private, would be subject to FASB rules, but the Board would have no enforcement powers of its own. Those powers would reside in the SEC with regard to filings with the Commission and in the AICPA with regard to the conduct of individual accountants. The state boards of accountancy would observe the rules in issuing licenses.

As 1973 drew to a close, two other significant events occurred. The aforementioned Statement No. 1, *Disclosure of Foreign Currency Translation Information,* important only because it was the FASB's first Statement, was adopted in a session that lasted late into the evening. The vote was 6–1. Overnight, however, John Queenan changed his negative ballot because he thought that unanimity on the Board's first Statement was more important than the reservations he had about it.

Ted O'glove, writer of the *Quality of Earnings* newsletter, had been campaigning for early resolution of the age-old materiality issue. When Statement No. 1 appeared, barely five months after the FASB officially replaced the APB, with a bit of boilerplate saying that "the provisions of this Statement need not be applied to immaterial items," O'glove threw up his hands. "The Board has failed its first test," he said, by not solving the materiality question before it did anything else.

Of greater significance than Statement No. 1 was a consensus of FASAC, which became evident at its December meeting, that rapidly rising inflation required action by the FASB on what was then known as general price level accounting. In a decision that proved to be portentious, the Board decided in January 1974 to add a topic to its agenda that would go through various vicissitudes on its way to becoming Statement No. 33, *Financial Reporting and Changing Prices*, almost six years later.

Marshall Armstrong called 1973 and the first half of 1974 a time of "filling the pipelines," that is gathering data that the Board would need in order to begin actual deliberations on the topics on its technical agenda. Seeing the pipelines nearly filled in the spring of 1974, Armstrong moved to reshape the organization to cope with new needs and circumstances. No longer would Board members be directly involved in research and the drafting of documents. Those activities would be carried out, or overseen, by staff project managers, subject to Board review and approval. Board members would concentrate on absorbing and evaluating information developed by the staff and on forming both individual and collective conclusions about the issues and subissues. Most of the technical advisers to Board members became project managers, replaced by less experienced technical assistants, and the rest of the research personnel were organized into a unified Technical Activities Division.

It was this reshuffling that first gave rise to a perception on the part of some constituents, reluctant to criticize the Board members directly, that unpopular decisions came about only because the Board was dominated by its staff. Despite frequent and detailed denials, that complaint persists to this day.

The logic of the staff reorganization was demonstrated by the Board's final numbers for 1974. Issued were two Statements of Financial Accounting Standards, seven exposure drafts of proposed Statements for public comment, and six discussion memorandums to provide the basis for public hearings. Adoption of Statement No. 2, *Accounting for Research and Development Costs*, was the most newsworthy event, but Interpretation No. 3 regarding an APB Opinion on pension plans also was significant because it was the FASB's first explicit response to federal legislation, the Employee Retirement Income Security Act (ERISA) that was signed by President Gerald Ford on Labor Day 1974. The Board's entanglement with ERISA would continue for 11 more years, giving rise to four standards, of which No. 87, prescribing *Employers' Accounting for Pensions*, was among the most controversial of all.

In 1975, another piece of federal legislation had an even more profound effect on the FASB than ERISA, though not as long-lasting. It was EPCA, the Energy Policy and Conservation Act, born of the severe shortages of petroleum and the consequent run-up of prices in 1973 and 1974.

Accounting for oil and gas exploration and production costs was a highly controversial topic on which the APB had thrown in its hand and which the FASB had declined to add to its original agenda. But when it became apparent, as the energy crisis continued in 1975, that legislation would be adopted, the Board added to its agenda a project on *Financial Accounting and Reporting in the Extractive Industries with Emphasis on Oil and Gas*.

As originally drafted, EPCA would have required the SEC to "prescribe accounting practices" for oil- and gas-producing companies. The FASB saw this as a threat to its turf and sprang into action. Though it has never sought, nor felt that it needed, lobbying "clout" in Washington, the Board has, on rare occasions, petitioned members of Congress and their staffs. This was the first. The objective was simply to ensure that the final legislation was worded so as not to preclude delegation of the standard-setting assignment by the SEC to the FASB, and in this the Board was successful—though the final language of the Act stipulated that the SEC would have to satisfy itself that practices developed by the FASB would be observed by oil and gas producers to the same extent as would result if the Commission itself "prescribed such practices by rule."

EPCA was enacted just before Christmas in 1975, giving the FASB and/or SEC until December 22, 1977, to issue the accounting rules. The Commission, still lacking the standard-setting structure of its own that the Securities Exchange Act of 1934 had empowered it to create, gladly turned to the technical expertise of the FASB. Although the standard was produced on time, the drama continued and intensified until the latter part of 1978—and economic and social consequences were what it was all about.

In the annual report for 1974, Marshall Armstrong was pictured with his elbow resting on a large stack of bound papers amounting to 9,087 pages of public records compiled in that year. These included position papers, letters of comment, and public hearing transcripts—only the beginning of an avalanche of paper that before long would defy quantification. Armstrong's expression in the photograph and his comments in the text of the report seemed to reflect satisfaction with this volume of input to the Board's process. In the 1975 report, however, the emphasis of his remarks shifted from the quantitative to the qualitative. "The Board finds itself to be the focal point for expressions of many divergent points of view," he said, "ranging from the highly theoretical to the intensely pragmatic, from the purely philosophical to the blatantly self-interested." He observed that this range of positions was evident not only with regard to specific issues but also with regard to the overall thrust of the Board's work.[22]

Among the public records with which Marshall Armstrong was pictured in the 1974 annual report were comment letters and a public hearing transcript on Accounting for Contingencies, a project that culminated in Statement No. 5 of the same title early in 1975. (As an original entry on the Board's technical agenda in 1973, it had been known as "accruing for future losses.")

In 1974 and 1975, not only was the FASB still exploring and experimenting with various ways to do its job, but the universe of individuals having a direct interest in the setting of standards was still learning how to interact with the Board. The public record on Accounting for Contingencies reflects this.

For many years, a jealously defended prerogative of corporate management had been freedom to use various accounting devices to "smooth" earnings, enhancing them in years when the flow was weak, damping them in years when there was a sharp upward thrust, so as to achieve a steady, year-by-year progression. No matter that the normal ebb and flow of economic activity, if accurately represented in the financial statements, was more likely to reveal for most companies an upward slope over a long period—but one characterized by craggy upthrusts and downturns as business conditions changed from year to year. Management had learned long ago that Wall Street gurus, no less than ordinary mortals, crave stability and predictability. "Please, no surprises" has long been Wall Street's advice to corporate management, but management has taken the advice rather more literally than intended, as was pointed out at the public hearing in the spring of 1974.

Among the favored devices for bringing about the desired smoothing were accounting accruals, often loosely called *reserves*, for such contingencies as losses resulting from litigation, expropriation of assets, uncollectibility of receivables, claims arising from product warranties or product defects, and most notably, self-insured risks. Property and casualty insurance companies also were in the habit of accruing for catastrophic losses resulting from explosions, hurricanes, tornadoes, earthquakes, and the like. The trouble with these practices, in the eyes of the FASB and other purists, was that such events did not occur regularly, and the magnitude of their impact could not be estimated in advance. Therefore, the amount of accrual could be adjusted from year to year to suit management's convenience in reaching a desired level of reported earnings.

Commentators on FASB proposals at the time, thinking that the Board was concerned primarily with consistency and uniformity of financial reporting, did not yet understand the extent to which the new standard-setting body would oppose income-smoothing techniques. But they would understand later, after the Statement on Contingencies was issued and after Don Kirk preached the gospel that "if in fact an enterprise's operations are subject to economic influences that are manifested in fluctuating earnings, financial statements should report those fluctuations and not obscure them."[23]

Meanwhile, in the public comment process on contingencies in 1974, both industrial corporations and insurance companies were quite candid about their perceived need to smooth earnings. For example, a major energy company maintained that regular accruals were preferable to reporting large losses falling in the periods in which they occurred because of the undesirability of fluctuating earnings. In a seeming contradiction, a very large industrial company observed that catastrophic losses, such as those resulting from hurricanes and tornadoes, would occur both regularly and unpredictably. Therefore, the fluctuations in earnings that would result from elimination of accruals would not be justified. The company also complained that the proposal must be based on a presumption that users of financial statements expected irregular patterns of earnings.

In fact, the Financial Analysts Federation observed that self-insurance is not really insurance at all and said that if management decides not to purchase insurance, it must permit the financial statements to reflect the facts of actual loss experience. To do otherwise, it added, would distort the reporting process.

Nevertheless, the Financial Executives Institute claimed in its comment letter that smoothing earnings to present a picture of stability of operating results was gaining support from the users of financial statements. The Institute's spokesman at the public hearing said, "Ultimately, down the road, we are going to have a substantial loss which will impact income in a given year, and you won't have provided for that kind of an income charge. This creates a distorting influence on your income statement in the year in which you have the high losses."

Insurance companies feared that they were being forced to purchase reinsurance for catastrophe risks. This concern was articulated for them in a letter from the late Senator and former Vice President Hubert H. Humphrey, then chairman of the Joint Economic Committee of Congress. In an instance of what is now called "constituent service," Senator Humphrey ventured into the as yet uncharted waters of economic and social consequences, saying he had been told that the proposed accounting method would have undesirable consequences. He said he had learned, presumably from an insurance industry source, that adoption of the proposed rule would place a burden on insurance companies and could have adverse effects on the U.S. balance of payments, U.S. tax revenues, and U.S. employment.

Nevertheless, Statement No. 5 was issued early in 1975, requiring that it must be probable that a loss has occurred at the date of a company's financial statements and that the amount of loss can be reasonably estimated before an accrual can be made. The Statement also said, "The Board believes that confusion exists between accounting accruals . . . and the reserving or setting aside of specific assets to be used for a particular purpose or contingency."[24] In fact, many of the comment letters and testifiers at the public hearing stated flatly that accruing and reserving were, in effect, the same thing. In covering FASB activities, some of the news media that should know better still make the same mistake.

Statement No. 5, along with No. 2, *Accounting for Research and Development Costs*, also is notable in that those two Statements marked the Board's first formal attempts to come to grips with the *concepts* of assets and liabilities, which would figure prominently in the development of a conceptual framework a few years later.

The standard on contingencies was followed six months later by an even more controversial Statement that brought concerns about volatility of earnings to the fore in a different way. The subject was accounting for the translation of foreign currency transactions and foreign currency financial statements, and this time the Board was seen to be creating a new and higher level of volatility in the earnings statement, not merely taking away a method of avoiding it.

Statement No. 8 required that exchange gains and losses resulting from translation be taken into income in the current period and not be deferred. Monetary assets and liabilities such as cash, receivables, and payables would be translated at the foreign exchange rate in effect at the balance sheet date, and other assets and liabilities would be translated at the rate in effect when the assets were acquired or the liabilities were incurred.

The standard generally was regarded as being conceptually sound, but the earnings volatility it introduced was considered unacceptable by most international companies. There also was concern that it would encourage uneconomic hedging of foreign exchange risk. Statement No. 8 was protested vigorously when it was adopted by a 6–1 vote in 1975 and even more widely and vociferously in 1976, the year it went into effect. In the spring of 1976, after receiving numerous requests to reconsider the standard, the Board decided not to do so on grounds that the concerns expressed had been considered fully in its deliberations and were addressed in an appendix to the Statement. Two years later, however, the Board issued a call for public comment on the efficacy of FASB standards that had been in effect for at least two years and noted particularly that the ones on contingencies and foreign currency had "generated many comments and questions." More than 200 comment letters were received and, to no one's surprise, Statement No. 8 drew the heaviest fire: 88 percent of the respondents expressed concerns with it, almost three times as many as cited the runner-up, Statement No. 5.

In opening a Board meeting to consider the responses, Don Kirk, by now chairman, remarked that No. 8 "covers the most complex and difficult-to-understand problem the Board has faced." He spoke with authority, for he had been the Board member honcho on the project when it was undertaken in 1973.

Although FASB-sponsored research by Roland E. Dukes of Cornell found no significant effect of Statement No. 8 on the stock prices of multinational companies,[25] other research sponsored by the Board (Thomas G. Evans, William R. Folks, Jr., and Michael Jilling, University of South Carolina) found that the Statement had some impact on the way companies managed their exposure to foreign exchange rate changes. However, the data were inconclusive as to whether there was a significant increase or decrease in after-tax cash flows.[26]

In this and other instances, Don Kirk publicly questioned the judgment of executives who said they would deliberately take uneconomic actions merely to make accounting numbers look better. Nevertheless, the Board finally decided early in 1979 to reconsider No. 8, but the Statement remained in effect until a replacement, No. 52, was forthcoming almost three years later. Statement No. 52, which calls for the use of the current exchange rate in translating from a foreign "functional currency" to U.S. dollars and includes those adjustments directly in shareholders' equity rather than in income, was relatively well received. It reduced earnings volatility significantly.

As can be seen in the brief descriptions of technical issues presented here, there is no way that accounting standards, though often more complex, can display the elegant logic and precision of mathematical formulas. Even the most determinedly purist standard setters must bend, at least a little, to the perceptions and wishes of their constituents, as the members of the FASB did in developing a new standard for foreign currency translation. But in doing so, they must consider how much credibility they can afford to lose with users of financial information—and particularly with the SEC and the U.S. Congress. As former Board member Victor H. Brown has pointed out, it is a matter of balance.

In his final speech as chairman of the FASB, Marshall Armstrong made some prescient comments about the Board's relationship with its corporate constituency.

There is nothing sinister about the efforts of corporate management to influence the Board's conclusions. On the contrary, those efforts ought to be recognized as a wholly legitimate part of the standard-setting process. Once the Board has acted, however, the corporate sector has conformed to its decisions. Even if they view some of the decisions with intense distaste, business executives have displayed an admirable restraint—not only faithfully complying with all the standards, but foregoing any attempt to overturn them by appealing to other authorities to intervene on their behalf.[27]

That was the good news. Armstrong also displayed an intuition about things to come.

This happy state of affairs may not, of course, continue indefinitely. The final result of the Board's deliberations on accounting for exploratory costs in the oil and gas industry, for example, could well provoke a campaign to repudiate the decision. No one can dispute the right of those who feel aggrieved by an action of the Board to strive to have it modified or rescinded. But if such tactics are too often adopted, the strength of the FASB could be fatally impaired.

Subsequent events more than justified Armstrong's apprehension, but meanwhile there were some housekeeping moves worthy of note. The Board suffered its first resignation. John Queenan, a veteran of the stand-ard-setting wars since the Committee on Accounting Procedure in the 1950s, opted to spend more time with his wife who was in ill health. He was replaced by Oscar S. Gellein, one of the acknowledged intellectuals of the public accounting profession and a member of the Trueblood Commit-tee on Objectives in 1971–73. Gellein, already retired for a few months, happened to have been an important partner in the same firm of which Queenan had been head, giving rise to an impression in some quarters that there was a "Haskins & Sells seat" on the Board. This was a stretch, as it has become fashionable to say, because there were still eight major accounting firms towering over all the others, and there were only seven places on the Board, with three at least tacitly allocated at that time to other disciplines.

With John Queenan gone, Bob Sprouse became vice chairman and would continue in that role until the end of his final term at the close of 1985.

New trustees of the Foundation, effective late in 1974, were Wilbert A. ("Wib") Walker, president of the United States Steel Corporation, and Philip L. Defliese, at that time managing partner of Coopers & Lybrand. Phil Defliese also was the last chairman of the Accounting Principles Board and subsequently, after he retired from Coopers and took up a teaching position at Columbia University, became a member of the Governmental Account-ing Standards Board.

There was a second realignment of the FASB staff, this time organizing it, in effect, into two separate staffs—one to deal with major long-term problems such as those already discussed above, and the other to handle "emerging problems," those of limited scope that arise out of the day-to-day experience of the public accounting firms as they encounter new kinds of accounting problems reflecting new kinds of business transactions. This development followed by several months the formation by the Board of a Screening Committee on Emerging Problems to advise it on such matters.

Another internal move of lasting significance was establishment of a Practice Fellow program that would bring first two, then later three or four, outstanding senior managers from public accounting firms to the Board each year for two years of intensive experience in dealing primarily with those same emerging problems. The Fellows also serve as consultants on a wide range of projects and, in a few cases, have been project managers on such major endeavors as accounting for income taxes.

Similar programs for accountants in industry and academe were insti-
tuted soon afterward. Though productive, they have not provided as vital
or consistent a pool of expertise from the outside world as the Practice
Fellow program has over the years. The reason is not the quality of the
people but the fact that industry employers and university faculties generally lack a depth of personnel comparable to that which allows large public
accounting firms the luxury of making outstanding people available for a
two-year tour of duty at the FASB.

On the technical side, a project on accounting by debtors and creditors
for debt restructurings was added to the agenda, and this would lead to an
extremely contentious dialogue with the banking industry, which felt
strongly enough about the issues to field its top guns at a public hearing in
1976.

Despite deep dissatisfaction with the original Statement on foreign
currency translation, which, after all, affected only a relatively small number of large companies that had multinational operations, Corporate America was remarkably tolerant of the FASB, as Marshall Armstrong noted in
his farewell address. It was still fearful of a government takeover of
standard setting, and it had good reason to be.

In 1976, subcommittees of both the U.S. Senate and House of Representatives worked toward publishing reports that would be dangerous to
the health of the FASB.

In 1975, the Board had made a first tentative step toward establishing a
presence in Washington. A one-room office was opened in one of those
places that provide office space and rudimentary secretarial and other
office services for largely absentee tenants. It was manned part-time by a
staff member who commuted from Connecticut. The primary mission was
one of liaison, not of lobbying. The main object was information exchange
between the FASB and those on Capitol Hill and in the departments and
agencies of the federal government who dealt with issues in which the
standard setters were interested and had acquired some knowledge. Three
years later, a more formal office, though still minimal, staffed by a full-time
resident representative and a part-time secretary, was opened. This modest
facility served the Board extremely well until the Foundation trustees,
under budget and other kinds of pressure, made a shortsighted decision to
close it down at the beginning of 1991.

NOTES

1. Attributed to Richard Hooker by Samuel Johnson in the Preface to
Johnson's *Dictionary of the English Language* (London, 1755).

2. See Jane Clapp, *Professional Ethics and Insignias* (Metuchen, N. J.: Scarecrow
Press, 1974).

3. W. A. Paton and A. C. Littleton, *An Introduction to Corporate Accounting Standards* (Sarasota, Fla.: American Accounting Association, 1940).

4. Bylaws of the Financial Accounting Foundation, Chapter A, Article II-A, Section 2, 1973.

5. Robert T. Sprouse and Maurice Moonitz, *A Tentative Set of Broad Accounting Principles for Business Enterprises* (New York: American Institute of Public Accountants, 1962).

6. Bylaws of the Financial Accounting Foundation, Chapter A, Article III-A, Section 3, 1973.

7. Certificate of Incorporation of the Financial Accounting Foundation, Third article, June 27, 1972.

8. Lee J. Seidler, "The Financial Accounting Standards Board: Goldfish in a Pool of Sharks," *Accountant's Magazine*, October 1973, 558.

9. Maurice Moonitz, "Why Is It So Difficult to Agree Upon a Set of Accounting Principles?" *Australian Accountant*, November 1968, 621.

10. Stephen A. Zeff, "The Rise of Economic Consequences" (Stanford University Lectures in Accounting, 1978).

11. Dale L. Gerboth, "Research, Intuition, and Politics in Accounting Inquiry," *Accounting Review*, July 1973, 475.

12. David M. Hawkins, "Financial Accounting, the Standards Board, and Economic Development" (Emanuel Saxe Distinguished Lecture at Baruch College, City University of New York, November 1973).

13. Marshall S. Armstrong, address to the Society of Business Writers, New York, May 1973.

14. Donald J. Kirk, "Private Standard Setting and Public Accountability," address to the Business Council, Hot Springs, Va., October 1979.

15. Donald J. Kirk, "Corporate Accounting and Accountability in Turbulent Times," John M. Olin Lecture, Fairfield University, Fairfield, Conn., May 1981; published as *FASB Viewpoints*, June 1, 1981.

16. Donald J. Kirk, "Can You Hear Me Now?" address to the Financial Executives Institute Conference on Current Financial Reporting Issues, New York, November 1985; published as *FASB Viewpoints*, December 9, 1985.

17. Dennis R. Beresford, "Financial Reporting: Comparability and Competition," address at Stern School of Business Administration, New York University, October 1990.

18. David Solomons, "The Politicization of Accounting," *Journal of Accountancy*, November 1978, 65.

19. Frederick Andrews, "Accounting Standards Panel Being Faulted as Moving Too Slowly on Urgent Problems," *Wall Street Journal*, October 9, 1973.

20. Securities and Exchange Commission, "Statement of Policy on the Establishment and Improvement of Accounting Principles and Standards," *Accounting Series Release No. 150*, December 20, 1973.

21. Rule 203 of the AICPA's Rules of Conduct provides a possible exception for rare instances in which literal application of a standard can be demonstrated to produce a misleading result, but a severe burden of proof is placed on the auditor.

22. Marshall S. Armstrong, Financial Accounting Standards Board Annual Report, 1975, 10.

23. Donald J. Kirk, paper delivered at Annual Alumni Business Conference, New York University Graduate School of Business Administration, May 1978; published as *FASB Viewpoints*, August 4, 1978.

24. FASB Statement No. 5, *Accounting for Contingencies*, March 1975, para. 61.

25. Roland E. Dukes, FASB Research Report, *An Empirical Investigation of the Effects of Statement of Financial Accounting Standards No. 8 on Security Return Behavior* (Stamford, Conn.: December 1978).

26. Thomas G. Evans, William R. Folks, Jr., and Michael Jilling, FASB Research Report, *The Impact of Statement of Financial Accounting Standards No. 8 on the Foreign Exchange Risk Management Practices of American Multinationals: An Economic Impact Study* (Stamford, Conn.: November 1978).

27. Marshall S. Armstrong, paper delivered at Butler University Financial Reporting Conference, December 1977; excerpted in *FASB Status Report*, January 5, 1978.

Chapter Three

A Baptism of Fire

Just as war has been said to be too important to be left to the generals, so with great respect I am suggesting that accounting rules are too important to be left only to the accountants.

Walter B. Wriston[1]
Former Chairman, Citicorp

Despite spirited debate that already had arisen over specific issues, the FASB in its first three years generally was remarked on with avuncular approval, followed by confessions of faith. The calm, however, was shattered in 1976 when the Board suddenly found that it was the target of heavy artillery trained on it from three different directions.

It had its first engagement with the massed firepower of the banking industry, the precursor of several passages at arms sparked by emerging and multiplying problems in the financial sector. In Washington, the staffs of subcommittees in both the Senate and House of Representatives were at work on reports that would, in effect, challenge the Board's legitimacy. And ostensibly within the Board's own camp, a major accounting firm first petitioned, then sued the SEC over the issue of whether its delegation of standard-setting authority to the FASB was legal.

In 1975, as debt was piling up and becoming more shaky, particularly in the real estate industry, the FASB was persuaded to add to its agenda a project of relatively narrow scope to consider accounting by the debtor when inability to meet the terms of an obligation brings about a "restructuring" of the debt, providing for a lower repayment, a stretched-out repayment period, and/or a lower interest rate. An exposure draft was issued and a public hearing held before year's end, but it was almost a nonevent: Only 63 comment letters were received and only five testifiers appeared at the public hearing, an all-time low.

Meanwhile, however, New York City was having a close encounter with bankruptcy, and the difficulties of other municipal, and even state, governmental units dramatized the fragility of many lenders' positions. Accordingly, at the close of 1975 the FASB abandoned its debtor-only project and focused its attention on formulating rules for the accounting and reporting by *both* debtors and creditors in "troubled debt" restructurings. That was when alarm bells began to ring throughout the banking industry.

The noise level increased markedly five months later when a 92-page discussion memorandum was published, setting forth the issues and a range of possible approaches to solving them.

In those early years, the public was not yet accustomed to the Board's modus operandi and often mistook the intent of the various classes of FASB publications. This was, and still is, particularly true where a project is of especially keen interest to an entire industry, most of whose members do not normally pay much attention to the standard-setting process. It also is particularly true of discussion memorandums, which are intended to be neutral documents setting forth the various issues within a project, along with possible alternative solutions to them. The purpose is simply to elicit information and comment from the public, but many persist in believing that if something is published under the imprint of the FASB, it must be a clear indication of how the Board intends to decide the issues.

The discussion memorandum "Accounting by Debtors and Creditors When Debt Is Restructured" was an extreme case, made even more difficult by a semantic misunderstanding. As used by accountants, the terms *current value accounting* and *present value accounting* imply a system under which all assets and liabilities would be revalued each time financial statements were issued. Few accountants, and certainly no members of the FASB in 1976, could foresee a time when such a system might be adopted. Opposition to it would be almost universal. The Board's intent was simply to consider ways of assigning a new value to restructured debt at the time of restructuring—a value whose basis then would remain constant in subsequent reporting periods.

There are, and have been for many years, certain items that may be reported in financial statements at current cost, or current market value, such as some inventories, investments in marketable securities, and assets that are expected to be sold at prices lower than previous carrying amounts. Against this background, the Board felt comfortable in setting forth in the discussion memorandum, without indicating a preference for any of them, five possible attributes that may be measured to determine the respective amounts for asset and debt when there is a restructuring. The first, and most obvious, was "historical entry value." The fourth, almost as innocuous, was "expected exit value in due course of business." But the other three were market value, present value of future cash flows based on the historical rate of interest, and present value of future cash flows based on the cost of money during the period the asset was expected to be held.[2] Hence, the alarm in the banking industry. Bankers could count, or thought they could: The score was 3–2 against them.

The table in the discussion memorandum in which these attributes were laid out in bloodlessly neutral language dominated the subsequent debate, to Marshall Armstrong's evident exasperation. The American Bankers Association (ABA) issued a call to arms, urging its 14,000 members to do battle against imminent invasion of their accounts by the dreaded "current value."[3] Of the 894 comment letters the FASB received, 721 were from banks, bank holding companies, and associations of same. The total number was a record that would endure until a group of electric utility companies organized a similar campaign a decade later, again missing the point that quality, not quantity, of argument was what the Board was looking for.

With regard to restructured debt, the major public accounting firms and many sophisticated industrial, commercial, and financial institutions weighed in as usual with careful and detailed analyses of the issues, but in sheer numbers, these were overwhelmed by simple cries for deliverance from the evils of current value. The letter from one small-town banker contained a single simple declarative sentence stating that he was opposed to current value. Another saw the proposal as creating nothing but problems and pleaded with the Board to concentrate on solving existing problems instead of creating new ones. Some were less polite. A letter from a country banker used a barnyard epithet to describe the proposal and expressed the hope that the FASB would "see the light" before it was too late.

The prospect of Armageddon also was viewed from on high. Arthur F. Burns, chairman of the Federal Reserve Board, expressed "deep concern" that current value accounting might be visited on the banking industry. He predicted that adoption of such an accounting rule would undermine the ability of banks to function effectively, thereby impeding the performance of the economy generally. Paul A. Volcker, who later succeeded Burns as chairman of the Fed but was then president of the Federal Reserve Bank of New York, argued that current value accounting could interfere with the efforts of banks to improve their capital positions, with similarly disastrous impact on the economy.

In opening the public hearing, Marshall Armstrong took pains to try to lay down a more realistic basis for discussion, but it was too late. The rhetoric of the testifiers already had been shaped by unfounded fear that banks might be required to revalue every asset and every liability every time they issued financial statements. For his pains, Armstrong received a

"Dear Marshall" letter from a onetime banker friend in his hometown of Indianapolis that, in effect, excoriated him for misrepresentation.

In characteristic fashion, Don Kirk went to the heart of the matter in questioning testifiers at the public hearing. An exchange with David Rockefeller, then chairman of the Chase Manhattan Bank, is illustrative:

Kirk: Mr. Rockefeller, I hope I can relieve the apprehension of some of the bankers. I don't know if I'll succeed, but certainly it's the intention of the FASB to solve this problem within the framework of historical cost accounting, and you'll find—

Rockefeller: But I didn't hear it.

Kirk: I may take away what I just gave, because as we study this project we see the perceptions of the historical cost system vary dramatically among the many respondents. . . . Some of the concepts which concern you, some people feel that they are firmly within the historical cost framework

Later in the same exchange:

Kirk: It's the potential fluctuations in earnings . . . that you feel would be misleading to your shareholders?

Rockefeller: Yes, I do. Because in many instances, and I say both with securities that are listed on the market and loans that are made by institutions temporarily in trouble, they would reflect losses perhaps at a given moment, which would be fully recovered, and we see no reason to inflict [*sic*] the profit and loss statements of our institutions with those temporary changes. If it's a permanent change, that's a different question.

Still later:

Kirk: Is it the . . . perception of shareholders that is of concern? Some people might argue that stretching out the maturity in effect represents an economic loss; that continuing a holding of something at less than a market rate or the period beyond which you originally intended to hold it is perceived by some to be an economic loss, measurable or not, but some people feel that it should be reflected now. Is it the shareholders' perception that is disturbing to you?

Rockefeller: Well, the shareholders' perceptions, there are two or three aspects to that. There's first of all that shareholders have expressed concern that New York banks have assumed such a large amount of City and State debt, given the fact that the City and State have been experiencing financial difficulties. I think we feel that we've been fully justified in that we expect a minimum of losses. However, it is a fact also that the shareholders are going to be further distressed if they see that we are being forced to write down in our portfolio investments as a result of stretching out which, in our judgment, is going to help the City survive and is in the best interests of not only the City, but also of the lenders to the City.

It remained for Walter B. Wriston, then chairman of Citicorp and Citibank, to ring the changes on a situation that was at the top of everyone's mind at the time. "If the banks that held the New York City obligations," he said, "had been required to record an immediate write-off of say, 25 percent of principal as a result of restructuring, that restructuring just might not have happened." He did not address the question of whether failing to report such write-offs constituted "fair presentation."

In the end, the Board issued Statement No. 15,[4] prescribing what the *New York Times* called a "conventional and relatively mild" accounting treatment that would be applied prospectively instead of retroactively as many bankers had feared. A lender would not recognize a loss from a restructuring unless the total of future payments of principal and interest would be less than the amount of the recorded investment before restructuring.

Don Kirk and Oscar Gellein dissented.

The Statement still is in effect but is generally regarded as one of the FASB's weaker efforts. Walter Schuetze, a long-time proponent of current value, left the Board just as the process that led to Statement 15 was beginning. Fifteen years later, as chief accountant of the SEC, he would say: "An entire generation of accountants has been retarded by Statement No. 15."[5]

Statement No. 15 enjoyed a flurry of notoriety in the mid-1980s when the increasingly desperate regulators of the savings and loan industry were grasping at straws to keep their fiefdom above water. Several of them testified before congressional committees that application of FASB Statement No. 15 provided a way for lending institutions to avoid recognizing loan losses. In testimony before the Subcommittee on Oversight and Investigations of the House Committee on Energy and Commerce in 1986, Don Kirk was at pains to explain why this wouldn't float. He pointed out that Statement No. 5, *Accounting for Contingencies*, requires financial institutions to evaluate the collectibility of amounts due under newly restructured terms. "If careful assessment of a loan receivable shows that full collection is still questionable after a restructuring," he said, "Statement 5 requires recognition of the loss if the loss has not already been recognized or if prior recognition was inadequate."[6]

For most of 1975 and 1976, the staff of the Subcommittee on Oversight and Investigations of the House Committee on Interstate and Foreign Commerce was kept busy accumulating many thousands of pages of documents and transcripts of public hearings that ultimately were processed into a 750-page report titled *Federal Regulation and Regulatory Reform*.

The report, which was approved by a 10–1 subcommittee vote, ranked nine federal regulatory agencies according to fidelity to their congressional mandate, quantity and quality of activity, effectiveness of enforcement programs, and quality of public participation. By these criteria, the SEC ranked at the top, but it was not exempt from severe criticism in one area—its permissiveness in allowing the private sector to establish standards for financial accounting and reporting.

The subcommittee concluded: "The results of the Commission's 1938 decision, by a 3–2 vote, to rely primarily on the private accounting profession to establish accounting principles has been disappointing at best." Then, after negative reviews of the AICPA's Committee on Accounting Procedure and Accounting Principles Board, it had this to say about the FASB:

The FASB has accomplished virtually nothing toward resolving fundamental accounting problems plaguing the profession. These include the plethora of optional "generally accepted" accounting principles, the ambiguities inherent in many of those principles, and the manifestations of private accountants' lack of independence with respect to their corporate clients. Considering the FASB's record, the SEC's continued reliance on the private accounting profession is questionable.

"Thus," the report concluded, "to the maximum extent practicable, the SEC should prescribe by rule a framework of uniform accounting principles."[7]

Though the subcommittee boasted of having heard 220 witnesses in 28 days of public hearings, these conclusions were based almost entirely on testimony by Abraham J. Briloff, Emanuel Saxe Distinguished Professor of Accounting at Baruch College in the City University of New York and longtime critic of accounting standards and the public accounting profession. Briloff told the subcommittee:

I have observed the ways in which it [FASB] has avoided the critical issues, vacillated on other controversial matters, and handed out special dispensations in order to obtain a consensus for a particular standard. I expected much, much more from a select body endowed with presumptive independence and supposedly possessed of intellectual might, integrity and intrepidity. In short, we have had a surfeit of compromise, of vulgar pragmatism, of pussy-footing and inching along.

Within days of the report's publication, Marshall Armstrong made what the *New York Times* characterized as a "stinging counterattack" in a seven-page letter to the subcommittee chairman, Representative John E. Moss.[8] Indeed, the language was stronger than is normally employed in such circumstances, and this dismayed some of Armstrong's colleagues. In the end, it proved effective, however.

The letter began by describing five major areas in which the subcommittee report was "highly misleading." Armstrong pointed out, among many other things, that one sentence of the Briloff testimony quoted above contained three allegations that were "utterly without foundation"—those having to do with avoidance of critical issues, vacillation on controversial matters, and handing out special dispensations. Armstrong said that the reason for the report's

failure to reflect reality is readily apparent: almost exclusive reliance for information and viewpoints about financial accounting standards on a single hearing witness, Professor Abraham J. Briloff. I find it puzzling in the extreme that only one witness was heard on the subject. . . . Certainly the Financial Accounting Standards Board, which has been at the center of every other discussion of standard setting that I have been aware of in the last three years, was not invited to testify. Indeed, we did not learn that a hearing had taken place until after the fact.

Armstrong charged that the subcommittee "failed to carry out a clear responsibility either to obtain in-depth and balanced testimony, or at least to verify the information provided by its star witness. Either exercise would have been instructive, and should have led to rather different conclusions."

Congressman Moss did introduce legislation, but it went nowhere. One year later, he turned out to be a staunch supporter of the FASB in a congressional battle over oil and gas accounting.

Briloff promised to reply to the Armstrong letter in "an appropriate forum" but never did.

Starting—and finishing—a few months after the Moss subcommittee in the House, the staff of the Subcommittee on Reports, Accounting, and Management of the Senate Committee on Government Operations conducted an investigation of the relationships among major public accounting firms, their corporate clients, the professional associations, and the private sector structure for establishing financial accounting standards. Published in January 1977 as a staff report, not an official report of the subcommittee, under the title *The Accounting Establishment*,[9] the Senate effort outdid its House counterpart in sheer volume by a wide margin— 1,760 pages to a mere 750.

The Accounting Establishment reflected the Prairie Populist bent of the subcommittee chairman, the late Senator Lee Metcalf of Montana, in its preoccupation with the size of the "Big Eight" accounting firms and the supposedly conspiratorial links between them, their "big-business" clients, the professional associations, and the FASB. The possibility of antitrust prosecution was suggested as an antidote. "The inability to divorce private influence from private control impairs all efforts to achieve public confidence in a system which vests public authority in private organizations," the report said. It recommended that Congress assume responsibility for establishing financial accounting standards either directly or through the General Accounting Office (GAO), which is an arm of the Congress, or a new body to be created by Congress. In the staff's view, the SEC had disqualified itself by delegating standard-setting authority to the private sector in the first place.

This time the Foundation led the public counterattack, which was a relatively bland demurrer to the report's conclusions. It remained for the FASB itself to deliver a coup de grâce, although it was one that would not capture the interest of the news media. Hearings that were held by the subcommittee a few months later were rendered almost pointless as far as accounting standard setting was concerned by an exhaustive piece of FASB staff research, incorporated in a joint Foundation-FASB submission to the subcommittee that demolished the report's central thesis.[10] Analysis of all comment letters, position papers, and public hearing testimony that had been received on the 12 subjects on which the FASB had issued Statements up to that time revealed a completely random pattern. There was no evidence that even large and powerful clients influenced accounting firms, that either accounting firms or corporations influenced their professional associations, or that any of them unduly influenced the FASB. The evidence for that research, of course, was limited to the years 1973–76. As will be seen in later chapters, there is reason to believe that different results would be obtained if similar research were conducted today.

In effect, however, the committee staff's case as of that time was disproved, and the official subcommittee report that was issued 11 months later in fact was mildly complimentary of the FASB.[11]

Though the FASB survived unscathed, even strengthened in the opinion of some, the interest the two subcommittees displayed in standard setting did have some significant effects. In furtherance of their oversight function, the trustees of the Financial Accounting Foundation are empowered to "conduct periodic reviews of the structure for establishing and improving financial accounting and reporting standards in such scope and at such times as the trustees shall determine."[12] As the "Moss Report" was published and the "Metcalf Report" was awaited, the FASB was nearing the end of its first five years of operation. It seemed like an appropriate time. Accordingly, the trustees' structure committee, chaired by Russell E. Palmer, then managing partner of Touche Ross & Co. (now part of Deloitte & Touche), was directed to conduct a comprehensive review of the Board's mission, structure, operations, and relations with relevant external groups—and was given only a little more than four months to do the job, with a report and recommendations due no later than April 30, 1977.

In a preface to its report, the committee said, "Approximately 2,000 hours of senior-level time has been devoted to the study. Much of that time was spent by the six members of the structure committee, all of whom are trustees, and each of whom represents one of the six sponsoring organizations of the FASB."[13]

Certain organizational changes that are described in Chapter 2 as having occurred in 1977 were direct results of the structure committee report, along with many others. Among those other changes were regular publication of "short- and longer-range plans for technical projects" and correspondence with other organizations regarding technical issues of broad interest; greater public accessibility to public records; "layman's language" summaries incorporated into Board publications; an expanded role for the Advisory Council; and greater attention to the problems of small business.

The net result was greater openness and responsiveness to the concerns of the Board's constituents. Subsequent structure committee reviews in 1979, 1982, and 1988 also have focused on the FASB's responsibilities to its constituents. No attention ever has been paid in an organized way by anyone to what the constituents' responsibilities may be if they're really serious about wanting to retain a self-regulatory standard-setting process in the private sector.

In 1976, a major accounting firm puzzled most observers and highlighted the question of constituent responsibilities. After fuming for nine months, along with all the other major firms, Arthur Andersen & Co. petitioned the SEC to rescind its Accounting Series Release 177, which required auditors to attest, when a client changed from one accounting method to another in an area where no specific rule existed, that the new method was "preferable" to the old. When the Commission declined to do so, Andersen sought an injunction against enforcement. If Andersen had stopped there, the profession would have been united behind it, because most accountants feared that they would be asked to make judgments under 177 that belonged in the purview of the FASB or AICPA, and that once having found a method to be preferable in one set of circumstances, they would have difficulty convincing clients that it was not preferable in other circumstances. Lurking in the background was fear of increased legal liability.

But Andersen did not stop there. It sailed on into choppier waters where the other firms were unwilling to send boats. It demanded rescission of ASR 150—the Commission's policy statement saying that FASB pronouncements had "substantial authoritative support" and practices contrary to them did not. Andersen and its feisty chairman, Harvey E. Kapnick, long known as a maverick, argued that the SEC could not legally require corporations to follow FASB rules without first adopting each one of them as its own, following the cumbersome procedural steps required by the Federal Administrative Procedure Act. Most observers, including the other major accounting firms, the FASB, and the SEC, believed that this would mean the end of standard setting in the private sector.

In a decision that has not received a great deal of attention since that time but was a significant victory for the concept of self-regulation as well as for the SEC and FASB, a federal district court in Chicago twice found the Andersen suit to be without merit, and that was the end of the legal assault on ASR 177 and 150.

Mr. Kapnick soldiered on for a while, however, rehashing his firm's argument and severely criticizing the FASB's structure and operations in a major speech that autumn that was galling enough for both Marshall Armstrong and the trustees to issue statements rebutting it.

In the end, however, Kapnick did score some points. Changes recommended by the structure committee in its 1977 report and implemented by the FASB the following year had the effect of making the Board's procedures more stringent than those required of government agencies by the Federal Administrative Procedure Act. And his vendetta against the FASB had an odd ending. In 1978, he was elected a trustee of the Financial Accounting Foundation, but he served only a year before his partners deposed him as head of Arthur Andersen, and he left the firm to become a banker.

At least one congressman was disappointed when Kapnick's suit was dismissed. Representative Charles A. Vanik, chairman of the Subcommittee on Oversight of the House Ways and Means Committee, had been stimulated enough by Kapnick's moves to order up draft legislation—and a draft speech to introduce it on the House floor. His theme was that the longtime relationship between the SEC and the accounting profession was being torn asunder by Arthur Andersen's action, and therefore the Commission's delegation of standard-setting authority to the private sector no longer was viable.

That was the beginning of the congressman's proposed speech. At the end, he would declaim that the SEC had tolerated confusion and ambiguity in accounting principles for too long and that the Commission would have to act promptly in view of the imminent collapse of the private sector's standard-setting efforts.

The speech never was delivered, of course, and the bill never introduced. The FASB staff already had provided documentation that should have been sufficient to disprove Vanik's thesis, and when the Andersen suit was, in effect, thrown out of court, the prospect of striking legislative sparks over the supposed misfeasance and nonfeasance of the private sector standard setters disappeared at the stroke of the judge's gavel.

Strengthened though the FASB may have been in retrospect, while they were going on, the Moss, Metcalf, and Andersen episodes gave rise to widespread uncertainty about the Board's life expectancy. This, in turn, created difficulty for the trustees in their search for someone to fill the vacancy on the Board resulting from the resignation of Walter Schuetze in the spring of 1976. Ralph E. Walters, director of professional standards for Touche Ross International (now part of Deloitte & Touche), finally agreed to accept appointment out of a sense of duty to his profession. The Board had operated with a vacancy for eight months—and the trustees' search had gone on for ten.

In the FASB's first five years of existence, the general price level in the United States rose more than 41 percent as measured by the Gross National Product (GNP) Implicit Price Deflator. Less than a year after the FASB began operations, members of its Advisory Council were urging the Board to examine the financial reporting implications of an accelerating rise in prices. In January 1974, Marshall Armstrong announced that a project entitled "Reporting the Effects of General Price-Level Changes" had been added to the agenda and a public hearing would be held by midyear. A current-cost approach was not then contemplated. The term *inflation accounting* was avoided scrupulously for two reasons: The prices of specific commodities and the assets of specific companies were changing at quite different rates; and downside changes in the general price level would have to be recognized in deflationary periods, even though such a circumstance was not foreseeable at the time.

In the comment letters and at the public hearing, the Board heard from most quarters, atypically, that something *should* be done, but there was wide divergence of opinion, as usual, as to *what* should be done.

At the end of 1974, the Board issued an exposure draft of a proposed Statement that would have required supplemental disclosure, outside the audited financial statements, of accounting information restated for changes in the "general purchasing power of the dollar," as indicated by the GNP Implicit Price Deflator. Because general purchasing power accounting was relatively untried in the United States, the Board said, the comment period would be an unprecedented 270 days. More significantly, the Board asked corporations to experiment during the long comment period with restatements of their actual financial results, and 101 companies cooperated.

Again, there was divergence of opinion, as illustrated in the comment letters of two future Board members. Robert A. Morgan, then controller of the Caterpillar Tractor Co., supported the proposal with some helpful but relatively minor suggestions for modification. Victor H. Brown, then controller of the Standard Oil Company of Indiana, expressed the belief that restatement in units of general purchasing power would not yield "useful or relevant information" and urged the Board to consider the possibility of requiring supplemental statements based on replacement costs.

The bankers' fear of their old bugaboo "current value" impelled them to line up in opposition to any action, but most commentators continued to see a need for some way of ending, or at least moderating, the upward distortion of most companies' reported earnings under inflationary conditions.

Results of the "field test," published more than a year later, showed that for most of the companies restated net income was lower than reported net income, in a few cases by as much as 60 or 70 percent. At the same time, companies in industries characterized by high debt-to-equity ratios, such as public utilities, showed higher net income on a price level–adjusted basis. In general, the participating companies' rates of return on stockholders' equity were lower when restated, their dividend payout ratios were higher, and their debt to equity ratios were lower. Clearly, there were wide discrepancies between financial results reported on the historical cost basis and what was going on in the real world. Subsequent findings by the FASB itself and independent sources confirmed these results, and even went beyond them.

Meanwhile, however, the FASB had suspended its project on financial reporting in units of general purchasing power. Early in 1976, the SEC sat down at the table and drew a hand. Sensing an urgent issue, and being unwilling to wait for the FASB's lengthy due process to play itself out, Sandy Burton got the Commission to issue ASR 190, which required approximately 1,200 large registrants to report the current replacement cost of their assets. Whereupon the FASB folded its general price level hand, at least for the time being.

That decision provided at least some temporary comfort to the bankers, who, along with others, had a great fear of the current value accounting that was thought to be lurking in the closet from whence the general purchasing power proposal had been brought forth. Whether in candor or out of carelessness, Walter Wriston seemed to contradict himself in a speech in which he ritually denounced current value but allowed that recording depreciation "on some kind of replacement value" would make sense because it would increase cash flows needed for capital investment.[14]

Several months before ASR 190 was issued, Burton wrote a guest editorial for *Business Week* in which he said that restatement in units of general purchasing power "may be affirmatively misleading rather than helpful to the users." He called it "Pu Pu accounting."[15]

In announcing its decision not to proceed, the Board referred to the SEC's replacement cost requirement and cited lack of understanding of general purchasing power information on the part of the public but promised to continue consideration of the subject in the measurement phase of its conceptual framework project. As Don Kirk later described the process:

It became clear to us that our constituents were generally strong in their belief that profits were overstated but were widely divided about whether profits should be adjusted for the change in the general rate of inflation or adjusted for the change in specific prices of inventory, plant, and equipment. . . . While the former might be considered more reliable information and the latter more relevant, there is useful information to be obtained from both methods.[16]

The result was that the venture in "inflation accounting" was revived and reintroduced to the public in December 1978 in the form of an exposure draft proposing that about 1,200 of the largest public companies (those with inventories, property, plant, and equipment of more than $125 million or total assets of more than $1 billion) be required to present as supplements to their financial statements information on income from continuing operations either on a current-cost basis or on the basis of historical cost adjusted for changes in the Consumer Price Index (CPI). The proposal encouraged use of current cost "unless historical cost/constant dollar information better reflects the effects of changing prices on the enterprise." The Board said it was providing this flexibility "in order to encourage experimentation that will help develop techniques for preparing and using data on the effects of price changes."

At the end of May, the Board sponsored a day-long conference in New York on reporting the effects of inflation, attended by 400 paying guests. A lineup of heavy hitters, including Paul McCracken, former chairman of the President's Council of Economic Advisers, Harold M. Williams, chairman of the SEC, and David Roderick, chairman of the United States Steel Corporation, cited a variety of reasons why some way for financial reports to portray realistically the ravages of inflation was badly needed.

The news media, for a change, were overwhelmingly supportive of the Board's effort. It was an issue whose implications were plain, even though the technical niceties of it were not, so they expressed their own opinions and eschewed their usual practice of fishing for provocative quotes from complainants. But commentators on the exposure draft, by and large, were not enthusiastic, providing early support for the Don Kirk theorem that desired changes in accounting become much less desirable when specific proposals are presented.

Many objected to the Board's expressed preference for current cost. Others complained that permitting two methods indicated that the Board was not completely convinced of the merits of either and that the flexibility would create "confusion" and "chaos." The flip side of that argument, expressed by one very large and prominent company, was that limiting the choice to two methods might inhibit rather than encourage experimentation. Heavy-industry and high-technology companies objected to use of the Consumer Price Index as not being germane to their businesses. Many complained that they had not been given enough time to study the proposal. One company with a strong balance sheet expressed the view that "gains" for others with high debt to equity ratios should be negated somehow so that highly leveraged companies would not appear to be more profitable under the constant dollar method than they really were.

Most disturbing—and predictive of future events—was that professional users of financial information, usually strong supporters of FASB projects, were cool to this one. The reason was that their interest in financial reporting is its value as a presumably reliable source of raw data that they can manipulate in their own ways to make their own analyses and projections. In their view, the trouble with price level–adjusted data was that they already had been manipulated in arbitrary ways by somebody else.

Statement No. 33, *Financial Reporting and Changing Prices,* was issued in September 1979. While continuing to emphasize experimentation, explicitly committing the Board to review of the Statement's application after five years, it required supplemental reporting of both current-cost and constant dollar information.

Adoption of No. 33 was not without ramifications in Washington. Before it could be made final, agreement had to be obtained from the Internal Revenue Service to amend its LIFO (last in, first out) inventory regulations so that supplemental or explanatory disclosure by a LIFO taxpayer of an earnings measurement on a basis other than historical cost would not violate the tax code. And shortly after the Statement was adopted, the SEC made good on its private assurances that ASR 190 would be phased out once an FASB standard was in place.

Meanwhile, there still was standard-setting work to be done on changing prices. Recognizing that Statement No. 33 was general in nature and that certain industries had specific measurement problems, the Board proceeded to develop standards on specialized assets in the mining, oil and gas, forest products, and real estate industries for issuance in 1980.

As the five-year trial period for changing prices disclosures neared its end, inflation was abating and such enthusiasm as there had been was waning. Some of the required disclosures were eliminated at the end of 1984, and two years later the whole exercise was made voluntary. This was disturbing to many, including Raymond C. Lauver, David Mosso, and Robert J. Swieringa, the three Board members who dissented. They argued, among other things, that inflation was not something that could be considered to be forever behind us; that when it returned, the cost of developing from scratch ways to cope with it in financial reporting would be unjustifiable since so much already had been invested; and that in the meantime, the FASB should devote some of its resources to improving techniques that in Statement No. 33 were admittedly imperfect.

None of the three chairmen of the FASB in its first two decades have been insensitive to the concerns, or gripes, of his constituency. Early in 1976, in response to the increasing noise level of the "economic consequences" argument, Armstrong instructed the staff to arrange for special research studies to detect any effects FASB standards were having on management behavior or securities markets. A half-dozen such studies were commissioned and published in the next six years. Most reported little or no economic effect. In response to Armstrong's charge, an open-ended call for research papers also went out to several hundred prominent researchers, and an FASB-sponsored conference was announced at which selected papers would be presented and would be published afterward. Twenty-two papers were received, most from academe, and 6 were considered to be worthy of publication in an FASB research report in 1978. Not surprisingly, the papers focused on the esoteric research interests of academics and did not address either the needs of the standard setters or the expressed fears of corporate management.

In 1976, the Securities Industry Association became the FASB's sixth sponsoring organization and immediately was entitled to place a member on the Foundation board of trustees. He was John C. Whitehead, then comanaging partner of Goldman, Sachs & Co., later deputy secretary of state.

NOTES

1. Walter B. Wriston, "Accounting to Whom for What?" address to the annual meeting of the National Association of Accountants, Miami, June 21, 1976.

2. FASB Discussion Memorandum, "Accounting by Debtors and Creditors When Debt Is Restructured," May 11, 1976.

3. Charles N. Stabler, "Bankers Warn of Drastic Effects if Change Is Ordered in Their Accounting Procedure," *Wall Street Journal*, July 23, 1976.

4. FASB Statement No. 15, *Accounting by Debtors and Creditors for Troubled Debt Restructurings*, June 1977.

5. Walter P. Schuetze, remarks at the Board Member Forum, a public meeting of past and present members of the FASB, Norwalk, Conn., May 18, 1993.

6. Donald J. Kirk, testimony before the U.S. House Subcommittee on Oversight and Investigations of the Committee on Energy and Commerce, April 24, 1986.

7. U.S. House, *Federal Regulations and Regulatory Reform*, report by the Subcommittee on Oversight and Investigations of the Committee on Interstate and Foreign Commerce (Washington, D.C.: GPO, October 1976).

8. Frederick Andrews, "Accounting Board Assails Criticism of Its Rule-Making," *New York Times*, October 21, 1976.

9. U.S. Senate, *The Accounting Establishment*, prepared by the staff of the Subcommittee on Reports, Accounting and Management, Committee on Government Operations (Washington, D.C.: GPO, December 1976).

10. *Statement of Position*, Financial Accounting Foundation and Financial Accounting Standards Board, April 14, 1977.

11. U.S. Senate, *Improving the Accountability of Publicly Owned Corporations and Their Auditors*, report by the Subcommittee on Reports, Accounting and Management, Committee on Government Operations (Washington, D.C.: GPO, November 1977).

12. Bylaws of the Financial Accounting Foundation, 1973.

13. *The Structure of Establishing Financial Accounting Standards*, report of the structure committee of the Financial Accounting Foundation, April 1977, 7.

14. Walter B. Wriston, "Accounting to Whom for What," address at the annual meeting of the National Association of Accountants, Miami, June 21, 1976.

15. John C. Burton, "Accounting that Allows for Inflation," *Business Week*, November 30, 1974, 71.

16. Donald J. Kirk, "Private Standard Setting and Public Accountability," address to the Business Council, Hot Springs, Va., October 1979; published in *FASB Viewpoints*, November 9, 1979.

Chapter Four

An Encounter with "No-Cost" Accounting

The art of life is passing losses on.

Robert Frost[1]

As noted in Chapter 2, the Energy Policy and Conservation Act of 1975 called for development by the SEC, or at its discretion by the FASB, of "accounting practices" that would yield data to become part of "a reliable energy data base related to the production of crude oil and natural gas" by December 22, 1977—24 months after passage of the Act. Discretion for the SEC to delegate this responsibility was hard-won through FASB representations to the House subcommittee responsible for the legislation, as was the 24–month time frame: The subcommittee initially wanted 12, a period into which the FASB's due process simply could not be fitted.

No explicit wording in the Act specified that one of the two methods of accounting then prevalent in the industry must be eliminated, but the intent was clear. Creation of a "reliable data base" implied a need for comparable data from the companies whose reports would be fed into that data base. Besides, the principal author of the relevant part of the Act, Representative John Moss, whom we met in Chapter 3, was at the same time quarterbacking a subcommittee report that would come down hard on the FASB for failing, in its brief three-year history, to eliminate all "accounting alternatives."

Nevertheless, interested parties later would argue that since the Act did not explicitly call for elimination of one or the other of the two methods, both should be allowed to continue despite the sharply different results they produced.

Had EPCA been enacted a decade earlier, there would have been little argument about the approach the standard should take. Although there were many variations on it, there was one principal way to account for exploration and development costs associated with oil and gas production. Under this method, known as "successful efforts," the costs known *not* to have resulted in proven reserves were charged to expense immediately, which meant that they had a negative impact on the income statement.

By the early 1960s a new technique known as "full-cost" accounting had caught the fancy of many smaller and midsize producing companies. Under this method, the costs of *un*successful efforts miraculously became amortizable assets. The potential for improving both balance sheet and income statement was obvious, although a large number of smaller companies continued to use the traditional accounting method—and generally did not encounter difficulty in attracting capital versus similar full-cost companies.

However, spokesmen for the hundreds of companies that had adopted full-cost (the total number of publicly owned U.S. producing companies was estimated at 1,500) pleaded that if their method was proscribed, they would no longer be able to raise capital and therefore would no longer be able to pursue new sources of oil and gas, and America would suffer. The SEC was glad enough to hand off to the FASB what quickly became the first full-blown controversy about the economic and social consequences of an accounting standard—and probably the most intensely politicized accounting argument ever.

As the rhetoric heated up during the FASB's deliberations, *Barron's* characterized the full-cost method as "no-cost accounting."[2]

While gearing up for those deliberations, the members of the FASB and their staff were well aware of what had gone before. In 1964, the AICPA had commissioned a partner of Price Waterhouse to study the issue and make recommendations to the APB. The result was Accounting Research Study No. 11, which essentially supported the prevalent successful efforts method. The mills at the AICPA ground extremely fine in those days, and it was not until 1969 that the report was published.[3] In 1970, the APB asked its committee on extractive industries to review ARS 11 and try to determine the appropriate accounting practices with a view to narrowing alternative practices in the extractive industries.

There followed a fine theological argument that led nowhere as the APB's death throes were upon it. Enter the FASB, which in setting its original agenda in 1973, perhaps in an excess of caution, or even wisdom, declined to consider oil and gas accounting. But, by the autumn of 1975, shortages of petroleum products and escalation of prices, coupled with an unsurprising concern in Congess about constituents' ability to continue their accustomed energy-based life-styles under those conditions, led to congressional consideration of the Energy Policy and Conservation Act.

While the legislation was being considered, but two months before it was enacted, the Board added to its agenda a project entitled "Financial Accounting and Reporting in the Extractive Industries." The announcement made it plain that the emphasis would be on exploration and development costs in the oil and gas industry, but ambivalence on this question later became evident. An advisory task force was appointed at about the same time President Ford signed the law in December, chaired by Horace Brock of North Texas State University, who also was retained as a consultant to the FASB. Only 2 of the 18 members were directly engaged in extractive industries other than oil and gas. The rest were a cross section of executives in the target industry, plus accountants, financial analysts, and investment bankers with special expertise in oil and gas.

On advice of the task force, the Board quickly concluded that the discussion memorandum it would develop as a basis for public comment would cover issues relevant to "companies engaged in the search for and production of all wasting (nonregenerative) resources." Development of that discussion memorandum took a full year, giving rise to fears in some quarters that the FASB might not be able to meet its congressionally mandated deadline, although Marshall Armstrong took pains to assure the world that the project was on schedule. When the discussion document finally appeared, it warned that inclusion of all extractive industries in it did not mean that the Board would issue a single Statement covering all extractive industries. In fact, the others were not included in the final Statement.[4]

The discussion memorandum, though a neutral document, and the public hearing based on it at the end of March 1977, provided a basis for one of the arguments that the full-costers brought forth late in the process and continued after the Statement was issued. The very neutrality of its more than 300 pages placed the full-costers at a disadvantage, they claimed, forcing them to shadowbox instead of striking at a known target. They demanded that the Board amend its schedule to provide a public hearing on the exposure draft, but that, of course, was not possible under the statutory deadline.

Shadowboxing was not evident in either the written comments on the discussion memorandum or testimony at the public hearing that followed. For example, two financial people on opposite sides of the issue landed heavy blows on targets that were quite visible.

John S. Chalsty, a managing director of Donaldson, Lufkin & Jenrette Securities, stated forthrightly that full-costing provided the most realistic and meaningful method of accounting for exploration and production costs and urged the FASB to endorse it. Shifting gears, he stated that the successful efforts method would render the reported earnings of exploration and production companies "essentially meaningless." He then rang the changes on the economic and social consequences theme by stating that in a time of energy shortage full-costing was needed to promote aggressive exploration, particularly among smaller companies that he said were the most active in searching for new U.S. reserves.

David Norr, an analyst with First Manhattan Co., scored with short, punchy declarative sentences to the effect that an unproductive exploratory well, or "dry hole" in the parlance of the industry, has none of the characteristics generally associated with an asset. He summed up by stating flatly that a dry hole is nothing but an expense and should be accounted for accordingly.

In contrast to Norr, the major accounting firms were even more prolix than usual. One Big Eight firm occupied 170 pages of the public record spelling out the reasons for its very reluctant support of successful efforts. Another took up 91 pages to express its support for full-cost. The Eight divided almost down the middle—three for successful efforts without much equivocation and one with a lot of equivocation; three for full cost; and one supporting neither but calling for a whole new approach.

Two major corporations whose primary businesses were outside the petroleum industry but that owned oil- and gas-producing subsidiaries also found themselves on opposite sides. The International Paper Company had acquired the 50–year-old General Crude Oil Company for $489 million early in 1975, and although the ostensible purpose of the acquisition was to exploit mineral rights related to timberlands owned by IPCo, General Crude was converted almost immediately to full-cost accounting to dress up its income statement and balance sheet. EPCA and "a reliable energy data base" were still almost a year in the future. When it began to appear that full-costing might be proscribed, IPCo management did not have to agonize over a decision to act. The controller submitted written comments on the discussion memorandum and testified at the public hearing, but that was only the beginning. Unlike many full-cost advocates who were willing to see successful efforts accounting continue as long as full-cost was allowed to survive, IPCo took the hard-line position that only one method should be permitted—the one they had imposed on General Crude.

Union Pacific Corporation was the owner of Champlin Petroleum Company and Rocky Mountain Energy Company, a producer of coal, soda ash, and uranium. In 1976, it realized more than 40 percent of its total revenues from those non-rail operations. Therefore, UPC was concerned with all extractive industries and advocated universal application of successful efforts, maintaining that the primary consideration in decisions about capitalization was the degree of association between costs and minerals actually discovered and developed. Successful efforts, it said, precluded accumulation of worthless investments by capitalizing only those costs that would eventually relate to the production of minerals. Costs not contributing to the production of minerals, Union Pacific concluded, should be charged to expense.

Two figures who are still prominent not only in the oil and gas industry but in the business community generally were articulate full-costers. T. Boone Pickens, the founder and chief executive officer (CEO) of Mesa Petroleum Co., was not yet the enfant terrible that he later became, but he made a colorful appearance at the public hearing. Marshall Armstrong started it badly by introducing him as "Mr. Perkins," but in his good old boy fashion, Pickens wasted no time in correcting the chairman—and in establishing empathy with the audience.

"You've heard I'm long-winded, I suppose," he began.

We'll hold it down. It says in my notes here I'm supposed to tell you that I'm not an accountant. I don't know whether that's good or bad. But I *am* a geologist, a petroleum geologist . . . and I formed Mesa Petroleum in 1964. At the time, in 1964, when we became a publicly-owned company is when we started with full-cost accounting.

He then described how assets had grown in 12 years from $4 million to $600 million and revenues from $1.5 million to $100 million.

Now, as far as I'm concerned, there's no way in the world we could have ever gotten from 1964 to 1976 with this kind of performance had we not been practicing full-cost accounting. In 1964, if I'd appeared before this group of gentlemen here with the FASB, I think I'd have probably been on my knees, pleading for full-cost accounting and telling you how much it meant to us, or would mean to us in the future to make Mesa Petroleum into a company that I believe to be a major factor in the domestic oil and gas business.

In Q and A, Oscar Gellein reviewed the dire consequences Pickens predicted if full-costing were eliminated.

Gellein: Would it be your view that the Board should be sure to design an accounting standard in this or in any other industry that would avoid things like that?

Pickens: I think it should be considered, yes.

Gellein: Would you turn it around and say that we should design an accounting standard that would encourage domestic exploration, encourage and enhance competition, encourage new entry, and do all we could through the accounting to eliminate, to mitigate, the energy crisis? In other words, does it work both ways?

Pickens's reply was difficult to parse. "I think it does," he said, but then added: "I think we need to add one more thing. I'm not in any way suggesting that you would depart from good accounting principles. I think that's understood by all of us that we have to have that full disclosure."

Thus, Pickens added his voice to the wistful illusion of many that somehow "good accounting" could produce many kinds of good economic and political results for many different interests while, at the same time, "telling it like it is."

J. Hugh Liedtke, CEO of the Pennzoil Corporation, was still a decade away from his classic demonstration of the "home court advantage" in despoiling mighty New York–based Texaco, Inc., in the friendly courts of Texas. He also seemed to think that accounting could produce all those good results—if only the FASB would show some imagination.

At the public hearing, Liedtke said:

It is my belief that the accounting profession has, in addition to merely entering figures in various accounts, an interpretive function and a public policy function which to some extent has been lost in recent years. . . . It seems to me that it is well-known within the industry that the accounting profession—this Board—is under very great pressure to come up with some single method of treating the oil and gas industry, of presenting to the public, to our public officials, to the regulators, the results and the status of the various companies. It is being asked to present a cookbook which says that you can cook an egg only one way, and if you do not cook it that way, you are under threat that the federal government, through the Securities and Exchange Commission, will make available to industry a cookbook that will tell you that you can only cook an egg a certain way.

He sought to enlist the standard setters in the cause of the full-costers. "I would hate to see this profession under duress," he said, "abandon its interpretive and policy-making function at this time."

It fell to Don Kirk to lead off the questioning of Liedtke. "I would like to pursue the public policy point," he said. Kirk then read a passage from Pennzoil's position paper asserting that "the ultimate conclusion of the Board should not be to mandate a single method of accounting that could seriously hamper the small companies in their access to capital markets" but that the FASB could "perform a useful public service by issuing an innovative, creative, and farsighted Statement which realistically recognizes the true economics involved in the discovery, exploration, and development of oil and gas reserves."

Kirk: Now you are suggesting what sounds like a two-tiered standard, or maybe a free-choice standard. I'm not sure whether it's two-tiered with full-costing applied to some companies and successful efforts to others, or whether it's free choice of which method should be selected. And secondly, you suggested that we do something innovative in creating the two tiers. I'd appreciate some insight into why it's a public service to institutionalize the two methods, unless they are specifically applied to specific circumstances.

Liedtke: Sir, I can't advise you technically. The one thing that I can say is that I know nothing in the law which commands this Board to come up with just one method. And, quite frankly, I think coming up with just one method under any political circumstance . . . is really a mistake. I think it tends to abandon not only the interpretive function, but the responsibility that the profession has. I would hope that the profession does not get itself forced into a position where it admits to the world that it has no interpretive function, that it doesn't have imagination.

Kirk: Some have been accused of being too imaginative.

Liedtke: Well, we live in a time where, unfortunately, many things and many professions are suspect.

Texaco itself was an interesting case. Alone among the major integrated companies, it had used the full-cost method for a while but concluded in the early 1970s that it was not appropriate, even though the company maintained during the controversy that "justification can be found for both full-cost and non-full-cost methods." Texaco's reasoning was that while historically U.S. oil companies could acquire an equity interest in overseas fields, it had become increasingly necessary to purchase drilling rights or enter into other contractual agreements that did not involve ownership. The company concluded that full-costing could no longer be justified under those conditions.

Many full-costers argued, however, that it was the increasing cost of acquiring rights, along with exploration and development, that made it necessary to capitalize. They also emphasized the point that exploration and development costs of companies engaged only in those activities were much higher relatively than the comparable costs for integrated companies that also had to account for heavy research, refining, distribution, and marketing expenditures. This disparity was magnified for full-cost companies, they said, because of the very high industrywide ratio of exploratory dry holes to producing wells.

The Ad Hoc Committee on Full Costing was a group of 33 of the larger independent, non-integrated producing companies that had come together in 1973 when the SEC was contemplating a rule that would not have proscribed anything but merely presumed that successful efforts was the "prevalent" accounting practice in the industry. The Ad Hoc Committee lived on and played a prominent part in the 1976–77 debate and the events that followed. The Committee sponsored research, submitted written comments on the discussion memorandum, and made a presentation at the public hearing.

Testifying at the hearing was Dean Bloyd, group vice president for accounting and administration of Tesoro Petroleum Corporation, who doubled as executive coordinator of the Ad Hoc Committee. He began by summarizing the results of an "impact study" conducted for the Committee by Touche Ross & Co. Fifty-four companies had responded to a mail questionnaire. In that sample were 36 using full-cost and 18 successful efforts.

"The study shows some very significant information," Bloyd said. "A full-cost company forced to use successful efforts accounting will lose 30 percent of the net capitalized cost of its oil and gas properties. It will lose 31 percent of its retained earnings, 16 percent of its shareholders' equity, and more than 20 percent of its annual reported net income." The successful efforts companies in the sample, on the other hand, if required to change to full-cost, "will enjoy increases in capitalized cost, retained earnings, and shareholders' equity of comparable amounts, and increased earnings of approximately seven-to-eight percent annually."

The Ad Hoc Committee also presented John H. Myers of Indiana University to summarize his research on behalf of the Committee. He said he found no theoretical basis for preferring one accounting method over the other, so "I chose to use an empirical approach." He set up a model company with identical transactions each year and applied both successful efforts and full-cost accounting to it. The model full-cost company showed greater net income and greater assets during the growth years, he said, but after maturity, both companies showed identical net income. Although he did not state it this way, his successful efforts company showed greater return on investment because its balance sheet was not burdened with unproductive "assets." Myers also noted that when his successful efforts model increased its drilling activity, there was an immediate decrease in reported net income. He was concerned by this. "At the very time the company was increasing its ability to face the future," he said, "the reported net income gave a negative indication."

Myers and other supporters of full-costing seemed to be saying that the traditional 12-month cycle of financial reporting should not be taken seriously. Don't worry about an increase in expenditures without an immediate corresponding increase in revenues. We didn't really spend more this year than we took in, because it will all work out just fine in the future.

The irony is that, in purely philosophical terms, Myers and his patrons may very well have been right, but in 1976 and 1977 the state of the accounting art provided no satisfactory way to measure those future benefits in relation to present sacrifices. As this is written, it still doesn't.

In the exposure draft it issued in July 1977, five months before the statutory deadline for a final ruling, the FASB, in effect, came down on the side of David Norr. It proposed that successful efforts be mandated as the single method of accounting for oil and gas exploration and development costs. There was no way, the Board concluded, that expenditures that produced no measurable economic benefit could be called assets. This conclusion was consistent with work then going forward on defining the elements of financial statements in the conceptual framework project. Statement of Concepts No. 3 eventually stated that an asset "embodies a probable future benefit that involves a capacity, singly or in combination with other assets, to contribute directly or indirectly to future net cash inflows."[5]

Nevertheless, it was a provocative position for the Board to take at the time, given the stakes in the game and the temper of its opponents. For about two months afterward, there was an eerie quiet—literally the calm before the storm. It was the period in which strategies and tactics were being decided and plans were being made by the determined defenders of full-cost accounting.

In March 1977, Marshall Armstrong, approaching the normal retirement age of 65, weary of the burdens of office, and hampered by a less-than-successful cataract operation, made known his decision to retire at the end of that year, more than a year and a half before expiration of the second term to which the trustees had appointed him in 1974. After several months of indecision, the trustees finally announced in late September the appointment of Don Kirk to succeed him, effective January 1, 1978. Only a week later, opponents of the Board's position on oil and gas launched a mortar attack in Washington. The timing was coincidental but ironic: Though direction and direct supervision of specific technical projects by Board members had ended in 1974, there continued to be an informal, unstructured pattern of Board members' involvement in projects according to their personal interests—and Kirk was the Board member most directly involved in the oil and gas project.

The CEO of the International Paper Company, J. Stanford Smith, had formerly been a senior executive of General Electric and while with GE had observed firsthand the benefits to a large corporation of having a savvy and aggressive presence in Washington. When he made the move to IPCo, he was determined to replicate GE's capability in that area, so when it became apparent that the FASB would seek to eliminate full-costing, Smith and IPCo were ready.

Neither International Paper nor General Crude was a member of the Ad Hoc Committee on Full Costing, but an alliance was formed without hesitation on either side. Though not integrated "majors," the Ad Hoc companies were large enterprises by any standard, and they had important political connections, particularly with senators and representatives from the oil-producing states. That web of influence, coupled with the paper company's large holdings of timberland in several states and wide-ranging contacts on Capitol Hill and in the federal administrative agencies, constituted a potent political force.

On October 6, Senator Floyd K. Haskell, a Colorado Democrat, with Senator Dewey Bartlett, Republican of Oklahoma, as cosponsor, introduced on the floor of the Senate a rider to an unrelated bill on regulation of public utilities that would amend Section 503 of the Energy Policy and Conservation Act in such a way that any oil and gas standard to be promulgated by the FASB would, in effect, be null and void. "Nothing in this section," the amendment stipulated, "shall be construed to establish or to affect the establishment of generally accepted accounting principles for financial reporting purposes."[6]

The Senate adopted what quickly came to be known as the "Haskell Amendment" by voice vote without a second thought and sent the utilities bill in which it was embedded on to a joint Senate-House conference committee.

On the same day, a letter went forth to the FASB from the office of Senator William Proxmire of Wisconsin, signed by him and four Wisconsin congressmen, requesting Kirk to comment on various points raised by objectors to the exposure draft. Several similar letters were received at Stamford in the following weeks, and all were responded to at length and in detail.

Capitol Hill was not the only focus of the full-costers' interest. High-level calls were made at the SEC to urge rejection of any standard specifying use of successful efforts only and to demand, at a minimum, that the Commission hold public hearings; on the Department of Energy to play on that agency's fear of any measure that might diminish or inhibit production of oil and gas; and on the Department of Justice and the Federal Trade Commission to play on their statutory concerns about anything alleged to be anticompetitive. Many on the receiving end of this attention said later that they had never seen such aggressive lobbying in their Washington careers. SEC Commissioner Roberta Karmel later described the issue as being "improperly politicized."[7] Meanwhile, representations continued to be made directly to the FASB, pleading for reconsideration of the conclusions set forth in the exposure draft. Intense deliberations on a final Statement, of course, were going on throughout this period.

In addition to examining and reexamining all the data it already had at hand, the Board commissioned two research studies on the potential impact that adoption of a successful efforts standard might have in the marketplace. In one, Thomas R. Dyckman of Cornell, aided by the FASB staff, studied market prices of the shares of 22 full-cost companies and 22 successful efforts companies for 11 weeks before and 11 weeks after issuance of the exposure draft. A slight negative effect on the shares of the full-cost companies was found in the week before and the week after issuance, but the market quickly adjusted, or "saw through," the effects of the proposed accounting change.[8] In the second study, telephone interviews were conducted under Horace Brock's direction with senior executive officers of 27 small and medium-size public companies of the successful efforts persuasion to ascertain whether they had encountered any difficulty in raising capital because of their accounting method. None was reported, although a few respondents feared there might be some problems in the future.[9]

In October and November, however, the most visible action was around the Senate-House conference committee. Members and their staffers were assiduously sought out, explained to, and handed briefing papers by both sides. Don Kirk spent almost full time on the matter for those two months, assisted by a senior member of the FASB staff and attorneys from the Washington office of the FAF's and FASB's law firm, Sullivan & Cromwell. It was the FASB's first and only concerted lobbying effort.

One company, when it was made aware of that activity, wrote to the chairman-designate questioning the FASB's right to take such action. The letter also contained a clumsy threat to sue, coupled with an allegation likening the Board to a judge tampering with a jury.

The FASB was not without supporters, however. Elmer B. Staats, the highly respected comptroller general of the United States, addressed a letter to members of the conference committee in which he sketched in some background and expressed strong support for the Board's efforts. He pointed out that for many years the accounting alternatives available to oil and gas producers had been a subject of controversy because transactions that were identical in nature and economic substance often were treated quite differently in producers' financial statements. The resulting lack of comparability, he said, had frustrated investors and policymakers alike, which was the reason for Section 503 of the Energy Policy and Conservation Act. In his view as an observer, he said, the FASB had done a commendable job of researching a difficult technical issue and providing a forum for public debate.

The redoubtable Congressman Moss sent a "Dear Colleague" letter to the conference committee members reminding them of his authorship of Section 503 and expressing "keen interest" in the Haskell Amendment because, in his view, its effect would be to negate the purpose of Section 503. He pointed out that the SEC already had proposed to adopt whatever decision the FASB made as a Commission rule that would require application of a uniform accounting standard for reports both to the Department of Energy and to the SEC under the federal securities laws.

A few days later, Chairman Harold M. Williams of the SEC wrote to Moss expressing opposition to the Haskell Amendment and assuring him of the Commission's expectation that the FASB's project would result in significant improvement in financial reporting. He added, however, that in recognition of intense interest in the issue the Commission would carefully examine the FASB's forthcoming pronouncement, solicit written comments on it, and hold public hearings early in 1978.

Finally, on December 1, the Haskell Amendment was rejected by the Senate-House conference committee. But that was only the end of the first battle in a political pressure war that would continue for nine more months. The SEC already had let it be known that its hearings would be de novo, meaning that it would look at the issue anew, even though it already had promulgated three Securities Act Releases, after the FASB exposure draft was issued, based on the assumption that the principles enunciated there would prevail in a final Statement. The Energy Department still was being coy at this stage, but it was fairly clear that it, too, would hold hearings.

On November 25, the Antitrust Division of the Department of Justice submitted a lengthy letter to the SEC commenting on the Commission's proposed rule-making related to the FASB's expected Statement. A copy of that document was conveyed to Don Kirk under a covering letter from Joe Sims, deputy assistant attorney general. (With a president who called himself Jimmy, why not a deputy assistant attorney general who went simply by the name of Joe?) Justice had taken the position, Sims wrote, that the Commission should not adopt the FASB proposed rules because "substantial" questions had been raised concerning the possible competitive effects of such action. He emphasized that the SEC had a statutory obligation to analyze possible effects on competition prior to adopting or approving a final rule.

Furthermore, Sims went on, to prevent the Commission's review of the issue from being "nugatory," Justice had respectfully recommended that the Commission seek the agreement of the FASB to refrain from adopting a final rule until the Commission had completed the required analysis. Therefore, he continued, the Department urged the FASB to postpone issuance of a standard until after the Commission completed its study. This advice, of course, ignored the congressionally mandated deadline for an oil and gas accounting standard, which by then was only three weeks in the future.

Kirk's reply was hand delivered to Sims on December 5—the very day Statement No. 19, *Financial Accounting and Reporting by Oil and Gas Producing Companies,* was promulgated. It was a stiff and formal letter, reminding Sims of the FASB's responsibility to establish accounting and financial reporting standards and to assist the Commission in meeting its obligations under Section 503 of Public Law 94–163 as well as under the federal securities laws. He assured Sims that the Board was going ahead with issuance of its standard for financial accounting and reporting by oil and gas companies and added that in the rigorous two-year process of developing the standard, the Board had considered carefully the views of all interested parties, including those opposed to the exposure draft. The final standard would include a complete record of the reasoning of the Board and the results of its research on possible effects of the standard on oil and gas producers. He also pointed out that the standard would not become effective for another year, and therefore the SEC would have ample time to consider and act on aspects of the matter that were within its jurisdiction.

The Energy Department hearings preceded those of the SEC by more than a month. Don Kirk, by now chairman of the FASB, was the first of 33 testifiers in two days. He pointed out that the Board's position on a variety of issues, not just oil and gas, had been that different accounting for the same facts and circumstances "impedes comparability and consistency of financial statements and significantly detracts from their usefulness." The facts and circumstances of oil and gas exploration, development, and production, he said, "are essentially the same regardless of the size of a company or whether its securities are publicly traded. Far from being anti-competitive," he added,

mandating one accounting method will eliminate inconsistency, noncomparability, and misunderstanding in the capital markets. By doing that, Statement 19 will foster competition in capital allocation by having oil and gas producers reporting comparable data and therefore reflecting the risks inherent in exploration as objectively and evenhandedly as possible.

He conceded that the Board's decision had not been unanimous. Three members dissented for different reasons, "but full-cost accounting as it is practiced today was unanimously rejected."

Kirk made many of the same points on the opening day of the SEC hearings, which occupied 12 days in Washington and Houston. "Accounting standards," he said, "should not be designed to take the peaks and valleys out of the periodic earnings of a high-risk business, particularly to facilitate the public offering of securities." He added that accounting standards should not "make the earnings pattern of an oil and gas exploration company look like a public utility. On the other hand, when a public utility or a company in some other unrelated industry gets into the oil and gas exploration business, its financial statements must reflect, not obscure, the new risks it has assumed."

He summed up by saying:

Successful efforts distinguishes among expenditures, considering those with discernible future benefits as assets, and those without as expenses. Therefore, it reflects risk by accounting for different circumstances differently and not making dissimilar circumstances appear similar. A principal defect of the full-cost method, a concept of accounting unique to the oil and gas industry, is that it obscures risks and conceals failures by treating the costs of abandoned properties and exploratory dry holes as assets.

Finally, Kirk attacked the claims of full-costers that Statement No. 19 would inhibit the ability of small independent companies to raise capital and would prevent new companies from entering the business. "Missing from those assertions," he said, "is an explanation of how an entire industry consisting of thousands of companies, both public and private, was able to raise capital and conduct effective exploration programs over the past 50 years or more—prior to the advent of full-costing."

From the moment the Haskell Amendment was defeated, the SEC had been at the center of the controversy. And in the end, the center did not hold.

For the next several months, the Commission pondered the situation and said nothing. Even the FASB's normally open lines of communication with commissioners and their staff yielded no clues as to what action, or actions, the SEC might take. By midsummer, the silence had begun to seem a little ominous. Then, in its meeting on August 29, the Commission wrapped up a package of three proposed rules, one final rule, and a Staff Accounting Bulletin that enabled it to straddle the issue instead of resolving it. At the same time, however, the net effect was to undercut the FASB, render Statement No. 19 almost meaningless, and leave everything as it had been before. But this package also held out the promise of a brilliant new solution to be invented by the SEC in about three years' time. The chimera was officially dubbed "Reserve Recognition Accounting," or RRA.

Sandy Burton, long since departed from Washington to become deputy mayor of New York for finance in the city's time of financial trouble, then professor and later dean of the business school at Columbia University, retained his talent for the well-turned phrase and catchy label. He quickly called the SEC's idea "Rah, Rah Accounting."

The basis for widespread cynicism, apart from the politicized history of the whole issue, was the fact that RRA apparently was going to be a value-based system—and methods for measuring either quantities or values of reserves in the ground were not sufficiently refined to produce reliable information for financial reports. Price estimates would be required, but who could predict the conditions under which the owner of a well would decide to produce its contents, when he would make that decision, and what price would prevail when he did?

The manner and tone of the SEC's announcement were puzzling. Every major argument made by the FASB before and after issuance of Statement No. 19 was affirmed by the Commission: the need for a single accounting method, unacceptability of recording unproductive expenses as assets, need to record like transactions in a like manner, irrelevance of claims that some companies would be disadvantaged in the capital markets, and most important, rejection of the claim that "economic consequences" should be given greater consideration than the need for evenhanded information.

There also was an oblique plea for "further initiatives or participation by the FASB in the continuing efforts relating to financial reporting for oil and gas producing activities."[10] What that might entail was not spelled out and was not clear for several weeks after the SEC announcement. The FASB felt itself under no further obligation with regard to the requirements of EPCA, but cognizant of the strictures imposed by the AICPA Rules of Conduct, the Board recognized that it would have to take some kind of action to release preparers and auditors of nonregistrant companies from the bind the SEC decision had placed them in. If it did not, full-cost companies not subject to SEC rules would have to switch to successful efforts if Statement No. 19 remained in place because the AICPA Rules of Conduct required auditors to adhere to FASB standards, while those that were SEC registrants would not be subject to such a requirement because the Commission's rule making specifically excluded them.

The solution was to leave Statement No. 19 in place because the SEC had decreed that successful efforts companies must be guided by its specific provisions but to suspend its effective date so full-costers of all sizes would not have to follow it.

Many observers assumed that the Commission had caved in to political pressure, and articles in the professional journals later expressed that view. All concerned within the Commission denied this for the record, but with varying degrees of conviction. The party line was that it had become a technical decision—that, in the words of the official announcement, "both traditional accounting methods—successful efforts and full-cost —fail to provide useful information on the financial position and operating results of oil and gas producers."[11]

Curiously, though, in a published interview with Donald E. Gorton of Wayne State University more than a decade later, Harold Williams seemed to play back some of the principal arguments used by the full-costers.

Statement 19 did seem, in a sense, rather than necessarily solving the issue . . . or addressing the issue in a way that really made progress in the solution of it . . . did in itself seem to me to be a political decision that would adversely affect a lot of the smaller independents. It would have had an adverse effect on that part of the industry that in some respects is the more aggressive and the more forthcoming in terms of exploration."[12]

This was a stark contradiction of the Commission's Accounting Series Release issued at the end of August 1978:

The economic and competitive consequences asserted by some commentators in this instance have been based on overstated and oversimplified presumptions. The Commission has concluded that any such impact of a requirement that companies should follow the successful efforts method would be short-lived and much less severe than predicted by these commentators. The Commission believes further that allocation of capital in the marketplace should be based on the competitive performance of companies and not on their accounting methods.[13]

Don Kirk learned of the SEC's decision not to support Statement No. 19 when he called Williams in the late afternoon of that memorable August 29 from a pay phone in Syracuse, New York, one of the stops on a college visitation trip he was making with his high school–age son. He was seated comfortably at his desk in Stamford, however, when he received the call two and a half years later informing him that the SEC had concluded that Reserve Recognition Accounting was not viable after all.[14] The Commission requested that the FASB undertake a project to simplify and rationalize disclosures then required under both successful efforts and full-costing without readdressing the basic question as to which accounting method should be a single standard. The Board obliged with Statement No. 69 in November 1982.

Many supporters of the FASB were thrown into a state resembling panic when the SEC declared, in effect, that Statement No. 19 was a dry hole. They feared that it was the beginning of the end for private sector standard setting. But in the low-key yet firm leadership style that characterized his chairmanship, Kirk rallied his troops and told the rest of the world, "I can assure you the Board is going about its other business as usual and without pause. We have a great deal to do in a limited time in order to maintain the private sector's role in standard setting. And we are doing our best to complete some very crucial projects in the near future."[15]

He was alluding to such things as the objectives of financial reporting and the rest of the conceptual framework, inflation accounting, which was described in the preceding chapter, and the first two standards relating to pensions, a subject that will loom large in this chronicle later on. While there continued to be tensions and disagreements with the SEC, and always will, they tend to be over esoteric details and are not life-threatening.

Oil and gas is the only instance in which the Commission has declined to support the FASB.

Since the late 1970s, the most serious threats to the Board's viability have come not from Congress, the SEC, or other federal agencies, but from the private sector itself.

In March 1979, only six months after the SEC decision on Statement No. 19, the International Paper Company sold General Crude to Gulf Oil Corporation for $650 million.

NOTES

1. Robert Frost, "The Ingenuities of Debt," in *The Poetry of Robert Frost*, ed. Edward Connery Lathem (New York: Henry Holt and Company, 1979), 399.

2. Alan Abelson, "Up & Down Wall Street," *Barron's*, July 18, 1977.

3. FASB Statement No. 19, *Financial Accounting and Reporting by Oil and Gas Producing Companies*, December 1977, par. 66 (background information).

4. FASB Statement No. 19, December 1977, par. 81 (background information).

5. FASB Concepts Statement No. 3 (as incorporated in Concepts Statement No. 6, *Elements of Financial Statements*), December 1985, par. 26.

6. Amendment to Energy Policy and Conservation Act of 1975 inserted in proposed Public Utilities Regulatory Act, October 6, 1977.

7. Donald E. Gorton, "The SEC Decision Not to Support SFAS 19: A Case Study of the Effect of Lobbying on Standard Setting," *Accounting Horizons*, March 1991, 30.

8. FASB Statement No. 19, December 1977, par. 90 (background information).

9. Ibid.

10. Harold M. Williams, statement in SEC news release, August 29, 1978.

11. SEC Accounting Series Release No. 253, "Adoption of Requirements for Financial Accounting and Reporting Practices for Oil and Gas Producing Activities," August 31, 1978.

12. Gorton, "The SEC Decision Not to Support SFAS 19," 38.

13. SEC, ASR 253, August 31, 1978.

14. This decision was made after private discussions with the FASB and experts in the oil and gas industry.

15. Donald J. Kirk, remarks to Southwestern Legal Foundation's Institute on Oil and Gas Accounting, September 7, 1978; excerpted in *Status Report*, September 14, 1978.

Chapter Five

Agent of Change in a Conservative Environment

To change all would be too much, and to change one is nothing.
Samuel Johnson[1]

Several years after the oil and gas debacle and after he left the SEC to head the J. Paul Getty Trust in California, Harold Williams remarked: "In both the accounting profession and the corporate community, potent forces exist which oppose any serious rethinking of traditional accounting conventions—even at the expense of the relevancy of the financial data those conventions yield."[2] Before he was chairman of the SEC, Williams had been a high-level corporate executive and business school dean for many years.

At about that time, David Mosso, then a new member of the FASB, told a group of Texas financial executives and CPAs that success of private sector standard setting would depend on how the business community views standards. "Are they rules of conduct," he asked, "designed to restrain unsocial behavior and arbitrate conflicts of interest? Or are they rules of measurement, designed to generalize and communicate as accurately as possible the complex results of economic events?"

Mosso observed that

rules of conduct call for a political process. Bargaining, horsetrading, logrolling, clout—describe it as you will, it is a power game. The stake in the game is business income and the object is to report it when you want it. The standard setter in this environment tries to write rules only when rules can't be avoided, and then to write them so the power is balanced. . . . Logical consistency and economic reality cannot be overriding objectives.

On the other hand, he said:

Rules of measurement call for a research process of observation and experimentation, a trial and error search for the dimensions of business income. The object is to
report it when it *is*. The standard setter tries to write rules that link the reporting of
income to the period in which it arises. It doesn't matter whether the business is
large or small, rich or poor, volatile or stable—if the income is there, report it, if not,
don't.[3]

Any form of standard setting can be expected to bring about some degree
of change. The difference is that the rules-of-conduct approach leads to
relatively small and infrequent changes determined on a case-by-case basis,
with each case subject to "bargaining, horsetrading, logrolling, and clout,"
while the rules-of-measurement approach implies deeper-running change
with a momentum of its own derived from developments in the marketplace and in the state of the accounting art. The standard setters also are
likely to be less susceptible to external pressure because they are chosen to
serve a purpose that is seen to be objective.

Even if they did not arrive at a recognition of this through analysis, many
issuers and auditors of financial information knew it intuitively and by the
late 1970s were becoming concerned about their relative powerlessness to
prevent unwanted change. Roger Smith, as chairman of General Motors
and of the Accounting Principles Task Force of the Business Roundtable,
indirectly voiced antipathy toward the rules-of-measurement approach
when he complained to Don Kirk that while he knew how to lobby for what
he wanted in Washington, he didn't know how to lobby the FASB.

Shortly before he resigned from the Board in 1987, Arthur R. Wyatt
described it as an institution that was "created to be an agent of change
[with] a broad constituency that strongly desires retention of the *status
quo*."[4] Art Wyatt resigned because he feared that institutional changes and
subtle shifts in the balance of power within the standard-setting structure
that began in the mid-1980s favored the status quo. Raymond C. Lauver
was driven by the same concerns when he resigned three years later. Those
changes will be described in following chapters.

Early in its history, before Mosso, Wyatt, and Lauver were appointed,
the Board recognized the need for logical consistency in its work and, as
noted in Chapter 2, mounted an ambitious effort to meet that need by
developing an orderly theoretical basis for financial accounting and reporting that it called a "conceptual framework." Dave Mosso was, and still is,
a strong supporter of that effort, but he has expressed misgivings about
characterizing it as a *constitution* for financial accounting and reporting, as
had been done in the news media and in some FASB publications, on the
grounds that the word implies a political rather than a measurement
approach to standard setting.

All of the 22 standards issued by the FASB in its first five years called for appreciable changes in financial reporting, if not for all companies in all industries, then at least for some classes of companies in some circumstances. The work on objectives of financial reporting, already far advanced, and plans for additional steps toward a conceptual framework held a promise—or threat—of profound changes over time for all issuers, auditors, and users of financial information.

In some quarters, this project was regarded with extreme wariness, but there also was caution about appearing to attack the idea of a conceptual framework overtly because the logic of seeking such a basis for decision making was difficult to assail. This meant that although the issues were extremely contentious, the debates were conducted in a lower key than those over specific standards, and the subject rarely broke into the public prints because the media tended to view it as too esoteric for popular consumption.

Most of the thoughtful, as distinct from merely fearful, arguments against the attempt to erect a conceptual framework stemmed from the "accounting-as-art" screed. Development of a framework would not be possible, one of the main arguments ran, because it had never been done before, even though there had been many attempts. And it had not been accomplished simply because accounting concepts were based on premises inductively arrived at, not on immutable natural laws. Therefore, it was said, accounting principles must arise from a continuous process of somehow deciding specific issues so as to generate a body of doctrine similar to what the lawyers call "case law."

It also was argued that with recent advances in technology it was possible for users of financial information to draw on data banks for raw data, then make of those data whatever their interests called for—and their expertise could handle. Users should be able to adjust to whatever data were made available to them. But this argument failed to acknowledge that there needed to be guidelines to ensure the reliability, relevance, and comparability of the basic data provided.

A recurring theme of defenders of the status quo was fear of current value accounting, and suspicion that the conceptual framework was a backdoor approach to it. This fear often was camouflaged by argument over the "asset and liability" approach to standard setting versus the "revenue and expense" view. The former held that earnings are a measure of the change in a company's net assets from one period to the next and thus placed greater emphasis on the balance sheet than on the income statement. Proponents of the revenue and expense view were concerned mainly with "proper matching of revenues and expenses" to avoid what they called "distortion of earnings." They believed that placing reserves and various kinds of deferred charges and credits on the balance sheet was justified to achieve "normalization" of earnings by smoothing the immediate effects of economic events.

This dichotomy led to some rather baroque language in comment letters and public hearing testimony. It is a peculiarity of accountants, especially of the corporate variety, that while they insist that accounting is an art, in the next breath many will argue even more vehemently for a rigidity that does not befit an art—that their preferred practices are based on "time-honored, historic concepts" with a standing only slightly below that of Holy Writ. The chief financial officer of one of the world's great corporations expressed fear that the framework would overturn a basis of accounting derived from concepts that were centuries old. He also asserted that users of financial information were not likely to accept data presented in ways that management itself questioned.

Another fear was that the framework would provide justification for relentless striving toward "standardization" or "uniformity" of financial reporting, code words for elimination of permissible alternative ways of accounting for the same or similar circumstances. Another of the world's great corporations maintained at the public hearing that

if a company has been in business for many years and has consistently followed a philosophy . . . which gives a fair presentation of its results, it seems unreasonable for it to be required to abandon its well thought-out procedures *solely because of an overriding desire for improvement*. There is a place in business for alternative approaches to business problems, and so it follows that there must be a corresponding basis for alternative accounting standards. (Emphasis added)

In the Q and A that followed, Oscar Gellein, who once had been the engagement partner on the General Motors audit for Haskins & Sells, was circumspect.

History is pretty replete with concerns about accounting alternatives. You can go back forty years. . . . Do you remember Congressman Staggers' request to the SEC in 1967? He virtually ordered the SEC to report back to Congress on the alternatives that were then in existence and, in effect, gave a mandate to the SEC to see what they could do about it. More recently, we have had Metcalf's staff report. We see investors, through analysts and investment advisers, continually complaining about alternatives. Have there been unwarranted alternatives?

Growing impatient with hollow answers, Board member John W. March ended the sequence by saying:

Neither General Motors nor this Board can change the mandate that the people in Congress have given us. I think that the sooner we wake up to the fact that alternatives must be eliminated, in many respects the better off we'll be because we can't have any progress, in my judgment, in public credibility unless that progress is made.

Some critics of the effort to erect a conceptual framework were more astringent than the GM representatives. Some were funnier. Some were both. Well versed though he was in the ins and outs of financial reporting, Ulyesse J. LeGrange, vice president and controller of Exxon U.S.A., was a natural orator in the southern tradition. Belying the popular image of accountants as dry-as-dust wearers of green eyeshades, he regaled a 1980 public conference in a calculated barefoot-boy style with his complaints about the conceptual framework.

Now, just on the odd chance that there are a few more slow learners in the audience who don't really comprehend all this stuff and can't, you know, get their arms around it all and feel totally comfortable with it, like some of the people here today apparently can, let me just try and make one point about a hole in this whole framework that bothers the hell out of me. And I think it's a hole we better try to fill pretty soon or this whole house of cards is going to fall down around our ears. . . . Every now and then somebody recognizes that maybe something to do with historical aspects, even historical cost, may have some relevance in this wonderful modern world in which we live, although there are others who think all of that historical stuff is a bunch of nonsense and we ought to throw it away and move on into the wonderful future that none of us can comprehend.

At the same conference, which was convened by the FASB, a future chairman of the Board also was among the critics. Denny Beresford, then speaking for Ernst & Whinney, told the 300 conferees:

Such broad concepts as objectives and qualitative characteristics will be of questionable value in resolving specific accounting problems. . . . To expect preparers—I should say auditors—to judge the preferability of accounting alternatives by looking to the objectives of financial reporting or by assessing such noble characteristics as relevance, understandability, or neutrality is wishful thinking.

The best he could say for the effort was that "it should result in a description of present accounting and reporting practices that is more understandable and widely recognized."[5]

The first Statement of Concepts, the one on objectives of financial reporting, was issued near the end of 1978, and the flavor of debate preceding adoption of that Statement is sampled in Chapter 2. Concepts Statement No. 1 identified "decision usefulness" of financial information as its overriding purpose, finally giving meaning, as far as financial accounting and reporting were concerned, to the Securities Act of 1933—almost a half a century after its enactment. Robert Sterling, a noted academician and author who spent two years at the FASB as a Faculty Fellow, would remark later that, "decision usefulness *is* the conceptual framework: all the rest is commentary."[6]

In retrospect, it seems clear that the SEC should have demanded that a statement of objectives consistent with the 1933 Act be completed within a reasonable time before it ceded the standard-setting function to the private sector, but the prominent lawyer, professor, and accounting critic Homer Kripke has provided some perspective on those times. Much later, he commented that "in the early 1930s, accounting was like the earth at the Creation, as described in the first chapter of Genesis, 'without form and void, and darkness was upon the face of the deep.' "[7] The question of objectives was not formally addressed until the Trueblood Committee was appointed more than three decades after the SEC's decision to rely on the private sector for financial accounting standard setting.

In surveying a cross-section of the FASB's constituencies almost 2 years after the first Concepts Statement was issued—and 47 years after passage of the 1933 Act—Louis Harris and Associates found that only small minorities of corporate chief executives and chief financial officers acknowledged "fulfillment of user needs" as the primary purpose of financial reporting, although auditors, investors, government officials, and leading academicians accepted it by large majorities.[8]

The 1980 Harris survey found skepticism that the conceptual framework as a whole would bring about major changes in financial reporting—and a lack of enthusiasm for anything but marginal change. It also uncovered a set of almost schizophrenic attitudes toward basic approaches to standard setting. Large majorities believed that it was both realistic and desirable to establish standards by developing public consensus, but even larger majorities said that "attempts to establish standards that are consistent with each other and with an overriding conceptual framework" were both realistic (83 percent) and desirable (91 percent).

From these findings, Don Kirk deduced somewhat optimistically that "practitioners and business managers are willing to [see us] spend money on a conceptual framework because they don't want a purely political system with the FASB acting as a power broker that compromises the positions of special interest groups."[9]

Though he is not known for being carried away by euphoria very often, Kirk's comment on the Harris survey was more sanguine than one he had made a year earlier in a speech to the Business Council (not to be confused with the Business Roundtable, although it is made up of many of the same people). "The central problem of the FASB," he said on that occasion, "is sifting through countless facts and countless perceptions of economic reality to find a way to direct the admittedly imperfect techniques of accounting toward producing information that is both reliable and relevant."[10]

Still ahead were five more Statements of Concepts, although No. 6 was merely a restatement of No. 3 (Elements of Financial Statements of Business Enterprises) to sweep in not-for-profit organizations. Thus, while there are six numbers, there are only five Statements extant in the Concepts series. They are:

- Objectives of Financial Reporting by Business Enterprises (No. 1)
- Qualitative Characteristics of Accounting Information (No. 2)
- Objectives of Financial Reporting by Nonbusiness Organizations (No. 4)
- Recognition and Measurement in Financial Statements of Business Enterprises (No. 5)
- Elements of Financial Statements (No. 6)

From the standpoint of business, the Statements on objectives, qualitative characteristics, and elements are the real pillars of the framework. While one still can get an argument in the more conservative neighborhoods about the primacy of decision usefulness as an objective of financial reporting, the proposition has found general acceptance over the years. It was difficult to argue against identifying relevance and reliability as the "primary decision-specific qualities," although there remains ample room for argument as to their relative weight in specific situations. And while there still can be debate over what specifically is and what is not an asset, even within the FASB itself, the definitions of elements provide a more meaningful basis for such debate than ever was available before. The framework never was intended to make all argument moot. Nor was it intended to be set in concrete, impervious to change forevermore.

The weak link in the series, generally recognized as such in the world at large and so acknowledged by members of the FASB itself, is recognition and measurement. This was where diehard defenders of historical cost—at all cost—dug in for their most determined stand. Some outside the FASB made it appear to be an all-or-nothing issue. Within the Board, as Don Kirk wrote in a guest editorial in *Management Accounting* while the struggle was going on, "no member of the Board or staff favors reporting only historical costs or only current prices in all circumstances."[11] In other words, it was both a matter of degree and of choice with regard to those classes of assets and those circumstances to which the respective measurement methods would be applied.

In that editorial, Kirk acknowledged that the Board was deadlocked on some major issues but described a special, organized effort that was being made to expand areas of common ground already identified. That effort included, among other things, development by the staff of a fairly lengthy series of purely fictitious "cases" to provide hypothetical, yet concrete, examples illustrating the conceptual issues the Board was considering. They were given semifacetious titles like "Health Spa," "Hula Hoop," "Lottery Ticket," and "Corn and Hogs." A few years later the cases were considered useful enough to be collected in a book,[12] and Board members who were involved in their consideration avowed that though the answers were extremely difficult to sort out, the cases were invaluable in helping to clarify the conceptual issues with which they were grappling at the time. Nevertheless, while that exercise was still going on, the *Wall Street Journal* solemnly reported in a critical page-one article that "the Board debated for months whether corn stored by a hog farmer should be priced at cost or adjusted for inflation." The *Journal* characterized this as "wasting time on minutiae."[13]

In his *Management Accounting* editorial, Don Kirk faced up to the practical question:

If agreement continues to elude us, it may be advisable for the Board to concentrate for a time on such major projects as pensions and income taxes—and continue to test the views of individual Board members on recognition and measurement questions against the difficult issues embedded in those projects."[14]

That's how dicey the situation was 18 months before the Statement on recognition and measurement was issued—and it was not a great deal better when the Statement finally appeared. It did not quite become necessary to put the project in mothballs, but almost. Art Wyatt, not a member of the FASB when recognition and measurement was deliberated or adopted, would say several years later that the parts of the framework dealing with objectives, qualitative characteristics, and elements were "very sound," but the further the Board went in developing a framework, the less of a foundation it had. "Too many provisions," he said, "one could read in equivocal ways, and that results in a framework that is squishy as you get down the road."[15]

Ralph Walters, who was at the center of the effort to rescue recognition and measurement, found the downside of his expectations realized in that Statement, namely, concepts that "merely embalm the *status quo*."[16]

Nevertheless, the conceptual framework as a whole has proven to be useful. It is looked to by succeeding waves of Board members for guidance, though they do not follow it slavishly or even as rigorously as they should. It is referred to increasingly by commentators on FASB proposals, though not always accurately or to the point. The sense within the FASB and its staff always has been that Statements of Concepts would not by themselves solve problems, but would merely help the standard setters in their efforts to solve them. In the annual report for 1979, Don Kirk predicted mildly that the framework would "impose a philosophical discipline on the standard setters themselves and, equally important, provide a common frame of reference for discussion of specific accounting issues."[17] A consistent theme of Kirk's chairmanship was that change must be evolutionary, not revolutionary. Though not attributed specifically to him, those words are written into the ambivalent Concepts Statement No. 5.

Over time, the FASB has been able to achieve widespread agreement on, or at least acquiescence in, the objectives, qualitative characteristics, and definitions of the elements of financial reporting, in part because it has thought longer and in a more organized way about those concepts than anyone else—and has subjected its conclusions to public comment and criticism by all who have an interest.

The cost of that effort, which accounted for as much as 40 percent of technical staff time at one point in the early 1980s came in for severe criticism in some quarters, despite Don Kirk's optimistic assessment of the Harris survey findings. Michael O. Alexander, still director of research and technical activities early in 1982, sought to turn the criticism around by focusing on the costs of *not* having a conceptual framework. After enumerating those costs in detail, he summed up by saying: "The real cost is found in the endless need for more and more rules. It is precisely that absence of an underlying and consistent conceptual framework that may cause us to need a standard or an accounting rule in order to resolve the issues and disputes that arise."[18]

Nevertheless, many of the same people who were complaining most bitterly about "standards overload" also rejected the idea of a conceptual framework.

Despite the inconclusiveness of Concepts No. 5, the members of the FASB who participated in development of the framework and had a commitment to it made clear their intent to avoid standard setting by consensus and to move toward a disciplined approach that promised less flexibility and more intellectual rigor in the standards. At the same time, however, they acknowledged a need for recognition of "reasonable practicalities." Among that group of Board members, avoidance of what they often called "ad hockery" was of major importance.

That stance was not popular with conservative constituents who continued to advocate more flexibility in financial reporting. Their plea was for "broad" standards that would allow plenty of room for "judgment" in their application. Don Kirk addressed their complaints on several occasions.

Broad accounting principles or standards are not enough when the Supreme Court believes that financial statements must be *accurate* and the public must *perceive* them as accurate; they are not enough when users of financial statements clamor for comparability and a U.S. Senate subcommittee calls for uniformity of accounting standards to be a major goal of standard setting. [The Supreme Court reference was to a 1984 decision in which the Court denied confidentiality for a major accounting firm's audit workpapers.]

Kirk then used the rules of golf as a metaphor.

You and I do not need those rules because we play every shot as it lays. It is because of those "other guys" that we have the rules. Nor do you and I search for ways to keep debt off the balance sheet or research and development costs and executive stock compensation off the income statement. We know the broad principle that liabilities should be in the balance sheet and expenses in the income statement.

As long as an accounting decision is perceived by preparers of financial statements as either winning or losing an advantage, the "other guys" in the financial reporting game will search for loopholes. . . . Broad principles like "follow accrual accounting," "practice full disclosure," and "let substance override form" in financial reporting, and "play it as it lays" in golf are just not enough to keep the game fair.[19]

A future chief accountant of the SEC, Walter Schuetze, would put it more succinctly a few years later. "General standards, it has been demonstrated," he said, "will not work—absolutely won't work."[20]

In those heady but difficult years when the framework, as it stands today, was being developed, spokespersons for the Board made a point of emphasizing that it was a "living document," subject to change as knowledge, theory, and experience advanced. Therefore, it would never be finished but would undergo changes and additions over the years. Unfortunately, however, nothing explicit has been done with it since the elements of financial statements of business enterprises were joined with those of not-for-profit enterprises in a single Statement of Concepts at the end of 1985.

The struggle over recognition and measurement in the early 1980s was both draining and discouraging for those who participated in it, but by now the personnel of the Board has changed completely. There is a minority of staunch supporters, however, and it is recognized officially that the projects on financial instruments and impairment of long-lived assets may yield important new insights on recognition and measurement, but it seems unlikely that there will be any specific activity directed to advancing the formal conceptual framework as long as the present "pragmatic" makeup of the Board obtains. The reasons for the prevailing pragmatism, and its implications, will be examined in later chapters.

In 1982, following one of the periodic reviews of FASB activity by the trustees' structure committee that found that the Board should strengthen its efforts to "communicate its mission to its constituents,"[21] a decision was made that a formal mission statement should be developed.

The heart and guts of the FASB's mission had been set forth in a mere 26 words by the founding trustees in 1973. It was, simply: "to establish and improve standards of financial accounting and reporting for the guidance and education of the public, including issuers, auditors, and users of financial information." Just as "decision usefulness" *is* the conceptual framework, those 26 words *are* the mission statement—and the rest is elaboration. But great pains were taken by the staff, the Board, the Advisory Council, and the trustees themselves over that elaboration.

The mission statement runs to more than 600 words and includes five operating principles and five precepts that the Board commits itself to follow in setting standards. The first principle springs directly from the conceptual framework: "To improve the usefulness of financial reporting by focusing on the primary characteristics of relevance and reliability and on the qualities of comparability and consistency." The other four principles have to do with keeping standards current to reflect changes in business, considering promptly any significant areas of deficiency in financial reporting, promoting international comparability of accounting standards, and improving the "common understanding of the nature and purposes of information contained in financial reports."[22]

There is little quarrel over the principles, but the five precepts quickly became so many cudgels with which dissaffected constituents could beat the FASB about the ears. They are:

- To be objective in decision making. [If the decision is not in my favor, ipso facto it cannot be objective.]
- To weigh carefully the views of its constituents. [You did not adopt my view, so obviously you did not weigh the views of constituents.]
- To promulgate standards only when the expected benefits exceed the perceived costs. [You blew that one: The costs of applying this proposed standard would be far greater than the benefits to my company.]
- To bring about needed changes in ways that minimize disruption to the continuity of reporting practice. [Have you taken a look at what your proposal could mean for my staff?]
- To review the effects of past decisions. [Hah! You still haven't rescinded Statement No. so-and-so that has caused me and my company so much pain, so how can you say you have a review procedure?]

The reader may be tempted to conclude that promulgating such a document was a public relations blunder, but not so: In the long run, the greatest strength that can be had by a quasi-public self-regulatory body living on sufferance of the regulated is an open process, openly communicated. Without the "sunshine" reforms of 1977 and 1978, this "bold experiment in self-regulation" probably would not have survived for as long as it has.

NOTES

1. Samuel Johnson, preface to the *Dictionary of the English Language* (London, 1755).

2. Harold M. Williams, "Where Do We Go from Here? Prospective and Prognosis" (paper delivered at the Arthur Young Professors Roundtable, Harriman, N.Y., May 5–7, 1983).

3. David Mosso, address to a joint meeting of the South Texas Chapter, Financial Executives Institute, and the San Antonio Chapter, Texas Society of CPAs, San Antonio; published as *FASB Viewpoints*, January 26, 1979.

4. Arthur R. Wyatt, "Standard Setting: Processes and Politics," address to a joint meeting of the FEI and Robert Morris Associates in Denver, May 1986; published as *FASB Viewpoints*, October 3, 1986.

5. Symposium on Conceptual Framework for Financial Accounting and Reporting, New York, June 24, 1980.

6. Robert Sterling, quoted by Donald J. Kirk in a paper delivered at the Arthur Young Professors Roundtable, Harriman, N.Y., May 5–7, 1983.

7. Homer Kripke, "Disclosure Beyond Accounting Disclosure: An Unsatisfied Need" (Emanuel Saxe Distinguished Lecture in Accounting, Baruch College, City University of New York, April 22, 1980).

8. Louis Harris and Associates, Inc., *A Study of the Attitudes Toward and an Assessment of the Financial Accounting Standards Board* (Stamford, Conn.: Financial Accounting Foundation, April 1980).

9. Donald J. Kirk, paper delivered at the annual meeting of the American Accounting Association, Boston, August 13, 1980; published as "Statement in Quotes," *Journal of Accountancy*, April 1981, 84.

10. Donald J. Kirk, "Private Standard Setting and Public Accountability," address to the Business Council, Hot Springs, Va., October 13, 1979.

11. Donald J. Kirk, "Significance of Accounting Concepts," guest editorial, *Management Accounting*, July 1983, 6.

12. L. Todd Johnson, ed., *The FASB Cases on Recognition and Measurement* (Norwalk, Conn.: Financial Accounting Standards Board, 1991).

13. Lee Berton, "FASB, Which Decides Accounting Questions, Sparks Much Criticism," *Wall Street Journal*, April 30, 1984.

14. Kirk, guest editorial.

15. Arthur R. Wyatt, participant, Board Member Forum, public meeting of present and past FASB members, Norwalk, Conn., September 1988.

16. Ralph E. Walters, participant, Board Member Forum, Norwalk, Conn., September 1988.

17. Donald J. Kirk, Annual Report of the Financial Accounting Standards Board, 1979, 13.

18. Michael O. Alexander, "The FASB's Conceptual Framework Project: After Eight Years, Is the End in Sight?" *FASB Viewpoints*, June 2, 1982.

19. Donald J. Kirk, "Enhancing Professionalism in Financial Reporting," *FASB Viewpoints*, June 28, 1984.

20. Walter P. Schuetze, participant, Board Member Forum, Norwalk, Conn., September 1988.

21. *Operating Efficiency of the FASB*, Report of the Structure Committee (Stamford, Conn.: Financial Accounting Foundation, August 1982).

22. FASB, *The Mission of the Financial Accounting Standards Board* (Stamford, Conn., 1983).

Chapter Six

What's Sauce for the Goose . . .

Nothing in progression can rest on its original plan. We may as well think of rocking a grown man in the cradle of an infant.

Edmund Burke[1]

In 1977, 1978, and 1979, the "agent of change" itself underwent some significant changes. Evident to all was a changing of the guard. In addition to Marshall Armstrong's retirement, it also became known early in 1977 that Arthur L. Litke and Robert E. Mays, whose terms expired at the same time, would retire at the end of that year. John W. March, a senior partner of Arthur Andersen & Co., Robert A. Morgan, controller of Caterpillar Tractor Co., and David Mosso, assistant secretary of the Treasury, were appointed to fill the vacancies, effective at the beginning of 1978.

In addition, there also was a new director of research and technical activities who was accorded a more important place than his predecessors. In large part as a result of the 1977 structure committee recommendations,[2] the position was upgraded to parity with the Board members, both in status and compensation. George Staubus had served as director while on leave from the faculty of the University of California at Berkeley as a Faculty Fellow. The new director was Michael O. Alexander, only 37 at the time, who had had a meteoric career as a partner of Touche Ross in Toronto and on the national accounting scene in Canada. His appointment, at the beginning of Don Kirk's first term as chairman, signaled a new emphasis on professionalism in the various staff functions and a determination of the new chairman to upgrade staff support for the Board. It also tended to add to the impression that the Board was driven by its staff.

Less visible but also of major importance were procedural and organizational changes brought about by the Foundation trustees and by the Board itself.

The most significant recommendation in the trustees' structure committee report was that the Standards Board and related bodies should "move into the sunshine," in other words, open their meetings to public observation, as federal agencies and commissions had recently been required to do by Act of Congress. A joint committee of trustees and FASB members was appointed soon after the report was published in the spring of 1977 to evaluate this and other recommendations. At first, there was concern among some Board members that meeting in public might have an inhibiting effect on their discussions of technical issues and that efficiency of the Board's operations would be diminished. Nevertheless, decisions were made that led to the opening of meetings of the FASB, its task forces and other related groups, the Advisory Council, and the Foundation board of trustees to public observers, effective at the beginning of 1978.[3]

Apprehensions about possible side effects quickly proved groundless. Debate in Board meetings continued to be vigorous and candid, and the need to make public announcements well in advance regarding meeting dates, times, and agendas imposed a discipline that actually made operations more orderly and efficient. In keeping with the spirit of "open decisions openly arrived at," the Board declines to meet as a body to discuss technical issues behind closed doors with any except governmental agencies that request such a meeting. To date, only one has—in the early days of the savings and loan crisis. Otherwise, closed-door meetings involved no more than three members of the Board, although this, as we shall see in Chapter 8, was a sore point with certain powerful corporations and the associations representing them.

Implementation of "sunshine" rules and related changes placed the FASB in the position of having a more open and democratic process than is required of federal agencies under the Administrative Procedure Act of 1947 and the Sunshine in Government Act of 1977.

At the same time those changes in "due process" were being made, the requirement that at least four of the seven FASB members be CPAs from public practice was dropped, and the AICPA was replaced as the sole elector of Foundation trustees, even though that designation had never carried more than symbolic weight. Since then, trustees have been chosen by a panel of electors representing all of the sponsoring organizations.[4]

Early in 1979, after Oscar Gellein resigned, Frank E. Block, a prominent financial analyst, former president of the Financial Analysts Federation, and vice president of what was then Bache Halsey Stuart Shields, Inc., was appointed to take his place. For the first time, former practicing CPAs were a minority on the Board.

The structure committee also made a recommendation that would have reverse reverberations more than a dozen years later. A month after the Standards Board found itself unable to muster the five affirmative votes needed to issue a standard (in this case, on prior period adjustments), the committee proposed that the voting requirement for issuance of FASB pronouncements be changed from a supermajority of 5–2 to a simple majority of 4–3.[5]

The supermajority requirement, which was consistent with Accounting Principles Board rules, had been recommended by the Wheat Committee on grounds that it would "reduce the likelihood of controversial rulings which may not enjoy wide support outside the Standards Board," an argument that would be dusted off a decade and a half after this, the first of several reconsiderations by the trustees. There also was an unspoken concern that if the four CPA members of the Board originally mandated by the bylaws voted as a bloc, they could override the judgments of the other three Board members and perpetuate control of standard setting by the AICPA. The structure committee reasoned that with the AICPA no longer guaranteed a majority of FASB members, there was no need for that safeguard.

"The Board should . . . be composed of the best people with knowledge of accounting, finance, and business, and a concern for the public interest, regardless of previous employment," the committee said. "If . . . no one constituent group is by plan committed to a majority of seats on the Board, we recommend that the five-of-seven voting requirement be eliminated. A simple majority should suffice for Board decisions." The report also observed that the 5–2 requirement "apparently has caused delays in reaching decisions. It could result in unproductive discussion and might even create the temptation to compromise the substance of a standard."[6]

The full board of trustees concurred in a unanimous vote.

In another significant decision, chairmanship of the Advisory Council was separated from that of the FASB, and Paul Kolton was engaged as permanent chairman. Kolton had served as chairman and CEO of the American Stock Exchange (Amex) for seven years, a period in which the Amex had overcome some previous negative developments and re-established its place as one of the major exchanges. As chairman of FASAC, he quickly demonstrated an ability to draw from that diverse body a variety of meaningful points of view for the FASB's consideration and to make its meetings more interesting to the Council members themselves than they had been before. At the same time, he served as an active director of a number of major corporations.

Kolton retired early in 1992, and his place was taken by E. Virgil Conway, a financial consultant, corporate director, and former chairman of the Seaman's Bank for Savings in New York.

Also as a result of the 1977 structure committee report, a limit of $50,000 was placed on annual contributions from a single firm, or 1 percent of the FASB's annual budget, whichever was less. This placed a cap on the largesse of the big accounting firms and diminished by more than $1 million their aggregate annual giving to the Foundation. The trustees vowed to replace this loss by broadening the base of support, but over the succeeding years, increases in revenues from publication sales have far outpaced increases in contributions.

In 1978, in response to representations from the commercial banking industry, an at-large trusteeship was created for that industry, despite the heartburn it had caused, and would continue to cause, for the FASB. William H. Dougherty, Jr., president of NCNB Corporation, the predecessor of Nationsbank, was elected to the slot following consultations with the American Bankers Association, Association of Bank Holding Companies, Association of Reserve City Bankers, the Bank Administration Institute, and Robert Morris Associates. The bankers would have liked to become a sponsoring organization, but it was not possible to select one of their national organizations to be that sponsor. In 1983 and 1984, Bill Dougherty would serve as president of the Foundation, and there has been a commercial banker on the board of trustees since 1978.

In terms of internal organization, a program to double the size and upgrade capabilities of the technical staff was completed in 1978, bringing the complement of professionals to more than 40. The staff again was consolidated in a single Research and Technical Activities (RTA) Division with Mike Alexander as director and J.T. Ball, the first technical specialist recruited by Marshall Armstrong, as assistant director in charge of the extensive activity on emerging problems and other issues of narrow scope. The technical assistants to Board members were transferred to the RTA Division, and drafting of documents became a staff responsibility, completing the move toward freeing Board members to concentrate on considering technical issues.

Prodded by the SEC, the Standards Board developed in 1978 a proposal for giving a higher authoritative status to resolutions of "industry accounting matters and accounting questions of limited application" that still were being dealt with by the Accounting Standards Executive Committee (AcSEC) of the AICPA. Late in 1978, in keeping with its sometimes slavish adherence to due process, the FASB issued for public comment a proposal to give its own authority to those parts of AICPA Statements of Position, Industry Accounting Guides, and Industry Audit Guides that might be deemed to contain accounting or financial reporting guidance. It would do this by extracting from those AICPA documents any "specialized accounting and reporting standards" and issuing them as FASB Statements. Hearing no persuasive arguments against such a proposition, the Board went ahead and issued in 1979 its Statement No. 32, saying that guidance contained in those AICPA documents would be considered "preferable" in determining whether an accounting change was appropriate until the FASB issued a pronouncement on the subject. Then the Board proceeded to extract the relevant material from the AICPA documents and repackage it into FASB Statements.

The result was a dozen Statements of Financial Accounting Standards in this area alone, 11 of which were promulgated in a period of 19 months when a total of 22 Statements rolled off the presses. Though none of the 11 "extractions" were of major importance, and the substance of all had previously been laid before the public in AICPA documents, this avalanche of "brown books," as FASB Statements had come to be called, did more than anything else to create an impression of "standards overload" that would plague the Board for years to come.

Until 1979, requests for guidance on minor implementation problems were handled by letter, and those letters were summarized in the FASB newsletter, *Status Report*. In 1979, a new class of FASB publication, the Technical Bulletin, was created to provide this material in a more orderly and retrievable form. The Bulletins would be prepared and issued by the staff and would clarify existing pronouncements without establishing new standards or amending those already in place. Though not formally reviewed by the Board, they would carry its implicit approval. Nineteen such Bulletins were issued by the end of 1979, placing another log on the fire of standards overload.

Of much greater significance in the standard-setting context was the issuance in 1980 of Statements on accounting and reporting by defined benefit pension plans and on employers' disclosures of pension information, although the latter was but a prelude to the real drama of the 1980s— the Board's often stormy effort to set standards for employers' reporting of pension costs in their financial statements.

In this period, interest was mounting in what items were on the Board's agenda and how they got there. Accordingly, in 1981 formal criteria were developed for making agenda decisions. From its beginning, the Board had been open to suggestions, particularly from the Advisory Council and the sponsoring organizations, regarding possible agenda topics. By the beginning of the 1980s, a need was perceived for a disciplined approach to evaluating such suggestions. The criteria that emerged included consideration of (1) the extent to which a problem was troublesome to users, preparers, and auditors of financial information; (2) the likelihood of developing solutions that would improve financial reporting; (3) the extent to which technically sound solutions could be developed, and (4) the extent to which a solution was likely to be accepted generally. Also to be considered was whether failure of the FASB to act might cause the SEC, or even Congress, to step in.

The first agenda additions to which these criteria were applied were the troublesome one on consolidations and what turned out to be the ultra troublesome one on accounting for income taxes.

By the late 1970s, the National Council on Governmental Accounting (NCGA), standard setter for state and local governmental entities, was undergoing pressures and criticisms similiar to those experienced by the Accounting Principles Board a decade earlier. The FASB added to the pressure in 1978 when it placed on its agenda a project on objectives of financial accounting and reporting by nonbusiness entities. Not surprisingly, this action captured the interest of organizations concerned with accounting and reporting by units of state and local government. Specifically, there was concern that a private sector body might be in a position to set standards for governmental units.

Then in May 1979, Senator Harrison Williams, later expelled from the Senate and jailed for bribe taking, introduced a "State and Local Government Accounting and Financial Reporting Standards Act" designed to establish a quasi-independent federal institute to set standards. If anything, the state and local government people were even more fearful of the Feds than they were of the private sector. Discussions began almost immediately between the FASB and FAF, on one hand, and a long list of organizations representing state, county, and municipal officials, on the other. The General Accounting Office, which had a keen interest in the accounting for federal grants at state and local levels, and the AICPA also participated.

At first, the FASB maintained that it had the capability to serve as a single standard setter for all kinds of entities—business, private not-for-profit, and governmental—and that a single standard-setting body was needed to avoid inevitable confusion and conflict over jurisdiction where constituencies overlapped. It turned out later that although the Board's assessment of accounting realities was clear enough, its reading of the political situation was not. It became apparent very soon that government officials could not accept a business-oriented group as rule maker. A long series of on-again, off-again negotiations followed until late 1982 when the FAF and interested governmental organizations reached agreement "in principle" on establishing a separate Governmental Accounting Standards Board under FAF auspices. These efforts had sufficed to forestall Senator Williams's bill, but the 1982 agreement quickly fell apart over the division of jurisdictional responsibilities between the FASB and a new standards board for governmental units, among other issues.

Bleak as the outlook was at that stage, neither side felt that it could simply fold its hand and walk away. On the government side, there was a realization that the NCGA, which was part of the Municipal Finance Officers Association, was not viable—and that funding for an independent standard-setting body would be difficult, if not impossible, to obtain. The

Foundation, for its part, recognized a need to place itself in the position to mediate the inevitable conflicts between private-sector and governmental standard-setting bodies. Negotiations resumed, and finally in January 1984, a "memorandum of understandings"[7] was approved by the FAF trustees as a basis for organizing the GASB.

The trustees regarded establishment of GASB as a major accomplishment, but in their eagerness to achieve it, they averted their eyes from the messiest issue. Don Kirk and his fellow FASB members, however, predicted serious problems for both private and public sector entities arising from the almost casual allocation of jurisdictional responsibilities between the two Boards. The agreement ignored the fact that some types of reporting entities, such as colleges, universities, and health care facilities, not only were prevalent in both the private and governmental sectors but also, to an increasing degree, drew on some of the same sources for financing. Therefore, their financial reporting practices should be comparable. However, the trustees agreed to organize the GASB with a mere "understanding" that the new Board would establish standards "for activities and transactions of state and local governmental entities," and the FASB would continue to do the same for all other entities.

The problem was exacerbated by the obvious fact that the FASB and its predecessors had issued many more standards than were in the arsenal of the NCGA, which GASB inherited—and FASB standards would obtain until and unless the GASB acted. On two occasions the GASB felt constrained to issue Statements advising its constituents not to follow certain FASB standards in areas where GASB expected to act but had not yet done so—in 1986 with regard to pension costs and in 1988 with regard to recognition of depreciation by not-for-profit organizations.

Despite urgent pleas from spokespersons for affected organizations, the loudest and most insistent coming from the National Association of College and University Business Officers (NACUBO), the trustees declined to acknowledge that there was a problem—but said that if there were, nothing would be done about it until 1988–89 when they were obligated by the so-called structure agreement to conduct major reviews of both the GASB and FASB.

Predictably, jurisdiction dominated the 1988–89 reviews of the two Boards—and it did not go away even after the trustees thought they had resolved it.

After the drastic turnover in membership of the FASB at the beginning of 1978, which had no precedent and has had no parallel since, the need to replace Board members was less than usual until 1985. The addition of Frank Block in 1979 already has been noted. Bob Morgan chose to retire as he reached the age of 65 at the end of 1982, and he was replaced by Victor H. Brown, executive vice president, chief financial officer, and a director of

Firestone Tire and Rubber. On the surface, Vic Brown appeared to be an ideal choice for membership on the FASB. He began his career as an academician, first at the Wharton School of the University of Pennsylvania, of which he is an alumnus. He then moved to the University of Buffalo, where he became head of the accounting faculty and, incidentally, acquired a Ph.D. in economics. Then he cast his lot with Touche Ross & Co., rising rapidly to national director of operations. Finally, rounding out his résumé before joining Firestone, he served for nearly a decade as vice president and controller of Standard Oil of Indiana (now Amoco).

Did his very substantial career as a business executive make an impression on corporate critics of the FASB? Not on all of them. As they heated up their attacks on the standard setters in the next few years, some in the business community chose to ignore his heavyweight corporate experience and categorize him as an academician. Those who were fixated on "representation" in what they viewed as a political process were frustrated because they couldn't decide whom he represented, so they assumed what they thought was the worst. Corporate America was showing early signs of a propensity for devouring its own that would become starkly evident a few years later.

Ralph Walters opted for retirement from the Board at the end of 1983, saying that he was seeking one more career change before it was time to retire for good. He was replaced by Raymond C. Lauver, national director of accounting services for Price Waterhouse. Ray Lauver had served on the Advisory Council, as a member of the FASB's screening committee on emerging problems, and on several project task forces. He also had been a director of the AICPA and chairman of AcSEC.

Art Wyatt, whom we already have met, was appointed to succeed John March, effective at the end of 1984.

After that, the next Board appointments would not become effective until 1986. One of those appointments would give rise to major controversy five years afterward, both within and outside the standard-setting structure—and raise serious questions about the proper role of Corporate America in the standard-setting process.

Meanwhile, louder and more insistent criticisms of the standard setters and their approach to standard setting were beginning to be heard. Some of these would be dealt with and would fade away, but most found fertile ground and have continued to grow over the years.

Aside from the initiatives of the Moss and Metcalf subcommittees in Congress, the first broadly based challenge to the FASB came not from (Big) Corporate America but from small businesses and more particularly the small accounting firms that purported to represent their interests before the FASB. Ironically, however, the complaints of small businesses, and especially the small public accounting firms that serve them, still reverberate in the protests of a powerful handful of the very largest corporations clustered in the very small Accounting Principles Task Force (APTF) of the Business Roundtable.

Like so many other ills of mankind, the concerns of small accounting firms are entangled in the slow evolution of laws and regulations. And as in so much of history, there is passion. In fact, in standard-setting circles, *concern* often is a synonym for *passion*.

The underlying problem is that there is a dissonance between the Securities Acts of the early 1930s, which focus on the information needs of investors in publicly owned companies, and the realities of life in the much larger universe of private companies and public companies with too few shareholders to come under the purview of the SEC. The large and the small are drawn together under the rubric of GAAP as specified by the AICPA in its Rules of Conduct. Although the FASB's focus necessarily is on the public investor because of the SEC's surveillance, its standards apply equally, under AICPA rules, to all companies, public and private, that may be called on to have their financial statements audited by public accountants. That call is most likely to come from local banks that lend to small companies—and in this regard, the bankers don't care whether a prospective borrower is large or small, subject to the Securities Acts or not.

The rub is that non-SEC registrants, because they are smaller, find that the cost of preparing GAAP financial statements, and having them audited, is proportionately greater than for larger public companies. More to the point, the time required of small-firm CPAs to keep current with new accounting rules is proportionately much greater than the time pressures on larger firms with their ability to assign specialists and delegate responsibility to them for following such things closely and advising the other accountants in the firm what they need to know. Thus, the question arose: Shouldn't there be "differential disclosure" and/or "differential measurement"? In other words, shouldn't GAAP be modified in some way for small public and private companies? The rallying cry of those who advocated an affirmative answer was "standards overload"—a cry that was taken up out of quite different motives by the Business Roundtable a decade later.

For small public accounting practitioners, the cry is more passionate than calculating. They are concerned, justifiably, that they must spend more time and effort than they sometimes can afford in familiarizing themselves with standards that they seldom have to apply because their clients, for the most part, do not need GAAP financial statements. The frequently heard claim that they have difficulty explaining their bills to GAAP-audited clients is less a concern about billing for work actually done than it is about the cost of time required to prepare themselves for such audits. It is difficult for any professional to justify billing for study time related to a specific assignment. Just as would be the case with their larger brethren a few years later, a relatively small number of vocal activists created waves of a disproportionate height, giving rise to an impression in some quarters that a spirit of rebellion was abroad in the land.

The issues related to small business and small practitioners were studied backward and forward over a period of more than seven years. Special committees of the AICPA completed reports in 1976, 1980, and 1983. The FASB issued a call for public comment in 1981 and commissioned an independent research project on which a report was published in 1983.[8] The staff also engaged in extensive research of its own, finding among many other things that small businesses were more amenable to being audited according to GAAP, and users of their financial reports were more dependent on GAAP reporting, than many small public accounting practitioners acknowledged.[9]

There also was reluctance on the part of many small business people, and some public accountants serving them, to accept the "second-class citizenship" status that the differential measurement idea implied. This finding was at least partially borne out by a 1985 Louis Harris and Associates survey that indicated a relatively high level of acceptance of standards by the executives of small companies, both public and private, suggesting that the smaller company people saw in standards the promise of a "level playing field" on which they might compete for capital against larger companies.[10]

Even the normally big business–oriented FEI Research Foundation sponsored a study of the financial reporting needs of small public companies and published a report in 1983. In sum, the efforts of the AICPA, FASB, and the FEI brought about a better understanding of the values of GAAP accounting for entities of all sizes, despite some inequities between large and small.

The FASB also made some standard-setting moves that alleviated the situation. In 1978, it formally exempted private companies from the requirements to report earnings per share and segment information, which had been particularly sore points. Later, it relieved them of the need to disclose pro forma results of operations for business combinations consummated under the purchase method and was careful to limit its inflation accounting experiment to larger companies. In 1984, a Small Business Advisory Group was formed. Perhaps more important, the Board committed itself to examine explicitly the implications to small business of each of its projects throughout the process of developing a standard and assigned a senior staff person to organize this aspect of its activity.

Problems remained, but the net result was determination on the part of all parties to do what they reasonably could to alleviate those problems over time. By the 1990s, spokespersons for small firms often were stronger defenders of standards in deliberations of the Emerging Issues Task Force (EITF) than the Big Six.

Meanwhile, pressure against the standard setters was building on another major front—and would continue to intensify from the early 1980s right up to the present.

NOTES

1. T. W. Copeland, ed., *The Correspondence of Edmund Burke*, "A Letter to the Sheriffs of Bristol," 1777 (London: 1958).

2. Financial Accounting Foundation, *The Structure of Establishing Financial Accounting Standards* (Stamford, Conn.: FAF, April 1977).

3. Ibid.

4. Ibid.

5. Ibid

6. Ibid.

7. "Agreement Concerning the Structure for a Governmental Accounting Standards Board (GASB)," *Status Report*, March 12, 1984.

8. A. Rashad Abdel-khalik and a team of five independent researchers, *Financial Reporting by Private Companies: Analysis and Diagnosis* (Stamford, Conn.: Financial Accounting Standards Board, 1983).

9. "Research Efforts and Highlights of Principal Findings," *Status Report*, November 22, 1983.

10. Louis Harris and Associates, Inc., *A Study of the Attitudes Toward and an Assessment of the Financial Accounting Standards Board* (Stamford, Conn.: FAF, 1985).

Chapter Seven

A Kaleidoscope of Complaints

There are no whole truths; all truths are half-truths. It is trying to treat them as whole truths that plays the devil.

Alfred North Whitehead[1]

The FASB entered the decade of the 1980s on an unexpected upbeat. Though it was undertaken with considerable trepidation because the sound of tom-toms up in the hills already was audible, an opinion survey by Louis Harris and Associates of a scientifically selected cross section of more than 400 constituents indicated that the Board had a broader and deeper base of approval than its more vocal critics would acknowledge. Because he had a special interest in accounting and finance, Harris personally constructed the questionnaire, directed the study, and analyzed the data.

In a survey that explored many aspects of standard setting, the "bottom line" was that 73 percent of all respondents gave the Board a positive rating overall. Fourteen percent were negative, and the rest were "not sure." Corporate chief financial officers were even more affirmative, at 82–18. Chief executives did not trail the total sample by much: They approved by 67–24.[2] But these findings did not still the drums of the unfriendly tribes.

Ignoring Lou Harris's long-proven professionalism, Roger Smith of General Motors and the Business Roundtable later insisted that Harris hadn't asked the right questions of the right people. He elaborated by saying that only the executives of very large companies were really in a position to evaluate the standard-setting function. This comment was at variance, however, with his dictum the year before that the standard-setting body should be more broadly based and responsive to all of its constituents.

On some of the basic issues in standard setting, members of the FASB often were bemused by the diametrically opposed claims of corporate preparers of financial information and the investment-oriented users of that information who, the Board had concluded, were of prime importance. Prominent among the issues dividing the contending parties was disagreement over who actually *were* the most important users of financial information—and whose views therefore were most deserving of the standard setters' attention.

Ever since the debates about objectives of financial reporting in the early 1970s, many in the corporate community had maintained that *they* were both preparers *and* the primary users of financial reports. In a paper delivered at the Wharton Symposium on Financial Reporting and Standard Setting in 1990, Gerald I. White, president of Grace & White and former chairman of the Financial Analysts Federation's financial accounting policy committee (before FAF became AIMR), said, "I find this view of financial reporting to be, at best, disingenuous." He acknowledged that preparers indeed are users but added, they are

very privileged ones at that. They have the ability to generate whatever financial and other data they require in whatever form they wish to have it. They do not need the FASB, the SEC, the AICPA, or any other body to obtain the information they desire. The external user, in contrast, is the beggar at the feast, dependent on whatever crumbs of information are made available.[3]

Writing in *Financial Executive* in 1990, John C. Jacobsen, vice president–finance, and William J. Ihlandfelt, assistant controller of the Shell Oil Company, maintained that the corporations' "dual role as both preparer and user results in a unique ability to recognize the needs of both." They pointed out that relatively little input on standard-setting proposals is provided by users and concluded that "the Board is being overly influenced by what it deems to be the needs of a rather narrow slice of its constituency, and a relatively unresponsive slice at that."[4]

Typically lacking in either sheer numbers of personnel, or numbers of personnel well enough versed in the technicalities of accounting, as distinct from the information needs of investors, to provide thought-out responses to FASB proposals, the user community has continued to disappoint and frustrate the standard setters by its paucity of response. And yet it has complained, along with Corporate America, that its views "are not heard." In a lengthy submission to the Foundation trustees' Oversight Committee in 1991, AIMR's Financial Accounting Policy Committee acknowledged the complaints of some preparers that their views were "not being heard" but added that analysts could make the same complaint just as strenuously but did not because they lacked the necessary time and resources.

The level of response to FASB proposals from academicians also is low—and for similar reasons.

Over the years, on the general run of projects, the group the standard setters categorize as "industry" has provided between 60 and 65 percent of responses to discussion memorandums and exposure drafts, although on certain projects it may exceed 80 percent. Representation at public hearings is in about the same proportion. Because only a handful of very large firms have the resources to respond regularly, the public accounting profession generally submits only about 15 to 20 percent of responses. The rest are scattered among various disciplines, with the mix varying by subject. Little significance can be attached to such figures, however. From the beginning, the standard setters have pointed out repeatedly that they are not interested in "counting noses" but may be swayed by a single tightly reasoned and well-documented argument.

Often overlooked by observers as a source of input to the standard setters is the Advisory Council. While individual Council members often submit written comments and participate in public hearings, discussions in FASAC meetings sometimes are more significant. Following a recommendation of the trustees' 1977 structure committee, the Council membership has been deliberately structured to mirror the constituency. For example, staff analysis conducted under Paul Kolton's direction showed that over a four-year period at the end of the 1980s almost a third of the Council members were from "business and industry," while nearly one-quarter were from "banking, insurance, and the securities industry." Public accounting provided a little more than one-fifth of the members, academe fewer than one-tenth, and a miscellany of backgrounds including securities law, not-for-profit institutions, and government accounted for the rest.

In the argument between issuers and users over primacy, Walter Schuetze, former member of the FASB, former member of FASAC, and future chief accountant of the SEC, had what normally might be regarded as the last word. In the charged atmosphere of contention over standards for financial accounting and reporting, however, it was not. In a roundup of opinions of eight leaders in the field published in *Financial Executive* in 1988, he stated squarely, as is his habit: "In the long run a standard-setting process that abandons the notion of the primacy of users will be in no one's interests."[5] A rebuttal came soon afterward. Writing in the *Journal of Corporate Accounting and Finance*, Merlin L. Alper, vice president and assistant controller of ITT Corporation, dismissed the users' claims to primary consideration, saying "users are often like the kid in a candy store, wanting everything he sees, even though he would only get sick if he attempted to eat it all."[6]

Not surprisingly, preparers and users expressed opposite views of the cost-benefit question. Corporate executives have consistently maintained that the benefits of a standard must clearly outweigh the costs (to themselves) of implementing it, though no concrete proposal of a method for adequate measurement of either benefits or costs has ever been put forward. Users, on the other hand, argue that they act on behalf of shareholders who bear pro rata shares of all corporate costs of doing business. Therefore, users, not managements, should be the arbiters where the cost of providing financial information is concerned.

Ivory tower is a term frequently used in corporate circles to describe the FASB. The Board is said to strive for "theoretical purity" in its standards and to ignore considerations of "pragmatism" or "practicality" from a business standpoint. When the Business Roundtable asked its members in a 1988 questionnaire whether the standard setters achieved a reasonable balance between theory and practical considerations, more than 90 percent of the responses were negative. Again, however, the professional users of financial reports had a different view of reality. Their professional association, AIMR, in a Position Paper published in 1992, stated: "Evidence demonstrates clearly that the FASB is not too theoretical. If anything, it is not theoretical enough, and such a trend makes analysis more difficult."[7] In his Wharton Symposium paper, Gerry White was more caustic. "Whatever criticisms one makes of the Board," he said "theoretical purity is one of the hardest to support." He cited the original Statement on foreign currency translation, which he admired, and its replacement, which was more acceptable to large corporations with overseas operations. "That the Board was willing to amend the standard so promptly suggests, I believe, a willingness to sacrifice good theory for preferred practice," he concluded.[8]

AIMR's 1992 Position Paper observed, "The fact that no group believes their interests are being completely served must mean that the FASB is doing a decent job of balancing the competing interests of each constituency group."[9]

Not all issues give rise to sharp differences between preparers and users, however—and on some the analysts' criticisms are more penetrating and harder for the standard setters to refute than those of the business community.

On the question of assets and liabilities versus earnings (or the balance sheet versus income statement), for example, the analysts' view provides some support for the "matching" advocates in the business community. This had long been a concern of the FEI and Business Roundtable, but AIMR came forward in its 1991 submission to the Financial Accounting Foundation with the observation that the standard setters showed concern for balance sheet presentation with little attention to how results are reported in the income statement. The letter expressed appreciation for the attention the FASB was giving the balance sheet but emphasized that the income statement is of equal importance.

Corporate America had been criticizing the FASB technical staff for several years as being ignorant of business decision making at best and "anti-business" at worst. The analysts' comments in their 1991 submission to the Oversight Committee of the Financial Accounting Foundation made a somewhat left-handed gesture of support for the staff, followed by a telling criticism. In general, AIMR said, the staff is competent but lacks sufficient understanding of how financial statements are used in the analytical process. At least some professional users of financial information were aware of intensive efforts by the FASB staff from time to time to gain understanding of analysts' decision making with regard to specific subjects, but AIMR concluded that the staff would benefit from exposure to analysts' decision processes and methodologies through internships in the research departments of broker-dealers, investment advisory firms, banks, insurance companies, or pension funds. That recommendation has not been acted on at this writing.

Historically, users of financial statements have had a keen interest in what they call "disaggregated data." Indeed, AIMR's 1992 Position Paper called such information "vital, essential, fundamental, indispensable and integral to the investment analysis process." In setting its original technical agenda in 1973, the Standards Board committed itself to a project on what it called "segment reporting" and issued Statement No. 14, *Financial Reporting for Segments of a Business Enterprise*, in 1976.[10] Analysts found this "helpful but inadequate," in the words of AIMR's Position Paper. "This situation has been exacerbated," the paper went on, "by issuance in 1987 of Statement . . . No. 94, *Consolidation of All Majority-Owned Subsidiaries*. That Statement has the good effect of presenting an overall report on complex economic entities and brings onto the consolidated balance sheet a large amount of debt that previously had not appeared there." But, the analysts went on, "its cost has been the loss of much detailed information about subsidiary operations quite different in character from those of the parent company."[11]

As part of their large and long-running project on "Consolidations and Related Matters," the standard setters commissioned a research study by Paul A. Pacter, a professor of accounting at the University of Connecticut and former staff member (later finance commissioner of the City of Stamford) who had been the principal researcher for Statement No. 14. It was the first step in a reexamination of that Statement and several related ones issued subsequently. Pacter's findings were published early in 1993,[12] and the report was to be followed later that year by a Board document soliciting public comments on whether and how to change existing requirements.

A second major concern of users has to do with the standard setters' inconsistency with regard to establishing effective dates and transition provisions for new standards, resulting in difficulty for the analysts in developing comparable information year by year. Some standards, AIMR pointed out, have not become fully effective for as long as five years after issuance. Such time lags have resulted in what AIMR called "destruction of financial data without commensurate improvement in the financial information provided."[13] Comparability of financial information had been identified by the FASB in Statement of Financial Accounting Concepts No. 2 as one of the "Primary Decision-Specific Qualities" of financial reporting.[14] Though its importance often is disputed by preparers of financial information, comparability of financial information has long been a major concern of analysts—and legislators.

Members of the FASB and its staff were accustomed to dodging "friendly fire" long before the term became familiar on the nightly news. Criticisms from preparers almost invariably were prefaced by pious expressions of belief in, and support for, private sector standard setting. "But . . . " And that is where the complaining would begin. Roger Smith, for example, began a determined move to bring the FASB under a significant measure of control by Corporate America in January 1983 by saying he thought that all chief executives believed it was more desirable to have the standard-setting function performed in the private sector rather than by a governmental agency. He added that CEOs were basically supportive both with words and with money, *but* this did not mean they were satisfied with some of the standard setters' decisions.

One of the things that bothered Smith and some of his like-minded followers most was the issue of what he called the FASB's basic goal of uniformity in setting standards. Smith's lieutenant for financial reporting at GM, Eugene H. Flegm, called it a "relentless thrust toward uniformity" in his 1984 book *Accounting: How to Meet the Challenges of Relevance and Regulation* and assigned almost equal blame for it to the FASB's predecessors, the CAP and the APB. "The discipline involved in having standard setters is quite beneficial," Flegm allowed, "so long as the standard setters only step in when a clear distortion or abuse of an accounting concept is involved." He charged that standard setters since the beginning in the late 1930s "have steadily marched toward the elimination of judgment and the mandating of a single method even when no clear abuse of alternative methods could be established."[15] It is difficult to reconcile this statement with the CAP's permissive identification of merely "acceptable procedures," but no matter. It doesn't reconcile, either, with the basic notion of standards of any kind, or with the thrust of Representative Harley Staggers's charge to the SEC in the 1960s, the concerns of the Moss and Metcalf committees in the 1970s, or the concerns of Representative Jonn D. Dingell in the 1980s—to say nothing of the consistent demands of investors and other users for financial information that would be comparable from one company, and one industry, to another.

The most frequently heard, and most shrill, complaint was that "the Board doesn't listen" to pleas for more "general" or permissive standards based on cost-benefit considerations and fear of claimed economic and social consequences. This goes to the heart of the question as to whether a select group of experts should be relied on to set standards for financial reporting or whether decisions should be determined by the interplay of pressures exerted by those parties that have the greatest interest in the outcome of a particular issue—and the greatest clout. This issue is discussed at greater length in Chapters 11 and 12.

Related to, and intertwined with, the "doesn't listen" complaint was dissatisfaction in many quarters with the way advisory task forces were used in connection with major standard-setting projects.

From the beginning, the members of task forces were deliberately chosen to bring to the FASB for its consideration the full spectrum of known points of view on each issue, and those positions generally have been represented by persons of recognized stature and expertise. From this diversity, the Board and its staff theoretically would be able to set forth a neutral discussion memorandum as a basis for public comment, including public hearing testimony. And indeed, that generally has been the case. However, the attempt to juxtapose stature and expertise with neutrality has proved to be naive. Task force members frequently have been frustrated or disillusioned by their mission within the Board's established procedure, believing that their expert opinions should influence final decisions to a greater extent than has occurred—or can occur—given the goal of having diverse points of view represented in each task force.

The most dramatic example of this tension was in the project that resulted in Statement No. 87, *Employers' Accounting for Pensions*, late in 1985.[16] The tension was heightened by fear on the part of some actuaries, who were well represented on the task force, that the project was merely a Trojan Horse behind which accountants were maneuvering to move in and take over the actuaries' functions in the administration of pension plans.

Several months after the Statement was issued, a major trade publication, *Pensions & Investment Age*, ran a page-one article that began by saying: "The lengthy process leading to adoption . . . of Statement 87, which placed pension obligations on corporate balance sheets, was a charade, some members of the advisory task force on the standard charge."[17] Despite that provocative lead, however, the article acknowledged that members of the task force were split almost evenly as to whether they would have voted for the Statement, which was about the way they might have been expected to come out, given the deliberate attempt to achieve a balance of views when they were appointed.

One purported piece of information that was given to the *Pensions & Investment Age* reporter but was not published because spokespersons for the FASB were able to refute it in advance was that the project manager had been "fired" because of the "unpopularity" of Statement No. 87. Timothy S. Lucas did leave the Board shortly after the Statement was issued, as many project managers do at the end of the lengthy, difficult, and emotionally draining process of getting a major standard in shape to be adopted. He became an investment banker for a while, but he was back at the FASB two years later as director of research and technical activities.

Nevertheless, the belief that task force members, whose function is defined as purely advisory in the FASB's Rules of Procedure and in separate Operating and Administrative Procedures for FASB Task Forces,[18] should vote on proposed standards and that their votes should have a strong, if not actually decisive, influence on the Board has not died.

Given the nature of standard setting, it is inevitable that any single entity or set of interests rarely, if ever, will see all its positions and preferences adopted. When strongly held views of constituents are rejected by the decision makers, even when good reasons are set forth for doing so, it is only human nature for convinced advocates of the rejected views to complain that their position was not properly considered.

It also is natural for grievances to accumulate—and give rise over time to proposals for ameliorating them.

The grievances that grew in the early 1980s had to do both with the Board's process and its judgment. There was great reluctance, however, to attack the members of the Board themselves. Corporate America was more or less united on the proposition that a private sector devil you knew was better than one the government might unleash, so it preferred to attribute the cause of decisions it did not like to a radically minded staff that was alleged to exert undue influence over the decision makers. The staff was said to be "a bunch of academics with no practical experience" or even "a bunch of kids just out of college." The first allegation bore no resemblance to reality. In fact, only rarely were there more than 2 members of the technical staff, out of 40 or more, whose backgrounds were primarily academic. The second was a reference to the four or five recent graduates who were brought in each year, on a highly selective basis, for a 12-month internship in which they were assigned to do the grunt work for senior staff members before moving on to permanent positions in public accounting, industry, and in a few cases, academe.

Claims that the Board was dominated by staff were a subject of wry humor for project managers who had been around for a while—and whom Board members had sent back to their word processors to redo draft proposals again and again.

Akin to the overload complaint, but more subtle, were claims that the Board was working on the wrong projects, or on projects that did not need attention. (It is sometimes stated more crudely that the Board adds topics to its agenda just to keep itself busy.) Even Denny Beresford who, when he was appointed to the FASB as its chairman, had had closer-in experience with it for more than a decade than almost anyone not actually a member of the organization, started with a notion that some agenda topics might not merit the Board's attention. Only a short time later, however, he was explaining that "the Board doesn't have nearly the resources needed to tackle all the accounting problems it is asked to address" and that requests to add topics to the agenda came from many sources, including users, auditors, regulators, and even preparers of financial information.

Beresford's predecessor, Don Kirk, may have diagnosed the frequently observed "If it ain't broke, don't fix it" syndrome correctly. "Widespread dissatisfaction with an accounting standard often disappears," he said, "when the alternatives are considered."

The flip side of "overload" was that the standard-setting process was too slow and that it should provide "timely guidance" as to the application of standards. Despite pleas for "broad" standards that would leave plenty of room for "judgment" in their application, many of the same people who advocated this approach to standard setting were among the most insistent, when the Board did write such a standard, that detailed guidance be provided as to how to apply it.

The 1982 report of the trustees' structure committee observed that many respondents to the questionnaire the committee had circulated said the Board should concern itself primarily with broad issues but that its standards, in the view of those respondents, "should provide clear accounting guidance" while at the same time leaving "room for judgment in determining the applications of those standards to particular situations." The trustees concluded that "there is a need for timely guidance on current accounting practice problems"[19] but what that entailed was not specified. Whatever it was, the report asked the FASB to develop a plan to achieve it.

J.T. Ball later remarked, "If you need the rule that is being issued, it is timely guidance: if you don't, it is standards overload."

At the beginning of its life, the FASB had hoped, like the APB before it, to concentrate on fundamental issues that might be described as "broad." But, like the APB, the FASB came to realize in a short time that its viability as standard setter depended almost equally on its ability to deal with "emerging problems"—those relatively narrow, but nonetheless difficult, ones that kept bubbling up out of the creativeness of day-to-day business and out of the tensions of day-to-day relations between preparers and auditors resulting from that creativeness. Though rightly revered for the wisdom of their precepts that were enunciated at the beginning of the 1940s, Paton and Littleton had long ago been upstaged by the action in the marketplace. Soon, as much as one-third of staff time was being devoted, under Ball's direction, to implementation and emerging issues.

Only two years into its standard-setting mission, the FASB realized in 1975 that it needed to develop antennae to help it know, understand, and react to what was going on out there in the workaday world. The Screening Committee on Emerging Problems was formed to help evaluate the importance and urgency of the problems that bubbled up—and whether and to what extent the Board could, or should, respond. In typical FASB fashion, the screening committee was made up of 15 members who covered all the bases within the Board's constituency.

Five years later, the screening committee was replaced by an Advisory Council committee on the FASB agenda. Two future Board members were among the original six members of that committee, Vic Brown and Denny Beresford. The latter, of course, became FASB chairman in 1987. But that committee also was superseded in the aftermath of the 1982 structure committee report.

Taking the FAF trustees' report as an assignment, the Board appointed a "blue ribbon" task force under the chairmanship of the late Robert C. Thompson, chief financial officer of Shell Oil and one of the more thoughtful corporate executives then taking an interest in the standard-setting process. The group's mission was to explore in depth the needs for timely guidance on implementation of accounting standards and on emerging issues "that have important financial reporting implications." Again, two future Board members served on the task force—Denny Beresford and Ray Lauver. The group issued an invitation to comment and held a public hearing before preparing a report that would have a profound effect on standard setting.

The task force made two principal recommendations. One was that the scope of Technical Bulletins should be broadened so they might deal with more issues. The other was that the FASB should establish a special advisory group of people from public accounting and industry who were in the best positions to be aware of emerging problems and their potential significance. This group would assist the Board in "identifying and defining financial reporting issues and in *developing possible solutions*" (emphasis added).[20]

Both recommendations were fraught with implications for the Board's due process and its mission. How far could it go in allowing the staff to issue accounting guidance? How far could it go in relying on an outside group to develop possible solutions to emerging problems? Recognizing the pitfalls, the Board moved cautiously. At the end of 1983, it issued an invitation to comment of its own, incorporating the proposals of the Thompson task force.[21]

Hearing no more than a routine murmur of disapproval in the public comment process, the Board proceeded in the spring of 1984 to expand the scope of Technical Bulletins, as recommended, to address areas not directly covered by existing pronouncements and to provide guidance that might differ from that prescribed by an existing pronouncement. To legitimize this leeway, it also decided that each topic to be covered by the staff in a proposed Technical Bulletin would be discussed by the Board at a public meeting and that no Technical Bulletin would be issued if a majority of Board members objected to it.

More significantly, the Board agreed to establish, "on an experimental basis," a separate task force to help in identifying implementation problems and emerging issues that might require FASB attention and—before referring them to the Board—to determine, if possible (only by overwhelming consensus), whether existing accounting rules, when properly applied, would suffice to solve them. Officially designated as the Emerging Issues Task Force in mid-1984, EITF would be made up of 15 persons, including the top technical partners of the Big Eight accounting firms, plus two from midrange or smaller firms, and in deference to the politics of the situation, two from the Financial Executives Institute, two from the (then) National Association of Accountants, and one representing the Business Roundtable. The latter was vice president and controller of the General Motors Corporation, whose chairman by then was taking a keen interest in accounting standards, both in his daytime job and as chairman of the Accounting Principles Task Force of the Roundtable. Political considerations overrode the fact that public accountants clearly were in the best position to know about emerging problems, and corporate executives were much less likely to have a broad awareness of such issues. Chairman of the group was James J. Leisenring, who had succeeded Mike Alexander as director of research and technical activities in 1982, and staff support was provided by the FASB.

Despite concessions to the concerns of preparers of financial information, the EITF and its parent soon were subject to complaints that de facto accounting standards were being established without due process. Never mind that the meetings were open to the public and their agendas were announced in advance, that copies of discussion papers were available on request in advance of meeting dates, or that only three dissents in the 15–member group could nullify a judgment by a majority of the group that an accounting rule already in place provided the answer to a problem if properly applied—and no new rules could be written by the EITF.

In spite of these tight limitations on its scope, the EITF quickly proved to be an effective instrument. It has been able to resolve, without sending on to the FASB, approximately two-thirds of the issues placed before it. The rest have either been taken up by the Board as full-fledged agenda topics or as parts of other projects, have been handled by the staff in Technical Bulletins, or have lost their urgency. In any case, the task force has significantly reduced the need for the FASB to issue new standards, despite the continuing proliferation of issues. Many of those who thought they saw de facto standard setting were among the most vehement protesters against standards overload.

When the AICPA yielded its preeminent rule-making role to make way for the FASB in 1973, it did not give up entirely its impulse to set standards. After a period of uncertainty as to what its function should be in this regard, the Institute's Accounting Standards Executive Committee in 1977 began to issue Statements of Position (SOPs) to provide guidance for AICPA members in areas not covered by the existing literature. At first, this caused consternation at the FASB because of potential confusion among both auditors and preparers as to the authoritative status of the new documents—and uncertainty on the Board's part about the Institute's intentions in seeming to reenter the standard-setting business.

Tension was eased temporarily by the FASB's decision, mentioned in Chapter 6, to clothe AICPA SOPs, Industry Accounting Guides, and those portions of Industry Audit Guides that had accounting implications in the raiment of FASB Statements of Accounting Standards. Although that effort never was completed, AcSEC turned its attention to preparing documents that identified issues for the Board's attention, rather than advising AICPA members what to do about them. The vehicle it chose was the Issues Paper, which was intended originally to be a neutral document, merely stating the urgency of an issue that AcSEC thought required resolution and setting forth the technical pros and cons. The serpent of competitive standard setting raised its head again, however, when Issues Papers began to include advisory opinions that *did* provide guidance of uncertain authoritativeness for AICPA members and therefore had the potential for confusion among preparers and auditors as to what guidance they should follow.

Again, the FASB and its supporters saw danger signals. What status, in relation to FASB Statements of Accounting Standards and Interpretations, should those advisory opinions have? Some were in direct conflict. So the Board urged AcSEC to omit opinions, however "advisory," from future Issues Papers and return to the use of SOPs—with the proviso that the FASB might explicitly decline to support the proposed document if it was in conflict with a current FASB project or one that was under consideration for addition to the agenda. From that time forward, the routine was intended to be that AcSEC would submit proposed SOPs and Issues Papers for formal review by the Board, with at least a tacit understanding that nothing would be issued if the FASB objected.

That tacit agreement was abrogated early in 1989, however, when the AICPA board of directors refused to approve a policy jointly recommended by AcSEC and FASB that would have required omission of advisory opinions from Issues Papers.

In human terms, it is understandable that the AICPA still sought ways to maintain some kind of role as standard setter. Two decades after the FASB took over that function, the leaders in public accounting still were people who grew up in the profession at a time when the Institute stood alone in the private sector as setter of standards. However well they may have recognized the political realities that compelled the AICPA to surrender this role in 1972, at least subconsciously some never have been wholly reconciled to that decision.

Therefore, it was not as surprising as it seemed at the time that another decision by the AICPA's directors a year later seemed to undercut still further the FASB's authority as standard setter. They decreed that it no longer would be necessary for AcSEC to obtain FASB approval before issuance of an Issues Paper. This heightened tensions once again. Norman Strauss, then chairman of AcSEC and former partner of Denny Beresford in the firm that now is known as Ernst & Young, sought to relieve those tensions in a speech to an FEI audience. "Why would AcSEC issue something if the FASB disagrees with us?" he asked rhetorically. "Well, the reality is we won't. We can, but it's almost impossible to conceive it will ever actually happen."[22] It was the familiar "benevolent dictator" defense, leaving unanswered the question of what would happen when there was a change in either personalities or circumstances. Nevertheless, relations between FASB and AICPA returned to normal and that worst-case scenario has not yet been played out.

Intertwined with the "overload" and "broad versus detailed" questions was a prevalent complaint about "complexity" in the standards. The Business Roundtable would play this to a fare-thee-well in 1987–91, which was a period in which several important—and admittedly complex—standards on difficult issues were promulgated. The Roundtable would find, at least for a time, a sympathetic ear at the SEC.

The financial analyst community, however, flatly rejected the complexity claim. AIMR and its spokespersons consistently stated that increasing complexity in standards merely was a reflection of the increasing complexity of business transactions. The Association's 1992 Position Paper went so far as to aver that "preparers don't do a good job of understanding and applying accounting standards."[23] Gerry White, in his Wharton Symposium paper, said: "The 'rocket scientists' who invent complex instruments have been working overtime; accounting and disclosure have been left behind."[24]

Nevertheless, it was true that, apart from the inherent complexities of many of the topics the Board addressed, including such subjects as pensions, income taxes, and postretirement health benefits, the standard setters themselves did contribute to the complexity problem by attempting to assuage the fears of corporate constituents about volatility of earnings. Jim Leisenring, who was appointed to the Board in 1987 and named vice chairman three months later, has pointed this out repeatedly.

For example, a good number of people say complexity equals cost, and I think we might intuitively agree to that. But I think maybe most people think some of the complexity in the standards is more than beneficial. If you take Statement 87 [pensions] and the one on other postemployment benefits, for example, an awful lot of the complexity is there to mitigate the volatility in earnings that would otherwise occur. . . . There's absolutely no doubt that an awful lot of the complexities in a good many of our standards are amortization devices, corridors and the like, that we have put in because people perceive these as benefits in mitigating volatility.[25]

In fact, built in to the pensions Statement was a 10 percent plus-or-minus "corridor," within which gains or losses in pension fund assets would not have to be recorded, and thus company contributions would not be affected. It was not the best accounting from a user's standpoint, to be sure, or even a literal-minded accountant's, but it was adopted to calm the nerves of corporate executives who had been unnerved by the prospect of a "pure" solution. The corridor, of course, greatly complicated computations of pension assets in relation to obligations. A similar device was adopted for the same reasons, and with the same results, in Statement No. 106 on health benefits.

In a public hearing on the remake of the ill-fated Statement No. 96 on accounting for income taxes, Tim Lucas probed one aspect of the complexity issue with a spokesman for the FEI, David Dusendschon, senior vice president of Kimberly-Clark. Lucas wanted to know why recognizing tax liabilities was more complex than recognizing assets related to foreign tax credits. This part of the hearing transcript reads as follows:

Mr. Lucas: But if complexity is solid grounds for not bothering to even look at the liability, unless there is a difference in complexity, I don't understand why we wouldn't apply the same test on the asset side.

Mr. Dusendschon: We responded, I think in the letter, that we appreciated the complexity and were glad that it was considered by the Board, but it wasn't the complexity issue that caused us to say it's not a liability, I mean. . . .

Mr. Lucas: So, it's not too complex?

Mr. Dusendschon: Right.

Mr. Lucas: To the liability. . . .

Mr. Dusendschon: It's complex, and we don't want to give up on that, but it's first and foremost not a liability in our view. But we are willing to fight through complexity when we are trying to record assets. (Laughter.)

Denny Beresford then observed that apparently there is such a thing as "good complexity versus bad complexity." That phrase quickly slipped into the jargon of standard setting.

Dave Dusendschon is a man of intelligence and wit. It was clear that he understood the irony of his response.

For critics of standards, *costs versus benefits* are words that trip lightly from the tongue and, superficially, have a ring of potentially great significance. But aggregate costs of applying a given standard can be estimated only within such wide parameters as to be meaningless, and benefits cannot be quantified at all because they accrue to society as a whole in the form of information that can be used in almost infinite numbers of unknowable ways. This has been reaffirmed every time thoughtful, as distinct from argumentative, attention has been given to the subject.

One such occasion was a meeting of the Advisory Council in 1990 in which the discussion was dominated by corporate people who generally are the most insistent on the feasibility of, and need for, meaningful cost-benefit analysis. Edward O'Brien, then president of the Securities Industry Association, came close to capturing the sense of the meeting when he said:

I think it is rather foolhardy, and it violates my sense of common sense in a way, to try to be too precise on cost-benefit analysis. We will never agree on a standard of costs, and we can never foresee the benefits. Therefore, why try to become as precise as some people would have you think we should be? That is not to say we should forget about it entirely.

In that last comment, O'Brien echoed the other participants who agreed that standard setters cannot ignore the subject but should always be mindful of it, bringing to bear their best informed judgment rather than any complex—and suspect—formulas to attempt to quantify costs and benefits.

"The subject," Ralph Walters said later, "is God, home, and motherhood. You can't be against it. But it's used mostly by people who want to put an obstacle in the way of change."[26]

For some, the magic key to cost-benefit analysis was "field testing." If only each proposed standard could be tested in "the real world," then the Board would be unlikely to make any more "mistakes" that cause complaints—or pain and inconvenience—on the part of preparers. Again, superficially, the idea had great appeal and indeed had been an important part of the standard-setting process on some projects in certain circumstances where testing was feasible, most notably on the extremely contentious projects on pensions and postemployment benefits. However, there were practical considerations of which those close to the process were well aware. But many others either were ignorant of those considerations or chose to ignore them.

Denny Beresford, impressed and somewhat shaken by demands for mandatory field testing on major projects when he assumed the FASB chairmanship in 1987, made a point of asking Paul Kolton to have the Advisory Council discuss the subject at an early meeting. This was done in July of that year, with results that were not surprising to close observers of the process.

The first problem was one of definition, which often is the case in arguments about accounting standards and the process leading up to them. Several definitions of field testing were suggested, ranging from solicited responses to an exposure draft focusing specifically, at the request of the standard setters, on implementation costs and economic consequences, to a statistically valid (and therefore so broad as to be unattainable) sample of companies' costs of applying a proposed standard.

The problem was that only small numbers of companies could be persuaded to go to the trouble (and expense) of participating in detailed field tests—and sometimes not enough were willing to participate to make such an exercise viable. Those that were able to participate generally were very large companies whose presence in the sample might tend to distort the results, especially as the companies were self-selected. That tendency, of course, was quite acceptable to many who were the most insistent advocates of field testing. (In a later FASAC meeting on the same subject, a member of the FASB staff made bold to point out that companies participating in field tests tend to focus on costs and ignore benefits. This probably reinforced the impression in some quarters that the staff had a radical cast of mind.)

At the time, there was pressure to force the Board into a straitjacket of required field testing for every major project or at least, as an FEI representative invited to the meeting to present the case said, "where a project is headed into uncharted waters."

It remained for Ray Lauver, with his talent for going to the heart of a matter, to point out that field testing in its various forms was merely a synonym for disciplined fact gathering and therefore "one of the ingredients of the due process procedure."

The sense of the meeting was that some form of field testing should be considered in connection with every project but that there was no need to change the bylaws to require such consideration. Whether or not to mount a formal field test, and in what form such a test might be mounted, should remain a decision of the Standards Board.

Five years after the first FASAC discussion of the subject, prodded by yet another committee of trustees, Beresford appointed a task force on field testing. At its initial meeting in 1992, this task force, while generally in favor of field testing, was no more able to define a field test or specify the circumstances in which one should be conducted than FASAC had been. Several of the comments seemed to verge on characterizing a field test as a public relations device. "It buys you a lot with the constituency," one corporate executive said. Though not opposed to field testing in principle, Peter Knutson, a professor at the Wharton School and consultant to organizations of securities analysts and bank credit officers, felt constrained to remind the group of some home truths. "A field test," he said, "slows down the process, is not inexpensive, can be biased, and is not statistically valid."

In 1986, the Foundation trustees had approved a report by one of their committees that concluded that differing definitions and perceptions of both costs and benefits made it impossible for any universally acceptable method of cost-benefit assessment to be developed.

Nevertheless, in a board of trustees meeting in 1990, by which time that body, in at least some respects, had become an adversary rather than an ally and supporter of the standard setters, the chairman of one of the Big Six accounting firms, in a quite adversarial manner, demanded of Denny Beresford: "Who is your cost-benefit man?" Failing to get a specific answer, he repeated the question—as though it were possible for there to be an expert in an area that is conceded by thoughtful and knowledgeable persons to be unknowable. It was as though the Business Roundtable had one of its members in the prompter's box.

Often, when specific kinds of information are under discussion, company spokespersons assert "Analysts never ask us for that." The assertion is sometimes puzzling, but James M. Meyer, an analyst with Janney, Montgomery, Scott, Inc., and a member of the task force on field testing, offered an explanation. "Users look for imprudent management," he said. "It probably is frustrating [for blue chip companies] to have to show they are prudent, and analysts tell the prudent ones they don't need that [particular kind of] information from them." Other things being equal, he added, "you're never going to hear a user ask for less information rather than more."

If they lose all other arguments, the final area for complaint by the disaffected is that the Board does not have a formal mechanism for post-enactment review of its standards. If only such a mechanism existed, the reasoning goes, "bad" standards could be eliminated quickly and easily.

In fact, the Rules of Procedure always have required the Board to consider a written request from any individual or organization to reexamine any existing pronouncement. That consideration must determine whether the information and reasoning presented in support of a request to reexamine had been considered adequately prior to issuance of the pronouncement and whether subsequent events might warrant review or reexamination. Although the answers are negative in most cases, a few amendments to standards have resulted from this process, and in one instance —accounting for income taxes—an entire standard was, in effect, nullifed before it ever became effective and subsequently was reissued in a substantially different form.

The irrepressible Lee Seidler, writing in *Financial Executive*, complained that the FASB's geographical location was too isolated and insulated. He demanded that it be moved "out of the woods." The "pastoral" Connecticut location was "far from the reality of financial markets and the problems of preparing, auditing, and analyzing financial statements," he wrote. No doubt a New York location would have seemed to be more convenient for special pleaders hoping to "do lunch" with Board members and staff—but that was one of the reasons for staying away from New York in the first place.

Seidler also observed that "in bucolic Connecticut" the standard setters "listen to presentations from staff and the outside world, leisurely deliberate and then issue their Statements in a process that is sometimes as relevant to the real world as eunuchs giving advice on sex."[27]

There were many other complaints and many variations on the ones cited above (except the last). In 1984, Roger Smith, acting in the name of the Business Roundtable, bundled them all up and attempted to use them as a battering ram.

NOTES

1. Alfred North Whitehead, quoted by Lucien Price in Prologue to *Dialogues* (Westport, Conn.: Greenwood Press, 1977), 16.

2. Louis Harris and Associates, Inc., *A Study of the Attitude Toward and an Assessment of the Financial Accounting Standards Board* (Stamford, Conn.: Financial Accounting Foundation, April 1980).

3. Gerald I. White, "The Coming Deregulation of Accounting Principles," paper delivered at a symposium sponsored by the American Institute of Certified Public Accountants on Financial Reporting and Standard Setting at the Wharton School, University of Pennsylvania, October 25–26, 1990 (hereafter cited as White, Wharton Symposium).

4. John C. Jacobsen and William J. Ihlandfelt, "The Rule-Making Process: A Time for Change?" *Financial Executive*, March–April 1990, 30.

5. Walter Schuetze, "Three Reasons Why Agreement on the FASB Is Unrealistic," *Financial Executive*, September–October 1988, 23.

6. Merlin L. Alper, "Is FASB Making the Grade?" *Journal of Corporate Accounting and Finance*, Winter 1991–92, 208.

7. Association for Investment Management and Research (AIMR), *Financial Reporting in the 1990s and Beyond: A Position Paper of the Association for Investment Management and Research*, October 1992 (hereafter cited as AIMR, Position Paper).

8. White, Wharton Symposium.

9. AIMR, Position Paper.

10. FASB Statement No. 14, *Financial Reporting for Segments of a Business Enterprise*, December 1976.

11. AIMR, Position Paper.

12. Paul Pacter, *Reporting Desegregated Information* (Norwalk, Conn.: Financial Accounting Standards Board, February 1993).

13. AIMR, Position Paper.

14. FASB Statement of Financial Accounting Concepts No. 2, *Qualitative Characteristics of Accounting Information*, May 1980.

15. Eugene H. Flegm, *Accounting: How to Meet the Challenges of Relevance and Regulation* (New York: John Wiley, 1984), 103.

16. FASB Statement No. 87, *Employers' Accounting for Pensions*, December 1985.

17. "FASB 87 Process Called a Charade," *Pensions & Investment Age*, April 14, 1986, 1.

18. Rules of Procedure, first issued in 1973 and amended in 1978, 1987, and 1991. Rules of Procedure incorporates the Rules of Procedure of the FASB, Certificate of Incorporation and Bylaws of the Financial Accounting Foundation, and Operating and Administrative Procedures for FASB Task Forces, though officially they are separate documents.

19. Financial Accounting Foundation, *Operating Efficiency of the FASB*, Stamford, Conn., August 1982.

20. Report of the FASB Task Force on Timely Financial Reporting Guidance, June 1983.

21. FASB, *Proposed Procedures for Implementing Recommendations of the FASB Task Force on Timely Financial Reporting Guidance*, December 27, 1983.

22. Norman N. Strauss, remarks to the FEI conference on current financial reporting issues, New York, November 1991.

23. AIMR, Position Paper.

24. White, Wharton Symposium.

25. James J. Leisenring, first Board Member Forum, an open meeting of past and present members of the FASB, Norwalk, Conn., September, 1988.

26. Ralph E. Walters, second Board Member Forum, Norwalk, Conn., May 1993.

27. Lee J. Seidler, "Move the FASB Out of the Woods," *Financial Executive*, September–October 1988, 24.

Chapter Eight

The Business Roundtable Steps Up to Bat

None can love freedom heartily but good men; the rest love not freedom but license.

John Milton[1]

A decade after Lee Seidler's gloomy prediction about the absence of a single, strong, self-interested constituency to defend the FASB, such as its predecessors had as senior committees of the AICPA, the new standard-setting organization seemed to be flourishing despite complaints and criticisms. The supposed weakness to which Seidler pointed was thought by many to be its greatest strength.

Underlying the almost universal euphoria that grew up around the Wheat Committee report in 1972, and the quick decisions by various key organizations to implement it, was a belief that the new standard-setting structure would provide a viable means for the private sector to retain an important and sensitive function and at the same time perform a valuable service for the public good in a responsible, politically acceptable manner. However, there were those who privately hoped, even assumed, that what was being erected was an attractive facade behind which they could play "let's pretend" about self-regulation.

As noted, the 1980 opinion survey found strong support for the standard-setting structure in all segments of its constituency. A repetition of that survey in 1985 would find even higher levels of approval, prompting Lou Harris, who again directed the survey and wrote the report, to tell the trustees and the Board in a meeting at Stamford: "If I were you, I'd be a bit embarrassed by the 87 to 11 percent positive rating. . . . You see, you have nowhere to go but down." He then added: "It just could be that the FASB has entered into its most difficult and treacherous era. . . . It is apparent that the constituents are not about to give up their God-given rights of remonstrance and even of recall, let alone the right to take exception to everything issued if necessary."[2]

Harris was prescient. Despite the heartening numbers generated by his interviewers and computers, a powerful negative force was beginning to be exerted by a tiny minority of the Board's constituents clustered in a handful of the largest and most imperial of America's corporations.

The Business Roundtable was founded in 1972 as a self-described "influential lobbying force." Early commentary in the business press hailed it as a long-needed countervailing voice for business in Washington. It soon became the power center for action by the largest corporations against such threats as unfavorable tax legislation, proposed federal regulations, and since 1976, accounting rules set in the private sector. In that year, Thomas A. Murphy, a founding trustee of the Financial Accounting Foundation and then CEO of General Motors, provided the impetus for formation of an Accounting Principles Task Force within the Roundtable and became its first chairman.

Membership in the Roundtable is personal and is limited to the chief executives of the 200 largest U.S. companies on *Fortune*'s list of 500, but at any given time its membership is a little less than 200 because of the normal turnover of CEOs within the charmed circle and a time lag in anointing the heads of those companies newly ascended to the top 200. Its task forces formulate positions that the policy-making executive committee routinely rubber-stamps, mindful of the etiquette among members of such an exclusive club and their disinclination to take issue with one another. In a typical year, the Accounting Principles Task Force includes only about 10 Roundtable members, sometimes less—and they tend to be the heads of companies that, for various reasons, have the highest level of discomfort with the financial reporting constraints imposed by GAAP.

In 1978, Tom Murphy decided it was time for members of the Task Force to sit down with the FASB to discuss matters that were bothering them. The Board readily agreed, stipulating only that under the recently adopted "sunshine" rule the meeting would have to be open to the public. It was, and a reporter for *Forbes* covered it. The resulting article was headlined "So Waddya Suggest?" Although the reporter was sympathetic to Roundtable complaints about the foreign currency standard then in force, he devoted most of his space to demonstrating the inability, or unwillingness, of the Roundtable members to suggest any constructive alternatives to it or to any of the other things they were complaining about.[3]

The Task Force remained eager to continue a dialogue with the Board, but this was the last time it would consent to meet in public.

Until 1982, the APTF-FASB relationship was characterized mainly by polite exchanges of long "Dear Don" and "Dear Tom" letters between Tom

Murphy and Don Kirk. Murphy wrote more in sorrow than in anger, and with nostalgia for the "principles" enunciated by Paton and Littleton before World War II, especially their centerpiece "matching" concept. Kirk attempted merely to elucidate the reasoning behind current FASB decisions. No converts were made at either end, but the exchange continued in a friendly, gentlemanly way even after Murphy retired, although Roger Smith later characterized Kirk's letters as "adversarial." Once Smith succeeded Murphy as chairman of both GM and the Task Force, the tone of the ongoing relationship changed radically.

Face-to-face meetings resumed but not in public. They were held at dinners, generally hosted by Smith at the Links Club in New York with no more than three Board members present in adherence to the sunshine rule. On one of those cozy yet chilly occasions, when Smith was enumerating the errors and shortcomings of the standard setters, Don Kirk sought to turn off the lecture by reminding him that he had been a member of the Wheat Committee that conceived and recommended an independent standard-setting structure. Smith acknowledged this and said he had hoped for "chicken salad" but had been severely disappointed because the Board recommended by the Wheat Committee had produced nothing but a less attractive by-product popularly associated with raising chickens.

From the beginning of this new phase of the relationship, the dialogue on the APTF side was less gentlemanly and more caustic—although a pretense was maintained that the Task Force was basically supportive and "only trying to help" the FASB. At the first private meeting, which was held in September 1982 soon after Smith became chairman, there was, as expected, extended probing about the sensitive project that eventually would require pension obligations to appear on the balance sheet as liabilities, and further expressions of the now-familiar fear that the conceptual framework was nothing but a smokescreen to conceal the Board's supposed determination to impose current value on the business community. There also were complaints that the Board was placing topics on its agenda that weren't "broke" and therefore didn't need "fixing." It was at this meeting that the agenda began to emerge as a major preoccupation of the APTF.

Moving swiftly, Smith next summoned the managing partners of the (then) Big Eight accounting firms to Detroit for a meeting with members of the APTF in January 1983. The same themes were sounded, but additional ground was covered. The FASB's emphasis on the information needs of external users of financial reports was questioned, as though the Securities Acts and the SEC had never existed. Its concern with assets and liabilities and the balance sheet was viewed with alarm as a door opener for eventual mandating of universal application of current value. The very nature of standard setting also was questioned. The idea was put forth that there should not be a body empowered to set standards for financial accounting and reporting at all. Instead, there should be a "court of appeals," in the private sector, of course, that would merely adjudicate accounting issues on a case-by-case basis.

The focal point of Smith's interest, however, was accounting for pension costs. It was made explicit enough in this meeting and in those with members of the FASB. It also was implicit in talk about "uniformity," "current value," and "emphasis on the balance sheet."

At the time of the Detroit meeting, the FASB had recently published its "Preliminary Views" on employers' accounting for pension costs that indicated that the Board was moving toward a standard that would require companies to show unfunded pension obligations as liabilities on their balance sheets. The reason for Smith's concern was starkly evident: By the time the Statement was issued at the end of 1985, GM had more than $2.5 billion of such obligations. Smith was not alone, of course; his problem was shared by the CEOs of many other companies, particularly in the "smoke-stack" segment of American industry where wages historically had been higher, work forces tended to be older, and pension promises exacted by labor unions were more generous than in most other sectors.

That, then, was the pièce de résistance of the meeting with accounting firm heads. Smith told his guests that it seemed apparent that the FASB had decided on a balance sheet approach and that the traditional matching of costs and revenues would be downgraded. It then would follow, he said, that more specific definitions of assets and liabilities would have to be made, and recognition of current values would be necessary. He blamed this presumed approach for the Board's initial conclusion that unfunded future pension obligations should be recorded as a liability. He had next-to-worst and worst-case predictions as to what might happen if the FASB persevered. Accounting for pension costs could, if the Board followed the course it appeared to be on, cause great harm to the business community and thereby weaken support for the standard setters. If this were to happen, he said, it could lead to a government takeover of the standard-setting function.

With regard to charges of overemphasizing the balance sheet, which Smith was not the only CEO to make, Don Kirk replied mildly:

There has been no deliberate or specific intent to do that, but it might be argued that we are finally giving the balance sheet the attention it deserves. Too often in the past, accounting standards were set by looking primarily at their effects on income, and the balance sheet was in danger of becoming a repository for residual deferred debits and credits that were not resources or obligations. We have developed definitions of assets and liabilities and are using those definitions to elevate the credibility and usefulness of the balance sheet.[4]

On the eve of the pension standard's adoption, Tim Lucas said in a *Wall Street Journal* interview that "many companies would still prefer the status quo . . . but under the new rule, financial statements will more accurately reflect the real economic cost of pension plans rather than the amount a company happens to have chosen to fund the plan during one year."[5]

Save for Charley Steele, the head of GM's own accounting firm, Deloitte, who also was a trustee of the Financial Accounting Foundation, the managing partners went away from their meeting with the APTF bemused. For them, the good times still were rolling. Attrition in the number of major audit clients due to mergers, acquisitions, and bankruptcies had yet to begin in earnest, and the big firms were not yet in an intensely competitive mode. By and large, they still were relatively independent-minded.

The court of appeals idea had been proposed originally more than a decade earlier by Leonard Spacek, a predecessor of Harvey Kapnick as head of Arthur Andersen & Co. Reasons for reviving the idea were sniffed out intuitively by the writer of the *Forbes* article in 1978. "In essence," he wrote:

Murphy was saying that since GM and other blue-chip companies follow decent conservative accounting principles to begin with, they should not be saddled with inflexible accounting rules capable of "surprising" management and shareholders. Let accounting principles bend to fit business and not vice versa.[6]

The writer of that piece, Lawrence Minard, then a young reporter, now is managing editor of the magazine.

The court of appeals notion was fleshed out and presented publicly in 1984 in Eugene Flegm's book *Accounting: How to Meet the Challenges of Relevance and Regulation*.[7] At the time, Flegm had an unimpressive title as deputy assistant controller of General Motors, but in fact he was the company's in-charge person and principal spokesman in the area of financial reporting. The "court" that he proposed the FASB should turn itself into apparently would exist for the sole purpose of adjudicating those troublesome little arguments between accounting firms and their clients. Since "good guys" like GM would rarely, if ever, be involved in such arguments, they would be virtually free and clear of any interference by standard setters. Generally applicable standards, as such, no longer would be set for anybody, and the seven "wise men" who had been assigned mistakenly to that task then could concentrate exclusively on harassing the perpetrators of the most egregious financial reporting lapses. From the separate judgments of the appeals court would emerge, over time, a series of decisions that would become something like a body of case law under which those who strayed from the straight and narrow would somehow be disciplined.

Aside from an occasional opportunistic reference to the possible impact of standards on small business, Smith was silent on social and economic consequences, but the pensions project provided plenty of opportunity for others to take up those cudgels.

Members of Congress soon began to receive letters—and copies of letters addressed to the FASB—claiming, among other things, that the Board's proposals might cause employers to discontinue their defined benefit pension plans and replace them with defined contribution plans that carried no promise of fixed income for retirees—and whose annual cost would not appear on the balance sheet. At a hearing before a subcommittee of the Senate Committee on Labor and Human Resources, one senator told Don Kirk that "some people have discussed possibly trying to cut your initiative off by statutory change."[8]

The CEO of a major industrial company, while emphasizing the point that a sharp increase in reported liabilities was unwarranted and would encourage shifts to defined contribution plans, also predicted that the sudden appearance without warning of a liability related to pension plans that had been in existence for many years might cause some people to question the credibility of the whole financial reporting process. In reply, Don Kirk wondered whether an accounting method that did *not* identify such obligations could be considered credible.

The executive vice president and comptroller of a well-known conglomerate warned that it was critical for the Board to proceed cautiously and to be aware that its conclusions could have a major impact on both the business community and the social welfare provisions for American workers. He called the pension proposals an ill-advised attempt to achieve theoretical purity that would diminish the usefulness and credibility of financial reporting.

Another *Forbes* article, by a different writer, advised readers: "Listen closely to the debates over pension accounting, and you might come to the conclusion that the corporate accounting community, generally speaking, thinks that the users of financial statements are fools." Dire predictions about consequences imply, he wrote, that investors either have grown accustomed to being misled for years by traditional methods of accounting for pension costs and are satisfied with such reporting "or they simply aren't smart enough to interpret the new numbers properly. Neither conclusion is attractive, yet that's what many of the opponents of the new pension accounting seem to be saying."[9]

Smith's next overt move against the standard setters was a request for a meeting with the Foundation trustees in 1984. Knowing that it was about time for another periodic review of FASB operations by the FAF structure committee, he suggested instead that a "blue ribbon" committee of prominent outsiders be designated to perform that task. He proposed three individuals for membership on that committee and later offered two other lists of three. Tom Murphy's name was on all the lists, accompanied by other like-minded individuals. Smith also had thoughtfully had his man Flegm draw up a proposed "charter" for the blue ribbon committee. That draft charter was remarkable in that it called for an unlimited scope of the review—and specifically charged the committee with reexamining the fundamentals of financial reporting and of the FASB's modus operandi, including, of course, the agenda selection process. It was a proposal that could have led to the undoing of everything the Wheat Committee, the organizers of the Financial Accounting Foundation, the trustees who had nurtured the standard-setting structure, and the Standards Board itself had accomplished in more than a dozen years.

Shaken, the trustees wavered for several weeks but eventually concluded that they could not cede to outside interests an oversight responsibility with which they were charged in the Foundation's bylaws. They bypassed their standing structure committee, however, and appointed a "special review committee," chaired by R. Leslie Ellis, retired group vice president of Armstrong World Industries, to conduct a comprehensive study of FASB operations, including the aforementioned Louis Harris opinion survey. The special committee was instructed to submit a preliminary report in July 1985.

Roger Smith expressed disappointment in a letter to Bill Dougherty, who was nearing the end of his term as president of the Foundation. He said that he and everyone else in the Roundtable supported the idea of having a private sector body establish standards for financial reporting, but he and all his peers believed the standard setters should represent the entire constituency. For this reason, he said, the Roundtable supported appointment of a blue ribbon committee, made up of Tom Murphy and two other like-minded elder statesmen in the accounting field, to consider ways in which the FASB could be strengthened and its productivity improved. Presumably, Smith was not thinking about "strengthening" in terms of potency or "productivity" in terms of quantity but rather in terms of acceptability to the APTF.

The trustees went ahead with their planned review, however, and it produced some noteworthy conclusions.

Meanwhile, following consultation with Smith, the Financial Executives Institute set out to do what it could to influence those conclusions. It established an ad hoc committee to "review the business community's role in the development of accounting standards." The committee's report, which its authors and many both inside and outside the FEI who saw it referred to as a "white paper,"[10] was a curious document. In a background section it attributed the APB's demise in large part to that Board's being rendered "relatively ineffective" by its inability to keep up with rapid proliferation of new business techniques and transactions. This observation was made at a time when many in the business community were deploring the standards overload created by the FASB in response to the same conditions. It acknowledged that Corporate America's concerns about standards "are far from monolithic in nature, as there are diverse business views on most accounting and reporting issues." In the next sentence, however, it said that "in many cases there are strong majority views, and there is a perception by the majority that their views have not been given adequate consideration in the standard-setting process."

The report took a gingerly approach to "a few mid-course corrections" the committee thought were needed in the process, but on its main point, it was emphatic:

The business community must play a more active and direct role in the standard-setting process itself if the private-sector concept is to survive. . . . To accomplish such increased representation the business community must have, and be able to demonstrate, the full support of FEI, the Business Roundtable, and other business organizations such as the NAA.

The discourse on representation ended with a demand for

appointment of at least two business-experienced executives to the FASB in the shortest possible time frame. This must be done promptly to maintain the FASB's credibility with the business community and to assure that the business community will continue to provide its financial and other support in maintaining the standard-setting function in the private sector.

In a clear call for politicization of the process for selecting members of the FASB, the committee urged that "in the future, the business community must not only identify outstanding candidates, but adequately communicate to the FAF board of trustees the broad-based business support for such candidates." The FEI followed this advice in the 1990 selection process with results that were an embarrassment to all concerned, as described in Chapter 10.

The committee concluded, "With relatively minor fine-tuning, the structure of the accounting standard-setting process appears generally appropriate." In other words, it will work just fine as soon as we get control of it.

The report had the explicit support of the Business Roundtable's Accounting Principles Task Force.

In addition to administering the second opinion survey by Louis Harris and Associates, the trustees' special review committee itself conducted interviews with "more than 50 persons having special knowledge of the FASB and its operations." The interviewees were a fairly accurately weighted cross section of close-in observers of the standard-setting process. A prevalent theme in those interviews was that members of the standard-setting Board should be selected on the basis of their ability to "serve the public interest," not to "represent" specific segments of the constituency.

Most impressive to members of the review committee were the comments of corporate executives in the sample. For example, one said: "It is important that any member of the FASB not consider himself a representative of any particular constituency, although it is important that there be different backgrounds and perspectives brought to bear on the problems being considered." Another thought it was most important that a person serving on the Board "should use his background and perspective in reaching solutions to problems, but that it should be done in the public interest, not just the interest of whatever part of the constituency he came from."[11]

Another significant finding that came out of the trustee interviews was that there was a general conviction among close-in observers of the standard-setting process that there needed to be a high level of technical accounting expertise among the standard setters, although it was not considered necessary for each one of the seven FASB members to be so equipped. The Wheat Committee and the original trustees of the Foundation had followed the same reasoning intuitively in considering the makeup of the Board, believing that empirical evidence indicated a much greater likelihood of finding technical expertise in the public accounting firms than in any of the other related disciplines. Indeed, of the 12 practicing CPAs appointed to the Board over the years, 5 had been responsible for accounting principles, professional standards, and/or research in their firms, and 1 held such responsibilities afterward. Under pressure from the business community for more "pragmatism" and "practicality" on the Board, however, the trustees agreed informally early in the 1990s to place greater emphasis on identifying practice partners for appointment.

As the review committee began its work in 1985, Rholan E. Larson, who had risen from managing partner of a successful regional public accounting firm in Minneapolis to chairman of the AICPA, was the newly installed president of the Financial Accounting Foundation. He was a man for whom caution and compromise were guiding principles. Although the committee observed that "there is very little evidence of deep dissatisfaction in any segment of the constituency," Larson caused to have included in the committee report the observation that "negative opinions appeared to be more intensely felt than positive opinions, as is generally the case with regard to almost any subject. Public opinion survey techniques are more effective in measuring breadth of opinion than they are in measuring intensity of feeling."[12]

The review committee fleshed out criteria for selection of FASB members that had merely been touched on by the 1982 structure committee report. They included knowledge of financial accounting and reporting; intellect, integrity, and discipline; judicial temperament; ability to work in a collegial atmosphere; communication skills; awareness of the financial reporting environment; and commitment to the FASB's mission. Most significantly, however, the committee provided a broad hint of what it regarded as the ideal "mix" of professional backgrounds among the seven members of the Standards Board. In deliberately obfuscated language, its report recommended that the trustees

continue to seek a Board make-up which includes a mix of backgrounds of members who have had major experience in public accounting, in business or industry, as a user of financial information, and as an accounting educator. . . . The Committee believes it would be preferable for particular emphasis to be given first to major experience in public accounting and second to major experience in business or industry."[13]

After doing some simple arithmetic, the translation was easy: three from public accounting, two from business or industry, one from the user community, and one from academe. It was a concession, but not the two additional places the FEI seemed to be demanding.

In its interviews with key constituents, the special review committee encountered a minority who believed that the due process followed by the Standards Board was "overly cumbersome and time-consuming," although the report was careful to point out that the FASB receives many requests for *more* due process. It did not attempt to sort out the motives of those who wanted faster action from those who wanted still more (and slower) due process, nor did it attempt to fathom the meaning of a few who complained that the sunshine rule impeded "negotiation." Instead, the committee merely recommended that the FASB and its staff be asked to assess within six months "the feasibility and desirability of shortening the due process and of modifying the 'sunshine' rule *within the original spirit of that rule*" (emphasis added).[14]

The "original spirit," as stated in the 1977 report of the trustees' structure committee, was that open meetings would be "part of the public involvement process. The Board needs that exposure so it can hear the logic of all of the conflicting views."[15] That this was not what was meant by "negotiation" already had become apparent, however.

The morning after the special review committee submitted its final, or "Phase II," report in early December 1985, Les Ellis and Rholan Larson conducted a meeting with representatives of the sponsoring organizations, plus Gene Flegm representing the Business Roundtable. The ostensible purpose was to present the committee's findings along with an in-depth look at the Harris survey results. Lou Harris had a conflict and could not participate, but that part of the presentation was made by Humphrey Taylor, president of Louis Harris and Associates.

Although it was meant to be a gathering of all the sponsoring organizations plus the Business Roundtable, it turned out to be in large part a reunion of the FEI's ad hoc committee.

In its impatience with any positive information about the FASB, the group was almost rude to Humphrey Taylor. It suffered his presentation for half an hour and then spent almost three hours probing for ways to assuage its grievances, even though it already had been given ample opportunity to air them in public. The scene conjured up an image of foxes circling a hen-house, sniffing out possible cracks and crevices that might be exploited to get at the quarry inside.

There was a suggestion, from an executive of a very important company, that the Board members should not have the privilege of selecting their own staff but that the trustees should do it for them to ensure that the business point of view would replace the perceived radicalism of the staff. Action, it was said by another, should be taken only within some undefined limits of "consent." In an oxymoron that seemed to ignore the nature of progress, one participant said the Board should not "rock the boat" but merely try to improve financial reporting.

The most pointed comment came from the spokesman for the Business Roundtable, Gene Flegm. The sunshine rule would have to go, he asserted. It was all right in theory, but it prevented business leaders from meeting with the standard setters behind closed doors. In other words, the real power centers must be able to deal with the Standards Board in terms of what each side can and cannot accept. This was the kind of evolution in standard setting that Don Kirk feared most, "a process of negotiation, horsetrading, logrolling . . . a process dominated by those appointed to represent particular interests."

In fact, the team of Smith and Flegm had attempted such a power play only a few weeks before.

At that stage, the principal issues in the Statement on employers' accounting for pensions had all been decided, and the document was merely undergoing some final adjustments regarding secondary questions. For more than a year, the "technical plan" published quarterly in *Status Report* had indicated that the Statement would be issued in the fourth quarter of 1985, which in FASB-speak generally meant right at the end of the quarter. It was on track to be published between Christmas and New Year's.

On October 27, Tim Lucas, then the project manager for pensions, received a phone call from Flegm in which the latter seemed to take it for granted that there would be another exposure draft modifying the Board's position, even though the public had been informed that the next step in the project would be a final Statement, and that this would be issued on schedule. After that next exposure draft, Flegm suggested, the Board should meet with representatives of the groups that were most interested in the project, such as the Motor Vehicle Manufacturers Association, the FEI, and AICPA, to work out a compromise that all parties could accept. A meeting of this kind would be difficult, Flegm continued, because of the sunshine rule. Decisions involving political compromises, he said, were more readily made in private. Solicitously, he indicated that *some* change in pension accounting could be made so it would not appear that the Board had caved in completely.

After being assured by Lucas that the Board was going ahead with issuing the Statement as planned, Flegm's final pitch was that before the Board made any final decision, Don Kirk should meet with Roger Smith in order to gain an understanding of what the auto industry could "live with."

On December 3, Smith wrote Kirk, once again expressing concern about effects that "radical" changes in pension accounting might have. While Flegm purported to be speaking for the auto industry, Smith had the Business Roundtable uppermost in mind. He proposed a meeting of the Task Force with Board and staff members before a final Statement was issued, and suggested January 10. That date, of course, was two weeks after more than 100,000 copies of the Statement would be distributed.

Kirk advised by return mail that the Statement would be released on schedule but that he would be glad to meet on January 10 to explain the document and the reasoning behind it. Smith responded promptly that he did not see any point in a meeting if the Statement already had been released. He concluded with a final plea for caution, more study, and further delay. The standard had been 11 years in the making.

In deference to the oft-proclaimed virtue of "management judgment," as well as to the recognized realities of financial reporting, the FASB could not presume to specify all details of all decisions about reporting on any subject, regardless of how important it was. As a practical matter, in both political and financial reporting terms, significant areas of judgment had to be left to corporate management. With regard to accounting for pension costs, those areas included certain key assumptions.

Near the end of the first quarter, 1990, GM announced that it was altering basic assumptions regarding its pension plans and hence the impact of those assumptions on the company's income statement. It was a time of rising life expectancies, but GM decided that its retirees would have life spans two years shorter than theretofore. It was a time of highly uncertain interest rates and investment returns in general, but GM chose to increase its estimate of the income to be earned from its pension funds from 10 to 11 percent. The result of these two adjustments was a diminution of the corporation's contributions to the funds and therefore a nearly 10 percent enhancement of reported earnings for the period. But 30 months later, near the end of the third quarter, 1992, the company had to 'fess up that its revised assumptions had not proved realistic, and there would have to be a charge to shareholders' equity that might approach $2 billion.

As a result of the 1985 special review committee report, the business community did secure an additional place on the Foundation board of trustees. In that year, the AICPA offered to give up the ex officio trusteeship that had been granted to its elected chief officer in the Foundation's original charter. On the committee's recommendation, the trustees accepted the AICPA's offer and amended the bylaws to add two at-large trustee positions with the tacit understanding that one would be filled by a person from the business community and the other by a public accountant.

As the review committee suggested, the FASB and its staff reviewed due process and "sunshine." The trustees left both in place on recommendation of yet another review committee that had been appointed to follow up in 1986 on loose ends left by the 1985 review. Les Ellis also was chairman of this committee, which observed in its report that "the rule has not proved to be overly cumbersome to the Board and alternatives would appear to create situations more time-consuming and less productive than presently produced."[16]

Early in 1990, the Seattle chapter of FEI staged a panel discussion that turned out, at least in part, to be a post mortem on the previously described events of 1985. The panel included Ronald H. Mead, a former national chairman of FEI who was senior vice president and treasurer of Security Pacific Bancorporation Northwest, and Loyd C. Heath, associate dean and professor of accounting at the University of Washington. Mead, obviously, was knowledgeable about the ways of FEI, and Heath's experience as a member of two FASB task forces and as an interested observer of the process qualified him to comment.

Mead described the extensive interface between FEI and FASB and summarized the familiar complaints about the Board's not listening, issuing too many standards, complexity of standards, insensitivity to the cost-benefit equation, and devotion to theory at the expense of practicality and ease of implementation. Citing the ad hoc committee, he said, "Even though the report contained excellent suggestions, the FASB has been slow in implementing them."

Heath emphasized two points. The first was that although financial statement preparers

have provided many useful comments on proposed standards, they have devoted too much of their effort to trying to control the standard-setting process. They have done this with delaying tactics and by trying to get control of the switches and levers used to set accounting standards rather than providing constructive input on FASB proposals.

His second point was simply that the input of preparers to the standard-setting process is "often ineffective because it is self-serving and shrill." He pointed out that the FASB is a regulatory organization, and therefore its members "must be responsible to the public, not to management or any other special interest group."

Indirectly, Heath was alluding to a research study commissioned by the FEI's own Financial Executives Research Foundation (FERF) entitled *Due Process and Participation at the FASB* by Stephen J. Mezias of the School of Organization and Management at Yale and Seungwha Chung of the Wharton School at the University of Pennsylvania. After examining mountains of input received by the standard setters from various sources, they concluded that submissions from financial executives "tend to emphasize pragmatic consideration rather than theory and oppose new standards on the basis that they represent too rapid a change or excessive standard setting." Perhaps, the authors concluded, "financial executives could increase the effectiveness of their letters by emphasizing the theoretical support for their positions rather than what might be perceived as issues of self-interest."[17]

In 1986, the trustees were faced with the problem of selecting a new chairman to succeed Don Kirk, who was not eligible for reappointment under the Foundation bylaws. The trustees were in a delicate position. They were under intense pressure from the Roundtable and the FEI to appoint people to the Standards Board who would be more "practical" and "reasonable" where business was concerned, and that eventually ruled out the two favored candidates from within the FASB, Jim Leisenring and Art Wyatt, who were articulate proponents of objective, neutral standard setting. Nevertheless, the trustees could not give the appearance of caving in to business community pressure without sacrificing the credibility of the entire standard-setting structure. After months of indecision, they pulled a card out of the middle of the deck that gave every appearance of being a winner. Denny Beresford seemed to many outsiders to be a perfectly logical choice. As a nonmember, he had as close an association with the Board as any individual could have. GM was pleased. In a congratulatory letter, Roger Smith contrasted his pleasure with the Beresford appointment with his concern about criticism of business participation by Don Kirk in a speech to the FEI current issues conference the previous autumn and Sandy Burton's charge of "preparer dominance" of standard setting in a speech at the annual meeting of the National Association of Accountants. Smith called preparer dominance an "illusion" and complained of a seeming implication that preparers of financial information could not be counted on to maintain the integrity of financial reporting.

Gene Flegm wrote that he hoped "a new era of cooperation and understanding based on mutual respect can begin." To some others, however, the prospect of such an era was chilling.

One member of the Standards Board, Art Wyatt, resigned in 1987, only halfway through his first term. In a letter to Rholan Larson, then still president of the Foundation, he charged the FAF trustees with taking the FASB down a path on which the views of preparers would have greater weight than the views of those striving to improve the fairness of financial reporting.

Roger Smith went on to higher office—as chairman of the whole Business Roundtable. But in his daytime job he was less successful. GM fell on hard times—and it was not because the FASB compelled it to display its unfunded pension liabilities on the balance sheet.

NOTES

1. John Milton, "Tenure of Kings and Magistrates" 1649, quoted in *Prose Selections* (New York: Odyssey Press, 1974), 269.

2. Louis Harris and Associates, Inc., *A Study of the Attitudes Toward and an Assessment of the Financial Accounting Standards Board* (Stamford, Conn.: Financial Accounting Foundation), 1985.

3. Lawrence Minard, "So Waddya Suggest?" *Forbes*, November 13, 1978.

4. Donald J. Kirk, quoted in "Comments and Issues," *Accounting Events and Trends*, Price Waterhouse, September–October 1983, 2.

5. Timothy S. Lucas, quoted in "Accounting Proposal Troubles Firms," *Wall Street Journal*, December 6, 1985.

6. Lawrence Minard, *Forbes*, November 13, 1978.

7. Eugene H. Flegm, *Accounting: How to Meet the Challenges of Relevance and Regulation* (New York: John Wiley, 1984), 124.

8. Senator Donald Nickles, transcript of hearing conducted by the U.S. Senate Labor Subcommittee of the Committee on Labor and Human Resources, March 21, 1983.

9. Christopher Power, "Critical Mass," *Forbes*, February 13, 1984, 166.

10. Financial Executives Institute, *The Business Community's Role in the Development of Accounting Standards*, July 18, 1985.

11. *Report of the Special Review Committee*, report to the board of trustees of the Financial Accounting Foundation, July 25, 1985, 9.

12. Ibid., 8.

13. Ibid., 18.

14. *Report of the Social Review Committee, Phase II*, report to the board of trustees of the Financial Accounting Foundation, December 3, 1985.

15. Financial Accounting Foundation, *The Structure of Establishing Financial Accounting Standards*, report of the structure committee, April 1977, 22.

16. *Report of the Social Committee*, report to the board of trustees of the Financial Accounting Foundation, December 4, 1986.

17. Financial Executives Research Foundation, *Due Process and Participation at the FASB: A Study of the Comment Period*, prepared by Stephen J. Mezias and Seungwha Chung, 1989.

Chapter Nine

Another Waltz 'Round the Table

Power is something of which I am convinced there is no innocence this side of the womb.

Nadine Gordimer[1]

Denny Beresford came to the chairmanship of the FASB with a long history of participation in the Board's process from a close-in, but nevertheless outside, position. As national director of accounting standards for the public accounting firm of Ernst & Whinney (now Ernst & Young), he had been a frequent testifier on behalf of his firm at FASB public hearings and a member of FASAC, the Emerging Issues Task Force, and two project task forces. He also had served as chairman of AICPA's Accounting Standards Executive Committee, which interacts closely with the FASB, and as one of two U.S. representatives on the International Accounting Standards Committee (IASC). And yet the complex process the FASB is required to follow and the conflicting pressures it must try to keep in balance make it impossible, no matter how "close in" he or she has been, for anyone who has not actually worked "within these walls" to understand fully how the process operates—and what the pressures and other considerations are.

This was pointed up by Clarence Sampson, who, in 11 years as chief accountant of the SEC before his appointment to the Board in 1987, had to maintain close liaison with the FASB. He said a few years later that in spite of his closeness over that long period, he had not realized until he got to Connecticut "the depth of . . . research, testing, and analysis that no one outside this organization can fully fathom, not even someone who is part of the scene."[2]

Beresford had a quick initiation as chairman. Within the first few months, he reported later

the CEO of a major corporation wrote me that "there seems to be a basic distrust [at the FASB] of the business community's motives for taking certain positions on accounting issues." The dean of a major business school was quoted in a prominent journal as saying that "the FASB is meeting the needs of businessmen rather than the needs of users."[3]

The business school dean he referred to was the former chief accountant of the SEC, Sandy Burton.

Beresford carried with him some preconceived notions, but he was wise enough to understand that once he got inside those walls, his views might change. They did. But before they did, there was some heartburn for both those who applauded his appointment and those who were disturbed by it. For example, in the months before he assumed the chairmanship, he alarmed some observers with cryptic remarks about reordering priorities and possibly dropping some topics from the technical agenda.

On the other hand, many of his go-slow supporters in the corporate world were taken aback by a *Wall Street Journal* headline in the first month of his regime: "FASB's Beresford Wants Rules Set Faster." Ironically, before his appointment he had criticized the Board for moving too slowly on its accounting for income taxes project. Statement No. 96 on that subject was issued at the end of his first year in office but caused such a firestorm of criticism that Statements 100, 103, and 108 had to be issued, delaying its effective date while the Board first debated whether to amend or replace it, and then how. Statement No. 109 superseding No. 96 finally was adopted early in 1992, more than four years after the initial standard was issued.

Beresford also brought with him, from his experience as a member of the IASC, a conviction that the FASB should play a stronger role in efforts to internationalize standards and to reduce differences among those that various national standard-setting committees were producing. Where Don Kirk had insisted that the FASB was compelled by its special position under U.S. securities laws and oversight by the SEC to devote its resources and energies exclusively to financial reporting by U.S. entities within the United States, while at the same time cooperating with international bodies in nondemanding ways, Beresford acknowledged mounting pressures for "international harmonization." But he was cautious about it. He pledged a reasonable level of participation in the international effort but not all-out commitment to it. This would become a major theme of his chairmanship.

That theme soon would be given force by an SEC that considered itself charged (politically) in the aftermath of the 1988 presidential election with considering ways that U.S. financial markets and U.S. companies could become more competitive with their foreign counterparts—a development that would cause new complications for the standard setters.

Some were surprised at the vigor with which Beresford soon began to articulate the Board's mission—and the candor with which he discussed controversy surrounding it. For example, he commented that the cost-benefit issue

is often a point of friction between the Board and many members of the preparer community who can directly observe the costs of accounting changes but find it difficult to relate to societal benefits because the latter are so diffuse and difficult to assess. The objective of full and fair disclosure expressed in the Securities Act of 1933 reflects a continuing consensus that capital market efficiency is enhanced by a free flow of credible financial information.[4]

He also acknowledged his early opposition to the conceptual framework, saying some years later: "When I was on the other side of things, I was not enthusiastic, but since I've been at the FASB, I've noticed it's a living document and is used. In fact, in some instances I ask the staff why there aren't more references to it in our documents."[5]

Though sometimes complained about, especially in the last years of Don Kirk's chairmanship, rhetoric does not greatly influence either attitudes or actions. Even when a chairman they considered "moderate" succeeded Kirk, members of the Business Roundtable Accounting Principles Task Force still grumbled about what they said were too detailed, too restrictive, and too many standards. The original statement on income tax accounting, even though it never became effective, exacerbated that view. It was the most visible in a series of very important, unusually complex—and contentious—pronouncements issued in a relatively short time. Among them were standards requiring consolidation of majority-owned subsidiaries and replacement of the familiar "statement of changes in financial position" in published financial statements with a statement of cash flows.

As Roger Smith became more preoccupied with the operational and financial problems of his own company, less was heard from him about the fine points of financial reporting. He was able to find time to serve as overall chairman of the Business Roundtable but yielded the chairmanship of the Accounting Principles Task Force in 1986 to the new CEO of another company that had a history of resistance to accounting standards and standard setters. His successor in that position was John S. Reed, who recently had succeeded Walter Wriston as the head of Citicorp.

Reed was a much more clever operator than Smith, at least in his role as chairman of the Roundtable Task Force. Where Smith was wont to use the battering ram, Reed preferred the political maneuver, backed up by more subtle but intimidating pressure. His first move was to present, for the record, a bill of particular complaints to the new chairman of the FASB in a lengthy letter in October 1987. The letter ostensibly was a suggested agenda for one of those meetings with the FASB chairman and a few of his cohorts a week later, but implicitly it was yet another attempt to lay down a basis for *negotiation* between the FASB and one particularly powerful business lobby.

Reed perpetuated the Smith argument that the only justification for writing new standards was evidence of widespread abuse of existing accounting practices. There was concern, he wrote, that the FASB had undertaken a total reworking of existing standards even though, he maintained, there was no evident need for doing so. Not content with warning that rapid change could disrupt preparers and the marketplace, he went on to claim that there also was concern that the standard setters might be overextending themselves by trying to deal with too many significant issues at once. And before detailing the APTF's concerns with specific issues, he suggested that the Board should make greater use of business as a resource by involving companies more often in field testing proposed rules early in the process.

In a dinner meeting six months later with the usual less-than-a-majority of FASB members, Reed made much of the possible economic and social consequences of standards and suggested that assessing those consequences should be the responsibility of some group other than the Board. He also mused that potential consequences should be assessed before a project is placed on the technical agenda. This was the birth of an idea that would grow up and be presented to the SEC the following autumn.

Reed's initial letter to Beresford was written at a time when the Board's project on postretirement health benefits was uppermost in the minds of other Roundtable members, even though more than three years would elapse before a standard was issued on the subject. However, in his rundown of specific issues that he said were bothering the Task Force, this was only number two. By this time, the realization had begun to settle in among corporate executives that their almost heedless granting of medical benefits in the past had created future obligations that would have to be labeled as liabilities on the balance sheet in larger dollar figures even than pensions, but just *how* this would be done still was a subject of intense debate. Nevertheless, Reed's number-one issue was accounting for the stock options that had begun to increase the compensation of top executives geometrically and, in some situations, even were granted to many lesser employees, but with no visible effect on the reported earnings of corporations granting them.

The FASB had added this topic to its agenda three years earlier and issued a discussion memorandum on it shortly afterward. However, by the time Reed wrote his letter, nothing much had happened because the Board encountered difficulty in settling on a suitable basis for determining the time at which to measure the value of stock options (grant date, vesting date, exercise date?) and an appropriate measurement method, so it decided in 1988 to defer a decision on stock compensation while it considered the broader problem of distinguishing between liabilities and equity within its project on financial instruments. What was difficult for the standard setters was the fact that when stock options were granted, there was no immediate expense to the corporation. It was clear, however, that there was a potential for dilution of shareholders' equity. Many corporate executives and accounting experts maintained that this dilution, if it occurred, would merely be the result of an agreement by shareholders to share the fruits of future growth in their equity with employees—not of a decision by management. This argument, along with the difficulty of measurement, often was used to discourage any effort to find a reasonable way to assign a cost that most thoughtful persons agreed was there somewhere.

It was not until amounts of income beyond the dreams of avarice were reported for a few top executives at the beginning of the 1990s, and were commented on widely and pejoratively in the news media, that Congress and the SEC began to prick up their ears—and the Board accelerated and intensified its efforts on stock compensation.

Meanwhile, Reed found plenty to occupy him in the area of financial reporting standards, even though, or perhaps because, Citicorp's own financial condition was headed south.

Early in 1988, he demanded a meeting with representatives of the Foundation trustees, pointedly excluding Board members. The venue had changed, along with the APTF's chairmanship, from the Links Club to the executive dining room atop Citicorp's Park Avenue headquarters in New York.

Reed sounded three major themes that would be repeated many times over the next two years. One was that too many matters were being considered by the FASB and too many standards were being issued. Another was that the Board's approach to standard setting was "purely conceptual" without adequate consideration of "practicality" from an industry standpoint. The third was a blanket complaint about "nonresponsiveness" to the views of industry in general. He also described a recent meeting of the Roundtable's Executive Committee at which, he claimed, there was a groundswell of support for an APTF effort to explore the possibility of having the SEC take over the standard-setting function and thus put the FASB out of business. This exploration would involve meetings with members of the SEC and with the managing partners of major accounting firms.

In a letter to Beresford reporting on the meeting the next day, Rholan Larson warned of underestimating the intensity of concerns within the Business Roundtable but also acknowledged the risk that Congress and the SEC might react negatively if there appeared to be excessive influence by industry. However, he urged care in differentiating "influence" from "input" received through the normal due process. Then he reminded Beresford of the ever-present danger of losing business support with the result that the standard-setting function might be taken over by government.

Two months later, following a meeting with the heads of the Big Eight accounting firms, Reed wrote to one of them reiterating the Roundtable's grievances and adding a new one. Increasingly, he said, the major accounting firms were using the FASB as a shield against their clients, which allowed the firms to avoid differences of opinion between auditor and client about applying specific accounting standards. This tendency, he said, was negating the relationships of the firms with their clients where standards were concerned. He tossed in an observation that the FASB was considering too many issues because it had too little else to do and emphasized again that some in the Roundtable thought it would be better to let the SEC be the standard setter because of the Commission's history of professionalism and responsiveness to the business community.

Intimidated, Rholan Larson decided that he, as president of the Foundation, would appoint a small "special advisory group" made up of a mixture of trustees and representatives of such outside organizations as the AICPA, FEI, and SEC to draw on their own knowledge, rather than any formal fact-gathering activity, in framing recommendations about the FASB and its process—and Foundation oversight of the Board. It was a kind of "belt and suspenders" approach as the board of trustees was committed to, and already was planning in great detail, an exhaustive review of both the FASB and GASB as required by the "structure agreement" on which formation of the GASB was based in 1984.

Two weeks after Larson made his plan known to his fellow trustees, the *Wall Street Journal* reported:

The Securities and Exchange Commission, under pressure from business, is quietly investigating whether the Financial Accounting Standards Board needs an overhaul. Since last May, individual members of the Business Roundtable, a powerful lobbying group, have been criticizing the FASB in meetings with managing partners of major accounting firms and SEC members.[6]

The article quoted the deputy chief accountant as saying his office "is currently monitoring suggestions raised that the FASB consider changes in the rule-making process."

This caused some throat clearing on Capitol Hill where Representative John D. Dingell, chairman of both the House Committee on Energy and Commerce and its Subcommittee on Oversight and Investigations, and arguably one of the half-dozen most powerful members of Congress, had been keeping a close watch on accounting and financial reporting matters for several years. Dingell wrote to SEC chairman David S. Ruder, advising him of the subcommittee's expectation that the SEC would use its powers aggressively to shield FASB from what he called "improper influence" by the business community and those federal agencies that had some quarrel with FASB pronouncements. He said that efforts by the Federal Energy Regulatory Commission and the Federal Home Loan Bank Board to undercut the work of the FASB where it applied to their regulated industries had proven that the process of setting fair standards works best when self-interested business and political interests could not control the outcome.

The Dingell letter delayed Reed's major offensive at the SEC, but in the meantime, he had been busy laying groundwork. In July he distributed two separate but similar questionnaires to each of the (then) 193 members of the Roundtable—one for the CEOs to complete and a longer one for their chief financial officers (CFOs) that in addition called for ratings of all the FASB's standards. There were five multiple-choice questions that reflected the Task Force's previously expressed concerns, and they elicited responses that were predictable but not completely supportive of Reed's thesis. There was one yes-or-no question that also asked for comments on whether "fundamental, structural changes should be considered." Despite the project's originally stated intent to explore the possibility of having the SEC take over standard setting, neither the Commission nor any other governmental possibility ever was mentioned.

Perceptions of a need for "fundamental, structural changes" were by no means overwhelming. The Task Force's report to the Roundtable membership observed

On the question of the need for change, 42% of the CEOs believed that the problems are so severe that major structural changes to the FASB are necessary. Somewhat less of the CFOs took this view (35%). We think that respondents may have been somewhat hesitant to call for major structural changes as they were concerned that this might be taken to mean that they were in favor of removing standard setting from the private sector.

In fact, none of the CEOs submitting comments supported standard setting by a governmental agency, and nearly a third explicitly rejected it. One went so far as to claim that the business community was unanimous in supporting the proposition that accounting standards should be established in the private, as opposed to the public, sector. The respondent went on to observe that the FASB still was structured essentially as had been recommended and agreed on in 1973. The only change that might be an improvement, he said, would be to return to the original 1973 requirement of a 5–2 affirmative vote for issuance of a standard rather than a simple 4–3 majority. That last suggestion would surface again two years later.

Meanwhile, Reed's campaign was running in bad luck. The Dingell letter, which found its way into the news media, was not an insurmountable obstacle, but it was an embarrassment. Several months before that, Edmund Coulson, who had succeeded Clarence Sampson as the SEC's chief accountant, expressed concern about the Roundtable's unrest in a letter to Rholan Larson in which he said he was aware of certain expressions made

by the business community that might be construed as an effort to curtail
the independence of the private sector standard-setting process. He concluded that such expressions were disturbing and counterproductive. He
added that the Commission was ready to assist in ensuring that the standard-setting activities remain independent from undue influence. He also
stressed that the mere appearance of undue influence was unacceptable.
The Foundation board of trustees, which was not exactly a pillar of strength,
nevertheless was showing little interest in surrendering its responsibilities
for FASB oversight. The survey of Roundtable members had resulted in
something less than a ringing endorsement of Reed's aims. And it was not
until October, only a month before the presidential election would effectively render David Ruder a "lame duck," that the APTF chairman finally
got a chance to make his big pitch to the SEC.

His proposition was startling in its boldness, even if the circumstances
were not propitious. The Roundtable would take the lead in organizing a
new Financial Accounting Standards Oversight Committee (FASOC) to be
made up of two corporate CEOs, the managing partners of two Big Eight
accounting firms, the president of the AICPA (which by then was a permanent staff position beholden to the Institute board of directors), an SEC
commissioner, and the chairman of the FASB. This group would have the
power to overrule proposed agenda items, cause reexamination of any
standard it did not like, and delete "unproductive"—whatever that word
could be made to mean—projects from the standard setter's agenda. And
because some items on the FASB agenda got there because the SEC wanted
them there, Reed's proposed FASOC would be empowered to make decisions that would be binding on the SEC.

Ruder made his reactions clear in the meeting, and in due course, he set
his impressions and conclusions down in a letter to Reed in which there
were polite expressions of gratification about opening avenues of communication between the corporate community and the Commission on financial accounting and reporting matters but an ice-cold rejection of Reed's
proposal. The proposed FASOC authority, Ruder pointed out, inevitably
would lead to an appearance that FASOC was the real standard setter, with
the FASB reduced to an innocuous role as mere technical adviser. He added
that the Commission could not support a decision-making authority in
FASOC that would enable such a body to overrule proposed FASB agenda
items for standard setting that would then become binding on the Commission.

Ruder elaborated on these views in a major speech in January 1989 that
was widely reported, but Reed had experienced another bit of negative
public exposure before 1988 was over. In a *Fortune* article about the FASB
in December, Carol J. Loomis, certainly the most thorough and possibly the
most astute of financial journalists, recounted this recent history. She had
written about Reed before in connection with Citicorp, and she interviewed

him for this article. "Sometimes when he is spinning the tale of FASB and where it went wrong," she said in concluding the piece,

Reed mentions that the U.S. has probably the best financial reporting system in the world. He sees this as a source of satisfaction, and as an argument for slowing the FASB way down. It could more logically be seen as evidence that we [the United States] are doing something right. Indeed, if you had a bank you thought was probably the best in the world, you might even be trying to make it better.[7]

Ironically, coming out of the Reagan era of deregulation, throughout which the SEC held reasonably steadfast to its historic mission of protecting investors, into a Bush administration whose inclinations were less clear and whose later overall record included at least partial revival of regulation in many areas, Reed and the Roundtable found fertile ground under the new regime at the SEC for their proposals, which were, in spirit and essential details, classically deregulatory. In fact, in the early days of the new pro-consul at the Commission, policy seemed to border on laissez faire. But later, the signals became sharply mixed.

President George Bush's choice for chairman of the Securities and Exchange Commission was one of the bright younger men in his conservative support group. Richard C. Breeden had been a member of Bush's vice presidential staff and then of the original Bush White House staff. His nomination to replace Ruder as SEC chairman did not go to the Senate until ten months into the Bush presidency. But, to borrow a phrase from the early days of the Reagan administration, Breeden "hit the ground running." He let it be known early on that his major interest was not the Commission's historical mission of investor protection but the "competitiveness" of American companies operating internationally and of American securities markets in attracting the registration of foreign-company securities for trading in the United States. In pursuing this course, he seemed to be moving what up until then had been an examplar of federal regulation for protection of the public into the same category as such agencies as the Interstate Commerce Commission, the Civil Aeronautics Board, the Atomic Energy Commission, the Nuclear Regulatory Commission, and of most recent notoriety, the Federal Home Loan Bank Board that had put themselves in harness to promote the interests of the very industries they were intended to regulate.

Almost immediately after Breeden's confirmation by the Senate, Reed sought to draw his attention to Roundtable concerns about financial reporting requirements. He wrote to complain about what he alleged to be increasing inefficiency of the standard-setting process and what he called the growing conceptual and academic nature of the standards themselves. He alleged that because many of the new standards resulted in presentation of a less favorable picture of corporate results than did accounting standards abroad—undeserved in many cases, he said—U.S. corporations had been placed at a competitive disadvantage in worldwide capital markets.

Reed attached a brief description of the Task Force's activities and a list of its members, of whom there were only seven that year, including himself—a tiny handful of powerful men who were in a position at least to appear to speak for all of American business.

As events unfolded in the ensuing year and a half, the new SEC posture gave rise to headlines like: "The Death of Securities Regulation" in the *Wall Street Journal*[8] and "The SEC and the Death of Disclosure" in the *New York Times*.[9] It was a period of consternation mixed with puzzlement for the standard setters and the financial community at large because the new regime at the Commission sent some sharply mixed signals, which perhaps is inevitable for public officials to do in a time of intense special interest politics. One thing quickly became clear, however: Breeden had resolved to identify, and presumably eradicate, what Commissioner Philip R. Lochner, Jr., characterized as "accounting rules that are so complicated and so costly, they may be a significant detriment to U.S. business."[10]

Lochner became the point man in what appeared to be an offensive against the very rules that, over time and with the Commission's encouragement, even prodding, had given American investors the best financial reporting system in the world. In June 1990, Lochner wrote an obsequious letter to John Reed in which he explained that Chairman Breeden had asked him to ascertain whether there were any actions the SEC could take that would reduce the complexity and costs of implementation of U.S. accounting rules. He was careful to add that such reduction should occur only while maintaining the investor protection and disclosure policies of the federal securities laws. He concluded by saying that he would be most interested in hearing the views of the business community about any particular problem areas that the Task Force might identify, as well as suggestions for action by the SEC on any other accounting matters.

This was the opening that Reed had been probing for. In his reply, he picked up on the theme of international competitiveness, asserting that complexity and rapid change in accounting and reporting requirements had a seriously negative impact on the efficiency and effectiveness of U.S. businesses. He alleged further that such requirements had not improved the quality of information available to investors and other users of financial information. Then, as though still smarting from the Carol Loomis *Fortune* article, he claimed that although for many years the United States had been far ahead of the rest of the world with respect to the development of financial reporting standards, it was unfortunate that while other countries moved toward better financial reporting, the United States had moved backward in significant ways. He cited such sore points as income taxes, cash flows, and consolidations, then added that if U.S. companies were to compete effectively in the global marketplace in the 1990s and beyond, they would need a more cost-effective approach to financial reporting. The Business Roundtable believed, he said, that accounting rule makers needed to reexamine the objectives of general-purpose financial statements and provide businesses with needed relief from what he called onerous reporting requirements and unrealistic accounting rules. In particular, he added, there needed to be a change in the standard setters' position that accounting theory must take precedence over what he called practical or public policy considerations, a position he claimed was hampering U.S. competitiveness.

In his 1990 Wharton Symposium paper, financial analyst Gerry White scoffed at the competitiveness allegation. "I have difficulty keeping a straight face when discussing this issue," he said.

I know of no evidence that any accounting or disclosure standard has harmed American business. . . . I assume that attempts have been made to document this harm, but we have never been provided with such documentation. The same people who demand cost-benefit analysis would have us accept such serious charges without any proof whatever.[11]

Although its views were not directly solicited by Lochner, the FEI chimed in anyway. P. Norman Roy, the Institute's president, complained that positions on issues that the FEI believed were thoughtful, responsive, and realistic were perceived by the standard setters to be inadequate and self-serving and were often rejected as such. He added a grace note to the effect that such an outcome was perplexing in view of what he called the excellent professional qualifications of the standard setters and their staff. In the FEI's view, he concluded, U.S. companies' competitiveness was negatively affected by the volume, complexity, and pervasiveness of U.S. accounting and financial reporting rules.

Attached to Roy's letter was a separate critique prepared by the FEI's Committee on Corporate Reporting (CCR) that complained of what it perceived as a trend at the FASB toward greater emphasis on theory and concepts instead of practical, "basic" accounting principles. A further complaint was that throughout many recent standards there was apparent reluctance on the standard setters' part to depend on management's judgment in applying "general concepts." The paper went on to describe eight standards that the Committee considered excessively "burdensome."

Another organization whose views had not been solicited, the Association for Investment Management and Research, nevertheless sent a delegation from its Financial Accounting Policy Committee to meet with Commissioner Lochner and "express support for the FASB, the current standard-setting process, and U.S. accounting and disclosure requirements." In her report to AIMR members, the committee chairperson, Patricia McConnell of Bear Stearns & Co., reminded them of the Association's efforts on behalf of "a U.S. accounting and disclosure system that is unparalleled in the world." That system, she said, "as well as the standard-setting process itself, is threatened with dismantlement." In fact, she added, "the SEC already has taken several significant steps toward dismantling the U.S. system," and cited several Commission initiatives that would allow foreign companies to sidestep U.S. disclosure requirements while issuing securities in this country. "Finally," she said, "the FASB itself appears to be weakening under the pressure of constant lobbying by business groups such as the Business Roundtable and the Financial Executives Institute."[12]

The Commission's new posture was a dramatic change from years of cooperation, even collaboration, with the private sector standard setters. In those years, the SEC on occasion had formally requested that the FASB undertake various projects, such as those on accounting for the costs of developing computer software for commercial purposes, and the complex subject of financial instruments and off-balance sheet financing. In furtherance of the "mutual non-surprise" policy enunciated by Sandy Burton in 1973, close liaison was maintained between the two organizations. Informally, their staffs were in almost daily contact by telephone on a wide range of matters. In a more formal mode, of course, the chief accountant participated in meetings of the Advisory Council and Emerging Issues Task Force, and the Board and Commission held periodic joint meetings, in public, to discuss matters of mutual concern. In addition, the respective chairmen met informally as circumstances required. The consistent thrust of these activities was toward improvement and refinement of the financial reporting system.

Observing this relationship, some private-sector commentators concluded that the FASB was little more than an arm of the SEC. However, the equation is more complicated, and the realities of it are more subtle, than this implies. It has always been clear that the SEC was the overseer of private sector standard-setting activity and that in certain circumstances, as in the oil and gas case, it might exercise its superior power under the law, rightly or wrongly. At the same time, it also was clear that it was in the Commission's interest to see that the FASB's viability was maintained, not only as standard setter but also as buffer between the Commission and the normal political pressures (as distinct from the intensity of the oil and gas controversy) brought to bear by registrants and by other governmental agencies and departments. In the paper he delivered at the Arthur Young Professors Roundtable in 1983, Don Kirk said that two requisites for maintaining a viable working relationship between the FASB and the SEC were "timely response by the FASB to valid concerns of the SEC, and restraint on the part of the SEC, to avoid the temptation to impose its preferences." Unrestrained action by the Commission would destroy the Board's effectiveness, he said, "just as the Board's implementing the preferences of the SEC will destroy the FASB's credibility."[13]

Over the years, these realities generally have been recognized by both sides.

Steve Zeff of Rice University, a member of the Advisory Council at the time of the Breeden-Lochner initiative, remarked at a Council meeting in which Commissioner Lochner participated:

The Securities and Exchange Commission may be at a historic turning point on accounting standards. After decades of urging standard-setting bodies to "narrow the areas of difference," to tackle novel and controversial accounting issues, and to expand disclosure requirements, the Commission now seems to believe that the standard setters have gone too far.

The Commission's posture, he added, "is ironic because the historic explanation for rigorous U.S. accounting standards has been the Commission's own policies and occasional exhortations that, if the standard setter did not heed the Commission's demands for stricter standards, the Commission itself would issue a release having the desired effect."[14]

Denny Beresford undertook to rebut both the Roundtable and FEI responses to Lochner in a single letter. He took special pains to address the question of "theoretical purity" raised by both. He pointed out that participants on all sides of standard-setting controversies are in the habit of evoking theory when they think their interpretation of the relevant theory supports the answer they prefer. A theoretically sound answer, he said, may be a practical one but not the desired one. On the other hand, when theoretical arguments in support of a desired answer are found to be without merit, the desired answer then is supported as a practical solution. He noted that two weeks before the FEI dispatched its response to Lochner, in another letter to the SEC regarding a proposal by the International Accounting Standards Committee to discontinue the use of LIFO (last-in, first-out) accounting for inventory as an acceptable alternative, the Institute argued that theoretical soundness was important in gaining acceptance of IASC standards and that there was no theoretical basis for the answer FEI did *not* desire.

Beresford also pointed out that of the eight standards the FEI cited as "burdensome," one had originated largely at the urging of FEI, another had been endorsed in toto, and the Board's position on many of the issues in the others had been supported by the Institute.

Meanwhile, the standard setters had received, by indirection, a somewhat contradictory "get tough" signal from Breeden. In testimony before the Senate Banking Committee in September 1990, he stated his determination that debt securities held by financial institutions would be required to be shown in financial statements at current market value rather than historical cost, as was the custom. He also said that if the private sector did not bring this about, the SEC would. It was a position that was politically delicate for the FASB—and anathema to most of the private sector along with the banking industry and therefore certain to arouse heated controversy.

At the time, the Accounting Standards Executive Committee of the AICPA was attempting to deal with the issue, but it proved unable to do so because of the accounting firms' pervasive ties with banks and other financial institutions. In fact, with the formal blessing of the major firms, AcSEC voted to pass the baton to the FASB. This put the standard setters on a collision course with the banking industry once again, for the bankers were determined that "mark-to-market" must not be adopted—and so were their regulators. The FASB, through no misstep of its own, suddenly was caught in a crossfire between the SEC, on one hand, and the Federal Reserve Board, the Comptroller of the Currency, and the Federal Deposit Insurance Corporation, on the other.

Breeden had expressed what turned out, unsurprisingly, to be an unrealistic desire for speed in getting the issue resolved. AcSEC took almost two months just to decide to get out of the way before finally handing off to the FASB—and the latter took two years trying to find a realistic compromise between the concerns of the SEC and those of the banking industry before coming up with a proposal that might produce a solution.

Meanwhile, contradictory signals still emanated from Breeden's SEC. Breeden and Lochner continued to press, at least for a while, for ways to simplify U.S. financial reporting in the interests of the international competitiveness of U.S. companies and securities markets, but increasingly there were signs of realization at the SEC that the Commission's historic (and legally mandated) mission of protecting the interests of investors and other users of financial information could not be ignored or even thrust into a secondary position in the list of priorities.

Over the next few months, Breeden's public comments suggested soul-searching about what the SEC's mission really was—or at least what the politics of the time seemed to demand of it. For example, two weeks after his Senate testimony he told the *Wall Street Journal*: "If accounting standards aren't adequate to give an accurate picture of a firm's condition, they're not doing the job they need to do."[15] A few weeks later, he told *Forbes*, "If you are in a volatile business, then your balance sheet and income statement should reflect that volatility." Words right out of the Don Kirk syllabus. And yet in the same interview, he said: "Over the past few years FASB has put out increasingly technical, detailed, and costly standards. . . . Unquestionably, the differences in accounting principles between the U.S. and other major countries create a significant disincentive for foreign companies to list in U.S. markets."[16]

In congressional testimony, Breeden opposed a plan by New York Stock Exchange chairman William Donaldson to obtain listing of 200 to 300 foreign companies by relaxing standards for financial accounting and reporting. There would be a risk, Breeden said. "Without this protection, investors might select a foreign company's stock, only to discover later that differences in accounting or auditing standard.: made the foreign stock look better."[17]

The validity of Breeden's observation was demonstrated late in 1993 when the highly publicized agreement by Daimler-Benz A.G. to report its results according to American GAAP in order to qualify for listing on the New York Stock Exchange brought about two dramatically different sets of figures. Under German accounting rules the company's loss in the first nine months was the Deutschmark equivalent of $105.4 million: Under GAAP it was $1.19 billion.[18]

It was difficult for the standard setters to know where the SEC chairman was coming from. It also was difficult for them to know where the Roundtable was coming from. Even as a hot banking issue, marketable securities, was occupying that industry's attention, little was heard from the Roundtable's Accounting Principles Task Force whose chairman was head of the nation's largest bank. He, of course, was occupied by such other matters as sharply declining profits, deep erosion in the quality of Citibank's assets, and public speculation that his directors might ask him to stand down as CEO.

"The Killer Cost Stalking Business" a *Fortune* headline called it.[19] A *Business Week* article was headed: "First Thing We Do Is Kill All the Accountants; Business Is Livid Over FASB Plan That Could Slash Corporate Net Worth by $1 Trillion."[20] The opening paragraph of a *Wall Street Journal* story quoted the CEO of a midsize machinery manufacturer as complaining that "pain is pain, evil is evil. It cannot be justified or excused by the principle of the greater common good."[21]

In the first two decades after World War II, hubris was the dominant mood of American business. The United States was the world's greatest economic power, and American corporations collectively were the engine that drove it. The prospects for perpetual growth and profit were so assured that companies grandly acquiesced in contracts with their unions that provided not only regular and generous wage increases but also what were then called "fringe benefits." The latter grew steadily in proportion to total compensation not only of unionized "blue-collar" workers but of white-collar employees, including executives, as well. The costs would be dealt with in the future. More recently, however, a sense of reality had begun to cause some squirming in Corporate America: By golly, some day a company has to pay for all that!

Nevertheless, to hear Corporate America tell it in the late 1980s when its attention finally was focused on the problem, the cause of the pain was not its own profligacy but the prospect of accounting rules that would enable shareholders and other users of financial statements to see not only the current but also the projected future costs of those medical and related health benefits so freely given so long ago. This was in a time of escalation of medical costs at a rate much greater than general inflation. A serious argument was put forward by many corporations that the offering of health benefits in union contracts, plus the glowing descriptions of them in brochures designed to attract new employees, whether union or nonunion, and to "orient" them once they were hired, coupled with the consistent providing of the benefits described over a long period of years, did not constitute a liability.

At first there were conflicting decisions by the courts in cases where companies sought to diminish their burdens in the face of rising medical costs—and retirees sought legal redress—but as such cases accumulated, it became clear that the weight of legal opinion was that employers had committed themselves. In other words, there was a liability.

Reluctantly, even some of the early opponents of FASB action on industry's admittedly huge health care obligations acknowledged that there needed to be some recognition of a liability. However, the measurement of that liability continued to be the subject of intense debate. If one believed in historical cost as the basis for financial reporting, it was difficult to imagine a method of reporting in which future costs were estimated. It was argued that such numbers would be "soft," not reliable enough to be included in financial statements. That was ground zero, but when it became apparent that the FASB would insist on a trade-off of maximum reliability to achieve reasonable relevance of such information, how it could be done—with minimum damage to balance sheets and income statements— became the dominant issue. The level of funding was not part of the equation, as it had been with pensions, because few health care plans were funded at all. It was almost entirely a "pay-as-you-go" proposition with companies reporting costs for the current year as expense but ignoring what were, for many of them, rapidly growing obligations for the future— something they could not do with regard to other kinds of long-term obligations.

There were long and tedious debates over such technical questions as the attribution period, or the span of an employee's service over which the postretirement benefit obligation of the employer is assigned; determining the future trend of health care costs; and the treatment of changes in established plans.

While these somewhat esoteric arguments were going on, however, public exposure of the issues through the FASB's drawn-out due process, augmented by extraordinary efforts on the part of the Board and its staff through speeches, interviews with the news media, and a widely distributed videotape, created an awareness even among some of the corporate executives who at first had been most vehemently opposed that there, indeed, was a liability and that some reasonable way of measuring and reporting it needed to be found. Due process demonstrated greater-than-usual value in this instance, slowly bringing a majority of constituents around to the view expressed in a *Business Week* editorial: "U.S. industry can't point a finger at anyone but itself for the problem. Certainly not at the FASB: It is just shining a little light into this can of worms."[22]

The contents of that can of worms were suggested by Carol Loomis in another *Fortune* article in which she invited her readers to imagine a worst case, from the corporate point of view, of a 60–year-old retiree with a life expectancy of 18 more years, a young second wife aged 30, and a young son aged 1. Under a typical health care plan, the retiree's former employer was committed to 88 years of health benefits whose costs were rapidly escalating.[23]

Late in the Board's final deliberations, the FEI attempted to call time-out and thus delay the game as GM and the Roundtable had tried to do on pensions, though not quite as brazenly. P. Norman Roy informed Beresford that although the FEI agreed that postretirement benefit costs should be recognized as a liability, the Institute could not agree with several specific points in the FASB proposal. He cited other opposing views and expressed fear that if the Board continued on the path it seemed to be following, the result would be a lack of "general acceptance" for a major standard. Roy predicted that this would accelerate what he called growing disillusion-ment and dissatisfaction with the FASB. He concluded by urging that the Board should meet with representatives of its major constituencies before adopting a final standard. Specifically, he requested such a meeting for the FEI's own Committee on Corporate Reporting in which issues of concern to Institute members could be discussed in detail.

The meticulously polite and mild-mannered Denny Beresford replied in what for him was a tone of irritation. He said the suggestion that the Board should discuss its direction with constituent groups implied that the stand-ard setters had not been doing this all along, an implication that he said was simply not correct. He enumerated a half a dozen of the most obvious groups with which such meetings had been held, including, several times, the FEI's Committee on Corporate Reporting.

The standard was issued on schedule just before Christmas 1990. Even as the Statement on pensions had been 11 years in the making, so had No. 106 on postretirement benefits.

Later, after corporations had faced up to Statement No. 106, it became almost a part of the conventional wisdom to aver, as many did, that the standard setters had done Corporate America a huge favor in pointing up the future costs of its commitment to postretirement health care—even though those costs could not be based on firm, precise historical figures but would have to be estimated and projected into the future. It was a concrete affirmation of the Board's belief, spelled out in Concepts Statement No. 2, that while relevance and reliability are the two primary qualities that make accounting information useful for decision making, and while "ideally, the choice of an accounting alternative should produce information that is both more reliable and more relevant, it may be necessary to sacrifice some of one quality for a gain in another."[24]

By this time, the focal point of Roundtable and FEI discontent was the 1987 Statement on accounting for income taxes. That standard, though it never became effective, would have called for a long, complex series of computations of future tax benefits and tax liabilities, but its greatest shortcoming from the corporations' standpoint was that it did not permit current recognition of tax benefits expected to be realized in future years. In effect, the corporations held that while they should not be required to include in the financial statements projections of pension and health care obligations in the future, they must be allowed to take future profitability for granted.

After four years of reconsideration, the Board came out with Statement No. 109 that did allow companies to recognize future tax assets as well as liabilities under most circumstances.

In the end, the defining issue of John Reed's chairmanship of the Round-table's Accounting Principles Task Force was not his own industry's worry about accounting for marketable securities, or the general concerns in Corporate America about postretirement benefits and income taxes, but instead the long-simmering question of how to account for generously priced options on huge blocks of stock granted to top and slightly-below-the-top executives and, in some cases, to directors. The corporations did not regard such grants as compensation, and therefore there was no charge to earnings. And there was no way for shareholders to discern the extent to which their stock was being diluted. By the end of 1993, Reed and his management team held options on 41,741,898 shares of Citicorp stock which by then were appreciating rapidly after an earlier swoon.[25]

The possibility that any cost could be assigned to anybody for stock options might spoil the game not only for some highly publicized "fat cats" who seemed to be receiving rewards that bore no reasonable relationship to their own performance or that of their companies but also for thousands of executives whose grants were relatively modest.

Although the standard setters had wrestled with stock compensation in the late 1980s without tangible result and had deferred definitive consideration of it until they could resolve certain theoretical issues underlying it, they were under pressure from various external sources to find solutions as the 1990s began. Fortunately, those pressures built up at a time when the FASB was just about ready, in the normal course of its work, to resume consideration of the matter anyway. In fact, a discussion memorandum entitled "Distinguishing Between Liability and Equity Instruments and Accounting for Instruments with Characteristics of Both" was issued in 1990 as part of the larger financial instruments project. This document dealt with some issues directly related to stock options and elicited more than 100 comment letters. It also was the subject of a public hearing. Most of the commentators, both in writing and at the hearing, urged retention of the status quo with regard to options.

As 1991 wound down, Breeden grumbled that "sometimes under the current disclosure system, you need to be a Ph.D. in finance to determine the value of an executive's compensation package." Six months later the SEC proposed a set of amendments to its proxy rules that included new disclosures regarding executive compensation. Part of the proposal was disclosure of a range of potential realizable stock option values based on various stock appreciation rates.

The chairman of the Senate Subcommittee on Oversight of Government Management, Carl Levin (Democrat, Michigan), introduced a bill entitled Stealth Compensation of Corporate Executives. Senator Levin held hearings early in 1992 at which FASB Vice Chairman Jim Leisenring testified. Attempting to explain the caution and conservatism with which the Board approached such issues, Leisenring stressed that the topic had not been dropped from the agenda or forgotten, as Levin had charged, but merely been delayed until the Board could satisfy itself that "any proposals it might develop would have solid conceptual grounding."

Such a studious approach was difficult for the senator to comprehend. He pressed for a commitment that the Board would act before the year was over, but Leisenring refused flatly, citing complexity of the technical issues involved and the time-consuming due process that would have to be followed once the Board thought it had found ways of resolving them. He estimated that it would take two years. "That's too long. I predict we're going to make your life easier," the senator replied—by enacting legislation. In concluding the session, Levin remarked that stock compensation was

a big issue, a particularly big issue in a recession, that has to do with the morale of workers and the morale of people in our country when they see CEO pay climb when their own pay is not even keeping up with inflation . . . . So Congress should act. We should act to require that the accounting rules here accurately reflect the value of these options to the people receiving them and the cost of these options to the companies that issue them.[26]

He did not indicate how or why he expected such accuracy to be achieved by Congress in a matter of months when the most highly qualified experts had been wrestling with the problem for years.

The participants in this drama were coming from several different directions. Standard setters had long been concerned that a significant amount of cost, not crucial for most companies but having a material effect on returns to shareholders in some, was not being accounted for in any meaningful way. The news media had created public awareness of what, in many cases, seemed unreasonable levels of compensation for corporate executives, and politicians had picked up on the issue. When the FASB convened an advisory task force that included partners of three of the Big Six accounting firms, however, all three acknowledged that they were receiving many inquiries from clients about it but none saw stock compensation as one of the major accounting issues of the day. And Pat McConnell of Bear Stearns and AIMR, while allowing that stock options were a form of compensation and therefore should somehow be recognized as a cost, signaled lack of interest by observing that no business failures had resulted from them.

Unlike other accounting issues, this one was regarded in the upper levels of the corporate community not so much as another potential limitation on management's freedom to report financial results as it saw fit but as a damper on personal income. In the world of smaller companies, particularly high-tech start-ups, it was seen as a potentially crippling limitation of their ability to attract and hold talented people without large, immediate outlays of cash.

John Reed soon hosted another of his dinners to express deep concern to the usual three members of the FASB plus the director of research. His message was that stock options were not to be tampered with. The standard setters indicated their commitment to proceed, however, so the Roundtable's net widened.

As employee benefit "packages" had expanded and grown more varied, a new profession had evolved, often within old-line actuarial consulting firms whose services originally were needed in connection with the design and administration of pension plans. As the prevalence and variety of broad-scale employee benefit plans grew, these firms found an additional niche as consultants on all phases of compensation—including arrangements made in the rarified atmosphere of the boardroom for CEOs and other high-level executives. And new firms sprang up to specialize in this burgeoning area.

Essentially, expertise in compensation consulting depends on ability to accumulate and manipulate masses of comparative data rather than on learning and theory. Nevertheless, an aura of professionalism grew up around the new discipline, and practitioners began to engage in some of the kinds of information exchange that characterize other professions, including the release of data to such professionally inclined groups as the FASB—and to the news media. The latter kind of activity included providing major assistance to such publications as *Fortune* and the *Wall Street Journal* in preparing special editorial features on executive compensation.

In the summer of 1992, word went out to the heads of the most prominent consulting firms from the CEOs of Business Roundtable companies who were their clients that such cooperation with either the FASB or the news media would not be looked on with favor. In general, this was handled with the proverbial velvet glove, but the implication was clear: Failure to take heed could result in the loss of important business.[27]

And the implication was not lost on certain trustees of the FAF. Although the Foundation bylaws explicitly proscribe interference with technical or agenda decisions of the FASB, a 1991 revision states that the trustees may "provide advice and counsel" to the Board on unspecified matters. Following their regular (open) meeting in October 1992, the trustees exercised this provision in a private session with the members of the Standards Board. The advice pressed on the standard setters by several, but not all, of the trustees was that it would be folly for the Board to adopt measurement rules for stock options in view of the Business Roundtable's opposition.

At least two of the more influential trustees then attempted to turn the Standards Board's claim of independence against it, but not without some opposition within the board of trustees. For example, one trustee wrote to Dennis D. Dammerman, senior vice president–finance of the General Electric Company and president-elect of the Foundation, that in his opinion the impact of stock options on the consciousness of the user community, if not the general public, created an issue that could not be ignored.

Dammerman replied curtly that the Board had forfeited its independence on the issue by overreacting to the SEC.

J. Michael Cook, chairman and CEO of Deloitte & Touche and chairman of the trustee's oversight committee, went much further. He addressed a letter to Senator Levin, Chairman Breeden of the SEC, and presumably just as a courtesy, to Denny Beresford at the FASB. He said he had observed interaction among Congress, the SEC, and the Standards Board that gave rise to concern about political influence on private sector standard setting. He then asserted that consensus was growing that increases in the value of stock options after they were granted did not constitute a cost, in the form of compensation expense, to companies granting them.

Cook then alluded to recently promulgated SEC disclosure rules regarding executive compensation that required some information about presumed values of stock options to recipients of the grants—but did not specify any method of assigning an actual cost to the granting company—or its shareholders. For Cook, however, that was enough to put investors in a position to understand and evaluate the benefits that individuals derive from options and the policies followed by the compensation committees and boards of directors of the companies concerned.

Cook concluded by wondering whether it wouldn't be in the public interest for the FASB to drop its stock compensation project. This in a letter from one of the most prominent trustees of the Financial Accounting Foundation to a U.S. senator and the chairman of the SEC. It was a clear-cut violation of the bylaw prohibition against trustee interference in agenda decisions.

Like others determined to score points versus the standard setters on various issues, Dammerman and Cook found it convenient to ignore certain facts of history. As long ago as 1982, the AICPA's Accounting Standards Executive Committee had asked the FASB to consider an Issues Paper on problems that already were apparent in stock options. Many other organizations and individuals had complained of inconsistencies that resulted from applying the Accounting Principles Board's 1972 Opinion No. 25 that specified the accounting that was then required. The Advisory Council was consulted, both in open meeting and by questionnaire. Finally, before stock compensation was added to the technical agenda early in 1984, it had to clear formidable hurdles represented in the previously described criteria for agenda decisions.

The SEC did not take an active interest until 1991, after the media, Senator Levin, and others had made an issue of it.

Meanwhile, the CEO and CFO of the Dover Corporation, not a Business Roundtable company but a $2 billion–plus manufacturer of industrial equipment with a long-term record of earnings increases more than double that of the Standard & Poor's industrial average, wrote to the controlling Business Roundtable Policy Committee: "It is ostrich-like to pretend that a stock option has no value at the time of grant. Corporate America undermines its credibility by trying to maintain this obvious fiction at a time when the spotlight of public, regulatory, and Congressional attention is focused on it."[28]

This was not, by any means, an idealistic position. Gary L. Roubos, the CEO, and John F. McNiff, CFO, were quite pragmatic about it. They added: "Pretending that option grants, however useful or appropriate, are somehow 'free' will increase the likelihood of our having to live with some other ideas becoming the rule." As possibilities, they cited nondeductibility of executive compensation above some arbitrary limit, shareholder votes on individual compensation packages, and changes in the tax law regarding option spreads at exercise date.

At about the same time, legendary investor Warren Buffett had tart words on the subject in his much-admired and oft-quoted annual letter to the shareholders of Berkshire Hathaway, Inc. "It seems to me that the realities of stock options can be summarized quite simply," he wrote. "If options aren't a form of compensation, what are they? If compensation isn't an expense, what is it? And, if expenses shouldn't go into the calculation of earnings, where in the world should they go?" Accountants and the SEC, he continued,

should be shamed by the fact that they have long let themselves be muscled by business executives on the option accounting issue. Additionally, the lobbying that executives engage in may have an unfortunate by-product: In my opinion, the business elite risks losing its credibility on issues of significance to society—about which it may have much of value to say—when it advocates the incredible on issues of significance to itself.

Public indignation about seemingly excessive compensation to the chief executives of certain companies, some with quite poor performance records, coupled with private sector concern about credibility of financial reporting with regard to stock options, revived in Congress the notion, dormant for more than a decade, that maybe standard setting could not be entrusted to the private sector after all. Representative Edward J. Markey, chairman of the House Telecommunications and Finance Subcommittee, issued a public statement in which he decried "ferocious hardball lobbying tactics and not-so-subtle threats" to the FASB and went on to observe:

The federal government allows the accounting profession to establish its own rules and standards, with limited federal oversight, because it has been promised that the profession can do so objectively and responsibly.... These reported threats raise serious doubts about the wisdom of delegating such broad and important responsibilities to the accounting profession in the first place.[29]

In mid-1993, the private sector accounting standard setters resolved to stop being muscled, sort of. They issued for public comment, on a 6–1 vote, a proposed standard that, if finally adopted, would eventually require stock options to be measured at fair value at the grant date, and to be recognized over the vesting period—but would allow three years of grace before such rigorous requirements would become fully effective.

NOTES

1. Attributed to [wire service] "News Summaries, December 31, 1979" in *Simpson's Contemporary Quotations*, compiled by James B. Simpson (Boston: Houghton Mifflin, 1988), 228.

2. A. Clarence Sampson, "The 'Process' in Due Process: A Behind-the-Scenes Look at Standards Setting," *Viewpoints*, October 14, 1991, 1.

3. Dennis R. Beresford, "Self-Regulation and the Consent of the Regulated," *Financial Executive*, September–October 1988, 21.

4. Dennis R. Beresford, "Notes from the Chairman," *Status Report*, September 30, 1990, 2.

5. Comments by Dennis R. Beresford at the Board Member Forum, Norwalk, Conn., May 1993.

6. Lee Berton and Thomas E. Ricks, "SEC, Reportedly Pressed by Business, Studies Need for an Overhaul of FASB," *Wall Street Journal*, August 3, 1988.

7. Carol J. Loomis, "Will 'FASBEE' Pinch Your Bottom Line?" *Fortune*, December 19, 1988, 98.

8. Saul S. Cohen, "The Death of Securities Regulation," *Wall Street Journal*, January 17, 1991, editorial page.

9. Floyd Norris, "The SEC and the Death of Disclosure," *New York Times*, June 11, 1991, business page.

10. Robin Goldwyn Blumenthal, "SEC Inquiry Examines Cost, Complexity of Accounting Rules to U.S. Companies," *Wall Street Journal*, July 20, 1990.

11. Gerald I. White, "The Coming Deregulation of Accounting Principles," paper delivered at a symposium sponsored by the American Institute of Certified Public Accountants at the Wharton School, University of Pennsylvania, October 25–26, 1990.

12. Comments of Patricia McConnell, chairman, Financial Accounting Policy Committee, Association for Investment Management and Research at Advocacy Meeting, New York, September 17, 1990.

13. Donald J. Kirk, "The FASB After Ten Years: An Insider's View," paper delivered at the Arthur Young Professors Roundtable recognizing the FASB's tenth anniversary, Harriman, N.Y., May 6–7, 1983.

14. Stephen A. Zeff, "Is the SEC at a Turning Point on Accounting Standards?" *Viewpoints*, November 30, 1990, 7.

15. Kevin G. Salwen and Robin Goldwyn Blumenthal, "Tackling Accounting, SEC Pushes Changes with Broad Impact," *Wall Street Journal*, September 27, 1990.

16. Dana Wechsler Linden, "If Life Is Volatile, Account for It," *Forbes*, November 12, 1990, 114.

17. Richard C. Breeden, testimony before the Subcommittee on Oversight and Investigations of the House Committee on Energy and Commerce, May 2, 1991.

18. Ferdinand Protzman, "Daimler-Benz Reports Sizable Loss," *New York Times*, December 16, 1993.

19. Carol J. Loomis, "The Killer Cost Stalking Business," *Fortune*, February 27, 1989, 58.

20. James R. Norman, "First Thing We Do Is Kill All the Accountants; Business Is Livid Over FASB Plan That Could Slash Corporate Net Worth by $1 Trillion," *Business Week*, September 12, 1988, 94.

21. Lee Berton, "FASB Finds Itself Under Heavy Attack," *Wall Street Journal*, December 19, 1989.

22. Unsigned editorial, "FASB Shines a Light Into a Can of Worms," *Business Week*, September 19, 1988, 182.

23. Carol J. Loomis, "The Killer Cost Stalking Business, *Fortune*, February 27, 1989, 58.

24. Financial Accounting Standards Board, Statement of Financial Accounting Concepts No .2, *Qualitative Characteristics of Accounting Information*, May 1980.

25. Citicorp Annual Report, 1993, 78.

26. Transcript of hearing conducted by the Subcommittee on Oversight of Government Management of the Senate Committee on Governmental Affairs, February 5, 1992.

27. Alison Leigh Cowan, "Executives Are Fuming Over Data About Their Pay," *New York Times*, August 25, 1992.

28. Alison Leigh Cowan, "Flap Over Value of Stock Options," *New York Times*, September 26, 1992.

29. News release issued by Representative Edward J. Markey's office, April 7, 1993.

Chapter Ten

The Trustees Go Into a "Prevent Defense"

The principles of a free constitution are irrevocably lost when the legislative power is nominated by the executive.

Edward Gibbon[1]

Football teams that are ahead by a few points late in a game often go into a "prevent defense," positioning their deep pass defenders far behind the line of scrimmage, virtually conceding completion of short passes. The trouble with this tactic, also known as a "sagging defense," is that opponents sometimes are able to complete enough short passes in a short enough time to steal the victory away.

From the time John Reed became chairman of the Roundtable's Accounting Principles Task Force, it seemed that the Foundation trustees weren't even waiting for the game clock to wind down before going into their defensive shell—and conceding too much.

The first major concession by the trustees, however, was not to the Roundtable or FEI or even to business interests in general. But it was symptomatic of a mind-set that was increasingly indifferent, if not antagonistic, to the basic mission of setting standards for private sector entities—and insensitive to the need for a clear mandate for the standard setters.

In the fall of 1988, the trustees conducted the exhaustive reviews of both the FASB and the GASB to which they had committed themselves in the structure agreement of 1984, which cleared the way for formation of the GASB. For most of the GASB's life up to 1988, the trustees had been ducking the issue, raised with increasing urgency, of how jurisdictional lines should be drawn between the two Boards. The battleground was, almost literally, a "no man's land" of what came to be known as "special entities," which included colleges and universities, health care facilities, and utilities, that had important institutions planted in both private and public sectors and were in competition with one another to obtain financing from some of the same sources.

As early as 1986, Don Kirk told the trustees bluntly that in failing to re-think and refine the simplistic jurisdictional split that was hastily agreed to in the 1984 structure agreement, they were "not stepping up to their responsibilities." The 1984 agreement was not satisfactory to either the FASB or the GASB, let alone to large numbers of constituents. Kirk and GASB chairman Jim Antonio both pointed out that the two Boards were at work on projects that could result in different standards affecting similar entities under the jurisdiction of different standard setters—and this was being done without malicious intent on the part of either Board but in the normal course of business under their existing mandates. The best the trustees were willing to do was to advise the two Boards to communicate with one another about the implications of their technical projects. Formal plans for such communication were called for, although informal commu-nication was a daily occurrence since the two Boards shared facilities in the same building, including an austere but adequate lunchroom.

The principal significance of the so-called five-year review, or so it was assumed, would be a serious effort to resolve the jurisdiction issue.

After ponderous procedures by two top-heavy, and to some extent interlocking, committees, their reports contained identical language in the respective sections on jurisdiction when issued early in 1989. Those sections had been considered long and intensely by both committees, which con-cluded jointly that, in general, jurisdiction should be determined on an ownership basis except that an "industry criterion" should apply to col-leges and universities, health care institutions, and utilities and that the FASB should be the standard setter in those areas, with the GASB empow-ered to specify the additional data that governmental responsibilities might require entities of those three types to provide.[2]

The state and local governmental constituency could not accept such a resolution, even though some of its best people had participated in formu-lating it. The perceived need for comparability of financial information furnished by essentially similar entities was given little weight. The argu-ments were stated as "a matter of principle," that "state governments are sovereign,"[3] and that "the integrity of government operations requires that these [special] entities be subject to a governmental standards board that has jurisdiction over all state and local governments."[4]

Determined to maintain both standard-setting bodies under the Foun-dation banner if at all possible, the trustees then began a course that resembled nothing so much as the path of the metal ball in an old-fashioned pinball machine as it caromed randomly off one pillar or post or wicket or gate after another. By now, John F. Ruffle, vice chairman of both J. P. Morgan

& Co. and the Morgan Guaranty Trust Company and a former chairman of the FEI, had succeeded Rholan Larson as president of the Foundation. He appointed yet another special committee to study jurisdiction, and it came up with an idea that was acceptable to virtually nobody. It was that the FASB would be presumed originally to be the standard setter for all special entities, whether publicly or privately owned, but the governing boards of government-owned entities in that group would have a onetime opportunity to make a nonrevocable choice as to which Board they would follow.

Somewhat out of patience with the general derision that greeted this proposal, the trustees soon gave up on it and reverted to a hard-line position. On October 30, 1989, they voted 12–2 to reinstate their original endorsement of the review committee recommendation that jurisdiction should be based on presumption of stronger "industry" affinity among special entities than ownership affinity. They were not prepared for the firestorm that followed.

Within a week, representatives of ten national associations of state and local governmental officials met in Washington and announced that they would cut off financial support for the GASB, form an entirely new standard-setting body, and petition the 50 state legislatures to designate that body as officially recognized and authoritative. (Many of the states already had so anointed the GASB.)

Ten days later, following a series of intense telephone conversations with leaders of the governmental organizations, and especially with South Carolina's comptroller general, Earle E. Morris, Jr., who had been a Foundation trustee and now was chairman of the GASB's Advisory Council, Jack Ruffle announced that he had been able to poll 13 of the 15 FAF trustees, and they now would support unanimously a retreat all the way back to the original 1984 structure agreement. The only face saver for the Foundation was a proviso that the GASB would be charged in its mission statement, then being drafted, with a responsibility to consider the "industry" affinities among special entities. "The GASB," the eventual agreement said, "should specifically evaluate similarities of special entities and of their activities and transactions in both the public and private sectors and the need, in certain instances, for comparability with the private sector."[5]

Although Ruffle said later that "there were no winners or losers," the National Association of College and University Business Officers considered itself to be a big loser—and did not hesitate to say so in public. In fact, a spokesperson predicted to the press that a militant segment of the membership henceforth would regard the standard-setting process as "a big farce."[6]

Shortly after the agreement was reached, one of the "name partners" of an Arkansas public accounting firm with an important segment of its clientele affected by the FASB/GASB jurisdiction issue wrote to Ruffle in a tone of anguish mixed with anger. He said his firm had been doing its best to keep clients informed about standard-setting matters so they could comply with reporting and disclosure requirements, but some clients could not understand how or why a decision made on October 30 could be reversed less than two weeks later. How, he asked, can the public be expected to react to that, and how can public accountants advise their clients properly in such an environment without appearing foolish?

The major drama of 1990 was a move to impede the setting of standards for Corporate America by making it more difficult for the standard setters to adopt them. The special advisory group appointed by Rholan Larson in 1988 in a nervous attempt to back up (or help to negate if the trustees found it desirable to do so) the findings of the broad-scale committee conducting the five-year review of the FASB also submitted its report early in 1989. In contrast to the five-year review reports that triggered the trustees' march up the hill and then back down on jurisdiction, the report of the special advisory group was largely a nonevent, but much was made of it anyway. In fact, more than two years after its issuance, the chairman of the FASB still felt compelled to report to the trustees each quarter on what the Board was doing about a series of mostly noncontroversial recommendations.

One that seemed to hold promise of having meaning, especially to the corporate community, was that a standing committee on oversight of the FASB and FASAC (significantly, the GASB and its Advisory Council were not under scrutiny in this exercise) should be established by the board of trustees. For more than a decade, the chairman and members of the FASB had been urging the trustees to pay more attention to, and familiarize themselves more fully with, standard-setting operations. For a time in the early 1980s there was an organized effort to schedule trustees to attend FASB meetings regularly as observers, but such attendance was rare. The oversight committee was formed, but after much huffing and puffing, nothing of significance has come of its specific recommendations.

The one matter considered but not agreed on by the special advisory group, however, turned out to have profound implications for the whole standard-setting process.

One of the members of the advisory group was John F. Quindlen, senior vice president and chief financial officer of E. I. du Pont de Nemours & Co. He had been chairman of the FEI's "ad hoc committee" that prepared the "white paper" in support of the Business Roundtable in 1985 and was elected by the board of trustees itself to fill an at-large position in mid-1988. It was one of several instances of trustee efforts to dampen criticism of standard setting by bringing critics "into the family."

Quindlen was an avowed advocate of ensuring "general acceptance" for standards by raising the hurdle they had to clear in order to be adopted. The most direct way to do this was by changing the FASB's voting requirement for issuance. As the advisory group took up its work, Quindlen immediately began to campaign for his cause. The group, however, was unable either to endorse or reject his proposal, even though it had been made by others in the past and had been given well-documented—and overwhelmingly negative—consideration by earlier boards of trustees. So the report merely noted that the group had considered the matter but had not been able to agree on a position regarding it.[7]

According to plan, the five-year review committee, whose report had been submitted only two months earlier, included in it observations on several matters for consideration by the special advisory group. One of them was the FASB voting requirement. The committee had this to say:

We considered the argument that respect [for FASB pronouncements] would be enhanced by changing the Board's voting requirements for adoption of a pronouncement from a simple majority of four-to-three to a supermajority of five-to-two. The concept that a simple majority carries an issue is typical of group decision making in this country. We therefore do not think constituents' attitudes toward an adopted standard would be significantly different because of the size of the majority that adopted it. In addition, a simple majority makes the conduct of business more efficient—avoiding, for example, both the delays that would sometimes arise in trying to fashion a supermajority and the compromises from that process that would tend to soften the edges of decisions on which constituents need clarity. It is true that a supermajority requirement would make mistakes less likely by making change less likely, but it would have the same effect on progress. Moreover, the appropriate safeguard against mistakes is well-crafted due process procedures, and they are already in place.[8]

This, essentially, was the reasoning on which the trustees based their unanimous decision in 1977 to change the voting requirement from supermajority to simple majority. It was the reasoning they accepted without a formal vote in 1979 when an interim review by their structure committee arrived at the same conclusion, and it was the reasoning they voted unanimously to support in 1982 when their structure committee formally reviewed a request by Ray J. Groves, the chairman of (then) Ernst & Whinney, to reinstate the supermajority voting requirement.

Groves was chairman of the 1988–89 special advisory group, and by that time, the environment had changed. Corporate America had luxuriated in ten years of a deregulatory, almost devil-may-care atmosphere in Washington that had steadily undermined tolerance of restraint in any form, whether exercised by the public or the private sector. For the public accounting firms, the news in that period had not been as good as it had been for corporations, but in a perverse and somewhat ambiguous way, it had a similar effect as far as attitudes toward standards were concerned. The universe of major auditing clients was shrinking as a result of rampant takeovers plus a few major bankruptcies, and competition for various kinds of consulting assignments was intensifying. The accounting profession was losing its gentility and learning how to be lean and mean. In such an environment, one took care not to be out of step with one's major clients. On the other hand, there was mounting concern about shareholder lawsuits against the accounting firms—and the growing practice among corporations of "shopping" several accounting firms for opinions on accounting issues if the anwer provided by their own auditor was not pleasing. Standards were a kind of crutch for the public accounting firms in those situations, but the net of it was that the need to please clients and hold on to audit engagements was greater than it had been in more than a half a century. This gave rise to a strange kind of cautious antagonism toward the standard setters.

On the corporate side, the voting issue was seen by many as an opportunity to slow down what they perceived as rampant standard setting. One trustee from the corporate world went so far as to say in a public meeting that a change in the voting requirement would "enhance the process by making change [in standards] more difficult." Others, including Quindlen, were more circumspect, insisting that the move would strengthen the standard setters by providing assurance that onerous standards could not "squeak through by one vote" and that there would be "general acceptance" out there in the world whenever a new rule was adopted. In fact, Quindlen insisted that the proposal had nothing to do with business concerns about the number or content of standards but was intended only to improve the "marketing" of them by assuring the customers that the standard setters were strongly united behind their product.

The notions of "general acceptance" and "marketing" of standards, of course, were based on the assumption that despite SEC policies and AICPA Rules of Conduct, adherence—or non-adherence—to standards was somehow a voluntary decision. They also ignored a mass of evidence that the distinction between a 4–3 and 5–2 vote in many cases was either misleading or virtually meaningless.

The trustees were presented with certain facts. One was that a 4–3 vote often did not reflect arithmetically or in any other sense the actual positions of the seven Board members on a particular standard. Given the room for opinion in arriving at positions on accounting issues, the standard setters often agreed on the basic principles involved but had reservations, or even outright disagreements, over subissues—and felt strongly enough to cast a negative vote in order to avail themselves of the privilege of writing a dissent that would be included in the standard. Members often did this even though they very likely would have voted to support the standard if one more vote had been needed for its passage. In such cases, the overriding consideration was that the new standard, despite shortcomings perceived in it, was an improvement over the status quo. Furthermore, this would be clear to anyone taking the trouble to read and analyze the dissents and the

"Basis for Conclusions" sections published as integral parts of the standards.

It was pointed out, for example, that although the failed Statement No.
19 on oil and gas was adopted by only a 4–3 vote, a fact that its opponents
made much of, all seven Board members were agreed on the basic decision
that successful efforts should be the single method of accounting. The hated
Statement No. 8 on foreign currency translation was adopted by a 6–1 vote,
but its replacement that was applauded and "generally accepted" passed
by only 4–3. It also appeared quite likely at the time this debate was going
on that it would not be possible to obtain enough votes to replace the most
unpopular of all FASB Statements, No. 96 on income taxes, under a 5–2
voting requirement, although a new Statement on the subject ultimately
did pass by 6–1.

Proponents of the supermajority requirement knew that it might occa-
sionally prevent adoption of something they favored, but they regarded
this as a minor and quite acceptable risk because their real interest was in
bringing about fewer and looser standards.

Ruffle suggested that the proposal for a voting change be exposed for
public comment, confident that the sheer number of letters from proponents would exceed those from people opposing it, and they did. But a
comment letter from Paul B. W. Miller of the University of Colorado at
Colorado Springs pointed up the essential facts of history. Miller was a close
observer of the standard-setting process, having served both as a Faculty
Fellow at the FASB and as an Academic Fellow at the SEC. He also was
coauthor, with Rodney J. Redding, of *The FASB: The People, the Process, and
the Politics*,[9] the first book published about the Board. Miller's letter described a more realistic picture of the financial reporting situation than the
supposedly heavy hitters of the corporate world and public accounting
profession—or even the SEC—could bring themselves to recognize.

The term "generally accepted accounting principles," Miller wrote,

> was representationally faithful only so long as there was no authoritative body
> empowered to impose its conclusions on others. This relatively unstructured con-
> sensus arrangement remained workable for nearly three decades, but came to a
> close with the 1965 action by the AICPA's Council that identified APB Opinions as
> having "substantial authoritative support."

The next key event, Miller pointed out, was the SEC's Accounting Series
Release No. 150 in 1973 that designated the FASB as the only authoritative
source for standards suitable for application in SEC filings. "Even though
the old terminology remains in the literature and in the auditor's report as
a vestige of the earlier system," Miller said, "these events show that the real
situation for the last 25 years is that principles are *authoritatively imposed*,
not 'generally accepted.' Thus, the argument that a supermajority is necessary to establish 'general acceptability' is anachronistic."[10]

The standard setters themselves produced a supermajority on the issue. All seven members of the Board wrote individually to the trustees supporting the simple majority rule. And the Advisory Council saw no need for change.

The trustee meeting at which the issue finally was decided seemed to hold some promise of being the accountants' version of *High Noon*, but in the end, it included only the scene in which most of the townspeople cop out—and in this version there was no Gary Cooper in sight. Only a minority spoke with conviction for either side. The rest were prepared to go with the flow—in other words, with forces emanating from outside the meeting room.

One of those external forces kept his weapon safely in its holster. Richard Breeden dramatically faxed a letter to Jack Ruffle while the meeting was going on, but to Ruffle's evident satisfaction, it took no position on the issue at hand. Breeden's only advice was that in order to be successful, private sector standard setting requires the ability to act promptly, to consider the views of interested constituencies, and to establish cost-effective standards designed to maintain the integrity of financial reporting. He made his customary bow to the competitive positions of U.S. companies and the U.S. capital markets and concluded by recommending only that in deciding on the FASB's voting procedures the trustees should determine which voting procedure best achieves the objectives he outlined. Over and out.

Philip Searle, retired chairman of SunBanks, Inc., and first chairman of the newly constituted FAF oversight committee, called the proposed change "Draconian" and urged that the trustees table the matter for a "defined period" to allow the oversight committee to study it. Thomas R. Dyckman of the Cornell University faculty argued that a 5–2 voting requirement would produce "mushier" standards and the case for such a requirement would have to be overwhelming in order to be credible. He also said that consideration of the matter at that time was inappropriate in view of the charge to the oversight committee.

Quindlen assured his fellow trustees that the matter was "no big deal" and the proposed change would not slow down the Board's production of needed standards. He said the change would cure an imagined problem of "control by one vote." Arden B. Engebretsen, the soon-to-be-retired vice chairman and chief financial officer of Hercules Incorporated, asserted that the FASB had gone a "bridge too far" in presuming to set standards at all, and that its proper mission was merely to identify and catalogue "accepted practices." It was a view of standard setting that was more than a quarter of a century out of date, but Engebretsen nevertheless was elected vice president of the Foundation the following year.

The trustees' vote was 11–5 to increase the voting requirement from a simple majority to a supermajority. Mission accomplished, Quindlen resigned from the board of trustees only a month later. He had been elected for a three-year term as an at-large trustee only two years earlier.

In a prescient comment to the FEI's annual conference on current financial reporting issues a year before he completed his final term on the FASB, Don Kirk referred to the FEI's "white paper" in support of Roger Smith and the Business Roundtable in 1985.

I am troubled by what I perceive as a strong inference . . . that more business representation on the Board will result in solutions more acceptable and more palatable to the business community. That expectation is contrary to the intent of the system, which is to pick the best-qualified individuals and charge them to put aside all interests but the broad public interest in credible, comparable financial reporting. I personally welcome more business participation in the process, more business backgrounds among Board members, but not *representation* of a particular constituent viewpoint. (Emphasis added)[11]

Kirk picked up on this theme again a year later in accepting the AICPA's Gold Medal Award for outstanding service to the accounting profession. "I would like to stress the need to guard jealously the independence of the Board," he said.

If financial reporting is to be credible, there must be public confidence that the standard-setting system is credible, that selection of Board members is based on merit and not the influence of special interests, and that standards are developed neutrally with the objective of relevant and reliable information, not purposeful manipulation.[12]

Kirk's remarks on those two occasions correctly foreshadowed the struggle for the FASB's soul that would go on at least for the next decade—if the Board were to survive that long.

The next major drama began in 1990, a year in which the trustees were confronted with the need either to reappoint or to replace two members of the Standards Board who were approaching the end of their initial five-year terms. Both were assumed by most observers to be shoo-ins for reappointment, and with good reason. In their first five years, both had established themselves as highly competent and generally well regarded standard setters. One was Robert J. Swieringa, an eminent and relatively young academician who had been on faculty at both Cornell and Stanford Universities. The other was C. Arthur Northrop, whose corporate credentials seemed impeccable. He had been treasurer, and before that controller, of International Business Machines (IBM), was a director of Intel Corporation, and had served as chairman of the FEI's Committee on International Liaison, vice chairman of its Committee on Corporate Reporting, and as trustee of the Financial Executives Research Foundation. It appeared to be an ideal appointment from Corporate America's point of view, and in fact, it was warmly praised at the time by Roger Smith.

But Art Northrop had made one mistake before his term even began. On the day his appointment was announced, he told a *Wall Street Journal* reporter that he was not accepting a mandate to represent the views of business alone but rather that he intended to work with the other members of the FASB to develop the best accounting rules possible.[13] The damage was compounded a week later when Don Kirk, addressing the FEI's annual conference on accounting and reporting issues, cited that statement of Northrop's with approval. Kirk concluded his speech by saying:

I am especially impressed by the views attributed to new Board member Arthur Northrop. . . . In my judgment, Art passed his first test as a member of the FASB with flying colors. He told the *Journal* that he won't represent the views of business alone on the FASB, but will work with other FASB members to develop the best accounting rules possible. My message is: "Let's keep it that way."[14]

As a result of a recommendation by the five-year review committee early in 1989, expiration of Board member terms was changed from December 31 to June 30 and existing terms were extended by six months. Bob Swieringa was reappointed routinely in October 1990, but Art Northrop was left twisting in the wind for another six months, in which time the FEI lobbied furiously to induce the trustees to dump a Board member whose appointment it had applauded five years earlier. Northrop's ultimate apostasy had been to vote in favor of Statement No. 94, which required consolidation in a parent company's financial statements of all majority-owned subsidiaries. This, of course, swept in the huge finance and insurance subsidiaries of some very large and influential manufacturing corporations—and the parent companies were not inclined to disclose anything that looked like responsibility for the debt of those subsidiaries.

No one, of course, dared be so crude as to cite a particular vote, or a well-publicized five-year-old newspaper quote, as counts in an indictment of an eminently well-qualified Board member, and certainly there were no questions of "character" such as often crop up in election campaigns. It was simply a matter, as FEI President P. Norman Roy put it, of his organization's perception that "business's point of view does not seem adequately reflected in the standards. I think that says it all."[15]

The trustees caved in to the FEI campaign. (At the time, industry accounted for more than 52 percent of those contributions to the Foundation that were earmarked for the FASB, and the FEI always had done a good job of mobilizing industry financial support, despite the troubles.) Northrop was dumped. Shaun F. O'Malley, chairman of Price Waterhouse and by now president of the Foundation, declined to explain the action but denied that the trustees had "caved in to anybody." Despite its success in getting rid of Northrop, the FEI was frustrated in its efforts to put across a handpicked replacement. The unsought publicity that attended Northrop's dumping intimidated the Foundation trustees to the extent that they actually rejected the FEI's candidate in an awkward contretemps that ultimately embarrassed all parties involved.

The financial executives had settled on Robert A. Orben, a member of their Committee on Corporate Reporting and former vice president–controller of the Cummins Engine Company, Inc., recently downgraded to vice president for accounting policy. He also had been responsible recently for some retroactive accounting changes at Cummins that were sharply criticized in the financial analyst community. Orben had been a member of FASAC in the early 1980s and was well known to several members of the FASB and its staff.

Although the trustees' selection committee had recommended Orben, the full board rejected him—and did so in a glare of news coverage, particularly by the *New York Times*, which had been paying close attention to the entire episode.

The FEI response was a curious mixture of rancor, recrimination, and paranoia that seemed to reflect an underlying but fallacious belief that the organization was fully entitled to choose whom it wanted to "represent" industry on the FASB. A memo reporting on the disaster went out from FEI headquarters to the members of the Committee on Corporate Reporting. The *New York Times*, it said, had obviously been fed information by sources that were antagonistic to the FEI and business in general. There was a suggestion that those sources might even be inside the FAF or FASB.

Attached was a list of 11 questions to be considered in thinking about possible action to combat what was perceived as a "smear campaign." One question whose answer had been set forth repeatedly over the years had to do with what interests the FASB was intended to serve. Another that the trustees' special committee dealt with at length in 1985, and their selection committee later elaborated on, was what criteria should be used in selecting members of the FASB. Of the seven qualities the trustees had identified as being essential in standard setters, the one to which the selection committee devoted the most space in its report was "judicial temperament." This was defined as lack of "bias or partiality" and "unwillingness to cater to demands of particular groups or organizations." Objectivity, the report summed up, "is the key trait."[16]

Another essential quality, the trustees had concluded, was "commitment to the FASB's mission." This statement in itself probably was the last really affirmative thing the trustees had to say about the standard-setting process.

Raymond H. Alleman, senior vice president–controller of ITT Corporation and a new Foundation trustee whose commitment to the FEI apparently was stronger than to the standard setters, responded to the FEI memo, first sympathizing with Bob Orben's unfortunate publicity, then worrying that this might discourage other business community candidates for FASB membership from coming forward. He then made a puzzling observation. The choice of members of both the FASB and FAF, he said, was quickly becoming politicized, with potentially destructive results. The statement was puzzling because it was the FEI, along with its Big Brother, the Business Roundtable, that was doing the politicizing.

In the immediate aftermath of the Orben rejection, Shaun O'Malley predicted that an appointment would be made in a month. It took six months. Eventually, Robert H. Northcutt, Jr., vice president and controller of Lockheed Corporation and an FEI stalwart, got the nod. He was a member of the Institute's influential Committee on Corporate Reporting and a member of the FASB's Advisory Council. In a jocular mood at an early joint meeting with the FEI Executive Committe as a member of the Board, he reported that when he last met with CCR, he was warned against "catching the Norwalk disease."

Before they became entangled in the case of *FEI v. Northrop*, the trustees managed, somewhat belatedly, to fill the vacancy on the FASB that was created when Ray Lauver resigned. The new member was Joseph V. Anania, a highly regarded practice partner from the Pittsburgh office of Price Waterhouse. And Denny Beresford was confirmed for a second term as chairman.

The trustees also embraced a new member of their group, nominated by the FEI, who brought with him fairly impressive credentials in the banking world. He was Thomas E. Jones, executive vice president of Citicorp—John Reed's point man in the Business Roundtable campaign against the standard setters.

Prior to the Northrop affair, there had been extreme reluctance on the part of even the bitterest critics of the FASB to attack, or even seem to criticize personally, the individual members of the Board. There had been, to be sure, a few cautious, indirect allusions to grievances, including a letter from P. Norman Roy to Denny Beresford complaining that two unnamed Board members had been less than respectful of some industry witnesses at a public hearing, but in general the critics' frustration still was directed, at least nominally, at the staff.

FEI v. Northrop made it clear, however, that a growing proportion of the standard setters' constituency was inclined to believe that standard setting indeed was nothing more than a game of "let's pretend"—and the players on that side of the table were growing more impatient with the FASB's continuing unwillingness, despite the pressures and restrictive changes, to go along with the game.

The trustees had tied themselves in knots—indeed, had become contortionists—trying to appease the critics of standard setting. But at some point there would have to be recognition of, and a facing up by all parties concerned, to the public intent to bring about reliable, relevant financial reporting. It was an intent that had been expressed clearly in the Securities Acts of 1933 and 1934 and had been evident in various ways throughout the six decades since then, but Corporate America had not yet caught on to the seemingly elementary fact that this public intent in the end would have to be the primary consideration, not corporate convenience.

Ironically, the supposed overseer of the standard-setting structure that the Wheat Committee had recommended in 1972, but not the standard-setting body itself, was showing many of the same weaknesses that, when perceived in the Accounting Principles Board, had led to appointment of the Wheat Committee in 1971. Like the APB, the board of trustees of the Financial Accounting Foundation is made up of persons who serve part-time, without compensation—and without giving up their primary means of livelihood.

The obvious potential for inattention, indifference, and conflict of interest that was inherent in this arrangement did not materialize in the first dozen years after the Foundation and Standards Board were organized. The trustees in that period were enthusiastic supporters of the idea of private sector standard setting, and they were strong allies of the standard setters in times of trouble. They also were conscientious overseers.

This began to change, however, in the early to mid-1980s as several influences brought about changes in the business and professional environment. One was the diminishing regard for federal regulation—or restraint of any kind—that was being exhibited in Washington. Another was the increase in competition among the major public accounting firms, not only for audit engagements but also for various forms of consulting work that was eroding their traditional attitude of independent-mindedness. Once proud of their professional objectivity and analytical abilities, they increasingly followed a practice of surveying their most important clients before taking a position on FASB proposals. Joe Anania commented at a conclave of past and present Board members in the spring of 1993 that "the Big Six are taking advocacy positions in the last few years that would have been strange for them before."[17]

Still another factor was the shortening of time frames in which executives did their thinking and planning as the financial markets became more demanding and the stalking of takeover targets grew bolder and more insistent. Finally, it was inevitable that with every passing year the standard setters, in the normal course of their work, would adopt more rules that would offend more people.

All the while, business was steadily increasing the numbers of its spokespersons on the board of trustees, but individual trustees were becoming less able (or willing) to devote sufficient time and attention to their Foundation responsibilities. At the same time, some were becoming more doctrinaire in their positions regarding issues before the standard setters. And they were increasingly torn by divided loyalties. It was difficult to focus conscientiously on the public's need for reliable, relevant financial information while at the same time worrying about how one's company's earnings would look in the next reporting period—or how one's client's wishes might be expressed at the next meeting.

Denny Beresford has denied publicly that the corporate community has gained influence over the FASB's deliberations on technical issues. In a literal sense, in terms of the Board's painstaking consideration of the details of any given issue, he is right. But in terms of the overall balance of power in the standard-setting structure, the atmosphere in which the standard setters work, and the trend lines and fault lines that are developing, he is overlooking some stark realities.

Of greatest concern is the growing determination on the part of some influential trustees who support the Business Roundtable view of standard setting to circumvent the explicit prohibition set forth in the bylaws against trustee interference in technical and agenda decisions of the standard setters. Less than a month after the contretemps over stock options, Dennis Dammerman, by then president-elect of the Foundation, became exercised over a *Wall Street Journal* story about a Statement the Board was about to issue that would amend two earlier standards so as to require recognition of an obligation to provide certain postemployment benefits if specific conditions were met. In a letter to the FASB chairman, he urged that the Board suspend its planned vote on the ballot draft. He asserted that such a radical accounting change [in fact, it was not "radical" at all] should not be adopted without further exposure and debate. He said constituents had come to expect full communication of possible consequences and solicitation of constituent views [which already had been done]. He then cited field testing as an "expected minimum" for such significant and complex standards [this was a minor one]. He went on to warn the FASB chairman that together they had to ensure that the Board would never abandon such an approach to standard setting. He concluded that "we," presumably the FASB chairman and the FAF president, still had work ahead of them before a standard could be finalized. It was a clear violation of the bylaw provision against trustee interference in the Board's technical decisions.

The barbarians were not at the gate: They were inside it.

One of Dammerman's predecessors as CFO of General Electric, Alva O. Way, was president of the Foundation in 1978 and 1979, a difficult period of transition in which significant changes in the makeup of the Board and its operating procedures took place. He was dedicated to the concept of independent standard setting and indefatigable in his support for the structure that had so painstakingly been erected to ensure it, including the "separation of church and state" clause in the bylaws that prohibited trustee interference in technical decisions of the standard setters. He was the first person from Corporate America to fill the post and still is regarded by knowledgeable observers as one of the most effective heads of the Foundation.

The contrast between the worldview of many CEOs and CFOs in the 1990s and that of Al Way and his boss, former GE chairman Reg Jones, and people like them, illustrates a disturbing development in American business, quite apart from issues of financial reporting. Less than a generation ago there still were some corporate leaders in whose view of the world the first priority of business was to develop and market goods or services that would provide benefits to customers in the near term, and thereby bring profit to their providers over the long haul. It was an expectation of corporate prosperity based on customer satisfaction over the long term.

Despite contemporary protestations of good intentions regarding customer satisfaction and quality of manufacture and service to customers, the new wave of corporate management generally has a narrow and short-term view, depending in large part on financial maneuvering. This view barely extends beyond the next quarterly report.

NOTES

1. Edward Gibbon, *Decline and Fall of the Roman Empire* (New York: Harcourt, Brace, 1960), 33.

2. Financial Accounting Foundation, *The Structure for Establishing Financial Accounting Standards* (Norwalk, Conn.: FAF, January 26, 1989); idem, *The Structure for Establishing Governmental Accounting Standards* (Norwalk, Conn.: FAF, January 26, 1989).

3. Relmond Van Daniker, quoted in the *New York Times*, November 6, 1989, and *Forbes*, December 11, 1989.

4. Press release, Academy for State and Local Government, quoted in *Securities Regulation and Law Report*, November 13, 1989.

5. Financial Accounting Foundation, 1989 Annual Report, 2.

6. Robin Jenkins, quoted in *Accounting Today*, December 4, 1989.

7. *Report of the Special Advisory Group* (Norwalk, Conn.: Financial Accounting Foundation, March 1989).

8. Financial Accounting Foundation, *The Structure for Establishing Financial Accounting Standards* (Norwalk, Conn.: FAF, January 26, 1989), 8.

9. Paul B. W. Miller and Rodney J. Redding, *The FASB: The People, the Process, and the Politics* (Homewood, Ill.: Richard D. Irwin, 1986).

10. Paul B. W. Miller, letter to the trustees of the Financial Accounting Foundation, January 16, 1990.

11. Donald J. Kirk, "Can You Hear Me Now? Two-Way Communications between the FASB and Its Constituents," address to Financial Executives Institute conference on current financial reporting issues, New York, November 6, 1985.

12. Donald J. Kirk, quoted in *Status Report*, December 23, 1986.

13. C. Arthur Northrop, quoted in *Wall Street Journal*, October 31, 1985.

14. Kirk, "Can You Hear Me Now?" address to FEI conference, November 6, 1985.

15. P. Norman Roy, quoted in *New York Times*, April 26, 1991.

16. Report of selection committee to the trustees of the Financial Accounting Foundation (unpublished), 1987.

17. Joseph V. Anania, comment at Board Member Forum, Norwalk, Conn., May 18, 1993.

Chapter Eleven

Accounting "Truth"—or Consequences?

Things and actions are what they are, and the consequences of them
will be what they will be: Why then should we desire to be deceived?
Bishop Joseph Butler
noted eighteenth-century clergyman[1]

In the early days of the FASB, Marshall Armstrong repeatedly warned against what he called "crusades to capture the Holy Grail of accounting truth." As a veteran of the Accounting Principles Board, he was well aware of the roadblocks and pitfalls, to say nothing of the hostile pagans, along the route.

Much later, after listening to "economic consequences" arguments throughout most of his dozen years on the Board, Bob Sprouse summarized in a 1987 article in *Accounting Horizons* the kinds of rule-making proposals that can be counted on to call forth such arguments:

Requiring expenditures to be treated as expenses rather than allowing them to be capitalized as assets *is predicted to cause a reduction in those expenditures to the detriment of society and the economy.*

Requiring certain obligations that presently may or may not be described in footnotes to be reported in the face of the balance sheet as liabilities *is predicted to cause violations of debt indentures; failures to meet regulatory requirements; increases in the cost of capital; and uses of different, less economic methods of financing.*

Requiring the full effects of transactions and events to be recognized when they occur rather than allowing those effects to be spread over several periods *tends to cause fluctuations in reported income that are predicted to lead to higher costs of capital, uneconomic hedging, or avoidance of otherwise economically sound transactions.*[2]

Oscar Gellein, also a survivor of many standard-setting scuffles, put it diplomatically. "Claims about that kind of effect [adverse impact on cash flow] have been made many times over many years to different standard setters on many issues," he said. "Evidence of the seriousness of the charge is sparse despite a long history of expressed concern."[3] Don Kirk made a similar observation in a response to Senator Bob Dole who had inquired about a constituent's complaint that certain FASB proposals surely would lead to financial disaster for electric utility companies. Over the years, Kirk replied, similar predictions had been made with regard to the effect of FASB proposals on various companies and industries. To the best of his knowledge, he said, the predicted consequences had not come about. He added the observation that financial markets are much too sophisticated to react in irrational ways to objective information.

In commenting on claims of disaster if mark-to-market accounting were to be adopted for marketable securities, Sandy Burton put it more colorfully: "When faced with accounting changes, people always say, 'Blood will run in the streets.' The world has not ended yet."[4]

Given that accounting "truth" comes in many shades, as we said at the outset, and exists in the eye of the beholder, as the subsequent narrative has implied, what claim can be made for the legitimacy of any "standard" established by mere mortals for the all-too-human activity of financial accounting and reporting? That question is a fulcrum on which Corporate America balances the lever it uses to try to influence specific outcomes of the standard-setting process. Few doubt the legitimacy of the FASB's structure or process, but many question the correctness of the answers it produces. Though not many corporate executives, or even public accountants, would admit to being philosophers, they, in effect, pose a philosophical question: What is truth? A corollary to that question is: How can mere mortals approach a reasonable, workable approximation of truth that can be accepted and acted on by all the players in a sensitive process of information development and dissemination?

The only viable answer is threefold. First, a completely neutral approach to the standard-setting process has to be decided on from the outset so as to avoid even the appearance of favoring one interest or set of interests over others. Second, an organizational structure and method of operation has to be created to carry out that approach, both in actuality and in the public's perception. Then the standard setters have to exercise best judgment—and all parties have to recognize that in the real world *best* has never meant *perfect*.

Denny Beresford noted the natural tendency of people to judge an institution on its product rather than its process. "That is fair enough," he said, up to a point. If the product is an automobile or a financial service or a laundry detergent, some subjectivity will creep into one's judgment, but there are fairly universal and objective criteria that apply. In contrast, there are no universally applicable objective criteria for judging accounting standards. Opinions are bound to vary all over the lot. Sure, there may seem to be a majority opposing or favoring a given standard or proposed standard. But when that seeming majority is analyzed, its views often reflect quite different reasons. Sometimes it even turns out that there is no true majority at all. Somebody has to take on the task of finding a solution that meets the objectives of financial reporting among many varying viewpoints.[5]

Oscar Gellein offered an idealized definition of financial reporting, and therefore of standard setting, at a symposium on the conceptual framework in 1980. "Financial reporting assists in the allocation of available resources to businesses and other enterprises," he said.

It makes no judgment about who should have the resources. It assumes, instead, that if the information reported about resource users is relevant and reliable for the kinds of decisions that resource providers make, there is a better chance that resources will be channeled to match their price with risk and return preferences.[6]

Two years earlier, Gellein had delivered a notable paper at the annual convention of the American Accounting Association. Its thesis was neatly summed up in a three-word title: "Neutrality Has Consequences." Financial reporting would be sterile and standard setting would have no purpose, he said, if the reporting had no results or impact. It should be useful in bringing about efficient allocation of resources but should not itself be the allocator.

If a . . . standard results in a more evenhanded portrayal by all enterprises of risks and returns, an impact on some enterprises is not unexpected. Some seekers of capital stand to lose short-run benefits of an undeserved competitive edge. The consequence of realignment of the capital market is fair and equitable treatment of seekers of capital and suppliers of capital. That is the consequence sought.[7]

Not all of the Board's constituents accept this proposition, of course. As Jim Leisenring points out, "Some use neutrality to mean we should deal only with the trivial and avoid all those consequences."[8]

Still others believe that an even more neutral posture for standard setters to take on any given issue is inaction. Art Wyatt addressed this while he was still a member of the FASB. "What few seem to understand," he said, "is that inaction when a significant accounting issue is identified also has consequences. For example, inaction by the Board on certain proposals made by savings and loan [S&L] association regulators would have permitted capital to be created artificially." Loans might have been extended and investments made in S&Ls where capital adequacy seemed to be sound, "when in fact the capital was artificial and overstated." Inaction by the standard setters, he concluded,

does not mean that no data will be presented relating to an issue, but rather that the data presented may in fact be misleading. When this is so, bad decisions can result and credibility of financial information generally can be impaired. That result produces an economic consequence just as new positions required by the Board produce economic consequences.[9]

Evenhanded treatment, Oscar Gellein said, "builds on objectives and concepts that continually search for real differences in risk and return, treats them differently, and avoids creating the appearance of difference where there is none."[10] That, of course, was the reason the FASB undertook to construct a conceptual framework. The perceived need for neutrality also was the reason the Board's designers and founders were at such pains to create a structure and process that would ensure a full and fair hearing for all interested parties.

It hardly needs to be said that for the structure and process to perform satisfactorily, they must be operated by persons of the highest intelligence, experience, and integrity. No one has ever charged seriously that any of the members of the FASB over the years have been lacking in any of those qualities. How, then, does one account for the very serious charges that the performance of the FASB is less than adequate, or even a total failure?

As we have seen, several perverse factors are at work that, taken together, brought down the predecessors of the present standard-setting arrangement and are showing signs of eventually negating the "bold experiment" that the private sector undertook in the early 1970s to preserve its own rule-making authority and to avoid being unduly subject to the clumsy hand of government.

The first of those factors is the subjective, imprecise nature of accounting itself, and the resulting diversity of opinion that arises on specific issues. This, of course, has corollaries in the diversity of opinion about political issues that are decided in Congress and the legal/political issues that are decided in the federal courts, including the Supreme Court. Inconsistency and imprecision in those areas, which generally are at least as great as in accounting, are remarked on often in the news media and elsewhere, but the imprecise decisions that are made in Congress and the courts have the imprimatur of an all-powerful federal government, and discontent with them generally results, as far as the public is concerned, in a kind of resigned recognition that the deals are done and there isn't much anyone can do about them. In extreme cases, there may be retribution at the next election, and some who are disaffected may seek redress in the courts but generally without much success. Public authority, whether it resides in legislative bodies or in the courts, is *public* authority—and usually is accepted as the final word if for no other reason than that the process of attempting to reverse it is perceived as too cumbersome. That is not the case with private sector standard setting.

A second perverse factor is self-interest on the part of those who ostensibly are regulated, the preparers and issuers of financial statements. That they have a legitimate interest in the outcomes of standard setting is undeniable, and their demands for greater participation in the process provided much of the impetus for formation of the FASB in 1972. But while the Securities Acts of the early 1930s and the efforts of standard-setting bodies since then, particularly the FASB since 1973, have emphasized the need for financial reporting that would be useful to a broad public, a vocal segment of Corporate America remains determined that it alone should be privileged to determine what information the users of financial statements should have and how that information should be presented.

A third factor is a literal-minded belief in the power of reported financial information as the end-all, be-all determinant of behavior, and a concomitant inability to recognize that the users of it, especially the more professional and influential ones, not only are adept at interpreting the data and applying "Kentucky windage" to them if they think that is called for but also have sources of information other than the published financial reports.

Another factor, as previously mentioned, is nostalgia for the good old days of "general acceptance" of accounting conventions, along with wider latitude for the exercise of "judgment" in their application rather than adherence to specific rules.

Still another is fear of having to reveal the consequences of management's mistakes, even those deeply embedded in the past.

Then, there simply is resistance to change of any kind.

Perhaps the most troubling factor, however, is a historic shift in America's political consciousness in recent decades. In the very period when public issues of all kinds have multiplied and grown in complexity at an unprecedented rate, an infatuation with something called "participatory democracy" has led Americans to forget how to delegate decisions on technical matters to panels of experts best equipped to deal with them. Selection of those experts, of course, is properly a part of the democratic process, but in all logic, the decisions they are called on to make cannot be if optimum results are to be obtained. America seems to have lost faith in its experts—and not without a modicum of reason. But despite occasional lapses by those experts, is the demos really better able to provide solutions to technical problems than those with special training and experience in the matters at hand?

In one of his first speeches as chairman of the FASB, Don Kirk sought to define the nature of the standard-setting process. He rejected both the view that it is essentially a legislative process and the view that it is essentially judicial but acknowledged that it has some of the elements of both.

There is in our governmental process a relatively new hybrid, the independent regulatory agency. The regulatory process, I believe, is the best available model for standard setting in the private sector. Across our country, legislative bodies have recognized that certain technical, but highly important, public interest matters require a mechanism responsive to the public need, but insulated as much as possible from the political process. The resulting regulatory process has both legislative and judicial qualities: It is legislative because it establishes authoritative rules consistent with a legislated mandate; it is judicial because it interprets its own rules.

This type of process, he added, generally requires "a body of experts whose experience enables them to act in the broad public interest under an explicit mandate."

In concluding that speech, Kirk predicted that if such a body of experts fails, "the standard-setting process can become one of legal negotiation, intergovernmental agency negotiation, or worse yet, a totally politicized process. Any of those possibilities would be devastating to business and the accounting profession, and certainly to the efficiency of our capital markets."[11]

Kirk's reasoning was that there is need for consistency of direction as new standards are promulgated and for predictability about the theoretical underpinnings of future changes. In a process of politicized negotiation, there can be neither consistency nor predictability.

Primary emphasis on economic and social consequences of standards, of course, demands that the process be in the political arena. And that arena calls for a wholly different set of skills than are now at work in standard setting. It calls for decision making by panels of politicians or political appointees rather than panels of professional specialists.

Neutrality is the quality that distinguishes technical decision making from political decision making. Near the end of his second year as chairman of the FASB, Denny Beresford commented:

Perhaps our critics have done us a service by elevating the discussion of accounting standards into the realm of "social consequences" and "public policy." On its face, this may seem to be a much more difficult issue for standard setters to respond to than evaluating economic consequences or merely comparing implementation costs [of standards] to perceived benefits, but I don't think it is.

He then pointed out that although many groups in society, including the political parties, labor unions, and business and professional associations, among many others, lay claim to "the public interest," none really can speak for it because it is unknowable. "They can only present their widely divergent claims," Beresford said, "to the voters, to the regulators, or to the legislators for a political resolution. In other words, public policy decisions are political decisions, made in response to the shifting winds of public opinion."

There is sometimes a fear, Beresford added,

that reliable, relevant financial information may bring about damaging consequences. But damaging to whom? Our democracy is based on free dissemination
of reliable information. Yes, at times that kind of information has had temporarily
damaging consequences for certain parties. But on balance, considering all interests,
and the future as well as the present, society has concluded in favor of freedom of
information. As a nation, we have had no reason in 200 years to fear disclosure of
reliable information other than military or diplomatic secrets. Why should we fear
it in financial reporting?[12]

Fear of economic consequences in the form of greater liabilities to be
reported on the balance sheet and larger accruals for employee pensions
was the driving force behind corporate opposition to issuance of the
standard on employers' accounting for the cost of pensions. But predictions
of what those consequences might turn out to be were far off the mark.
Within a few months, a strong rally in the stock market greatly diminished
the amounts that would have to be deducted from earnings to fund pension
plans, prompting GM's Gene Flegm to tell the *New York Times* that the
pension standard, which he and his company had fought bitterly to the
very end, "may be the most popular statement ever published by the
FASB"[13] and that GM was considering adoption of it in advance of the
required date.

At about the same time, a survey by the large consulting firm of William
M. Mercer-Meidinger, which had opposed the standard vigorously, found
that of the 508 companies in the sample, 56 percent expressed satisfaction
with the new rule, and two-thirds said they were unconcerned about the
effect on the investment community's perception of their companies.

Dave Mosso recalled that in at least one instance, a proposed standard
requiring loss recognition for abandoned nuclear power plants, people and
organizations in the same industry took both sides of the economic consequences issue. Some maintained that the proposal, if adopted, would lower
electric rates to a disastrous level that would force utilities into bankruptcy,
and others said it would raise rates to a level that would impose an
unconscionable burden on consumers. The standard was adopted in 1986,
and neither result has been observed to date.

The savings and loan debacle of the 1980s is, or rather should be, the
reductio ad absurdum of the economic and social consequences argument.
The underlying reasons for the sickness of that industry have been well
publicized, and so have the astonishing legislative and regulatory measures that its pervasive political influence was able to obtain to prop it up—

long past the time when a large segment of the industry should have collapsed and been swept away.

Less well known were the frantic efforts to use what Don Kirk called "accounting legerdemain" to paper over the widening cracks—and to conceal the true economic and social consequences of mismanagement, political favoritism, and in many cases, outright fraud.

As for the underlying causes, first there was the bandwagon of deregulation at the beginning of the 1980s, on which the S&L industry and its minions in Washington jumped eagerly. Minimum net worth requirements, meaning the amount of capital needed to support loans outstanding, were reduced by 40 percent in two years. The ceiling on Federal Deposit Insurance was raised from $40,000 to $100,000 per account, increasing the temptation to risk deposited money on ever-more speculative loans because the government would protect depositors from any catastrophic losses that might result. A requirement that an S&L have at least 400 shareholders, designed to prevent conflicts of interest between deposit-taking lenders and high-flying borrowers, was eliminated. The result was that an individual with a controlling interest in an S&L could, in theory at least, lend to himself as a real estate developer. And it became common practice to inflate outrageously the appraisals of real estate on which the depositors' money was loaned.

As these measures lured S&Ls deeper into the quicksand of speculative lending, and the consequences of that speculation began to become apparent, the regulators' early efforts to cope with the situation involved deferral of loan losses over unrealistically long periods and transparent paper-shuffling charades to create the appearance of capital where there was none. When these measures failed to suffice, the industry and its lobbyists exerted pressure on Congress and the Federal Home Loan Bank Board for relief from what had been fairly stringent regulatory reporting requirements. Originally, those requirements were designed to ensure solvency, but now they were seen as an obstacle to keeping shipwrecked S&Ls afloat.

As a result of Washington's tenderness toward the S&Ls, regulatory accounting practices (RAP), which historically had been more stringent than GAAP in some respects, were steadily softened to provide more leeway for troubled institutions, at least in their reporting to regulators. At the same time, pressure was being exerted on the private sector standard setters to bend GAAP for public financial reporting to suit the convenience of those, both in and outside the Beltway, who were trying every which way to make the weakest members of the S&L industry appear to be solvent when in truth they were not.

Throughout the 1980s, the FASB accumulated a thick file of its carefully reasoned and documented responses to such proposals in the form of testimony before congressional committees, comment letters on regulatory proposals, and responses to queries from interested senators and congressmen and members of the staffs of congressional committees. In each of these communications, the Board was careful to acknowledge that Congress and the regulators had the authority to do as they saw fit with regard to regulatory requirements. The theme throughout was that if public policy-makers were convinced that relief was needed, legislation and / or regulatory rules should be relaxed but that financial reports made available to the public must not be perverted by "accounting gimmicks." For example, in writing to the chairman of the House Banking Committee in 1987 to comment on the proposed Thrift Forbearance and Supervisory Reform Act, Jim Leisenring asserted:

If the intent of the Congress . . . is to permit the continued operation of thrift institutions that do not meet previously defined requirements for capital adequacy, the FASB . . . believes that objective is better achieved through forbearance of supervisory action to enforce the minimum capital requirements than through modifications to financial statements. . . . Modifying financial statements, even if designed only for regulatory purposes, so that they are no longer a faithful representation of an enterprise's financial position and [its] results of operations is likely to further impair the credibility of financial reporting by thrift institutions."[14]

The FASB's position was its familiar plain-vanilla one that investors and other users of financial information had a right to know what the real condition of any entity in any industry was and that if they did, they would make appropriate decisions. Some people hoped that if the facts of the savings and loan industry were widely enough known, the public would not continue to tolerate the complacency of regulators and Congress that was allowing, even encouraging, the losses to grow geometrically over a period of only a few years. That hope was in vain, however. Disguised as "public policy," the scam continued.

For their pains, the standard setters were excoriated by congressmen and senators beholden to the S&L industry for being "insensitive to the industry's problems" and by the president of the industry's lobbying organization, the United States League of Savings Institutions, for "a long history of conflict with public policy." *Forbes* lamented that "no accounting proposal allows thrifts a chance to survive and at the same time present the public with an honest description of their financial situation."[15] Don Kirk's retort was succinct. The objectives the magazine wished for, he said, were mutually exclusive.

Decisions in Washington to keep hundreds of terminally ill S&Ls alive, of course, were made on the basis of the wishful and drastically watered-down regulatory accounting practices that produced financial reports showing that, by and large, all was well in the S&L industry. The number of *billions* of dollars that were added to the taxpayers' tab every month that the supposed economic and social consequences of the S&Ls' malaise continued to dominate policy in Washington is not yet known, but that it is a matter of billions is by now a certainty.

In this instance, neutrality in regulatory reporting, if Congress and the regulators had had the perspicacity and courage (one is tempted to say integrity) to resist the siren song of economic and social consequences, might have saved the taxpayers an amount that is estimated to exceed $500 billion over the next decade.

In concluding his landmark AAA paper on consequences of accounting standards, Oscar Gellein recalled the then-recent skirmish with commercial bankers over restructured debt. "We were told," he said, "that [our] proposal affecting bank financial statements could shake the confidence of bank depositors, cause a run on the banks, and trigger all of the dire circumstances attending weakened confidence in the nation's banking system." He then wondered whether a change in financial reporting really could have any of those results. "One has to ask further," he said, "whether financial statements should be designed to avoid those results by obscuring uncertainties and circumstances, knowledge of which is needed by investors and creditors to assess risks and prospects of return."

Gellein's answer clearly was no, and in an echo of David Solomons's image of the neutral mapmaker, he invoked the example of the barometer. The barometer, he said,

produces a reading for someone else to use in assessing the prospect of storm or clemency. The barometer has an impact if it causes someone to buy an umbrella, or not to buy an umbrella. . . . The barometer is useful if it describes what it purports to show and measures that accurately—that is, if it is neutral. But suppose those who designed the barometer decided that the public interest would be served better if forebodings of storm were minimized, and accordingly a bias toward clemency was built into the calibrations of the barometer.

He then described the perverse consequences of faulty information.

Some would get wet because they did not have umbrellas, others would beseech for rain not knowing that it was on its way, clouds would be seeded needlessly, and worst of all, some persons would not duck into storm cellars or batten down the hatches soon enough to protect against imminent storm. And so it is with financial reporting.[16]

A necessary concomitant of neutrality in standard setting is independence of the standard setters. Paul Kolton predicted in his valedictory as chairman of the Advisory Council that maintaining it would be the Board's biggest continuing problem. "People will continue to try to whittle away at it," he said. "Independence is never secured for good."

Denny Beresford observed that the FASB's independence "is a source of frustration for many constituents who are accustomed to finding ways of exerting influence in other situations." He recounted Roger Smith's complaint that he did not know how to lobby the FASB. "Let me ask you," Beresford said to an audience of corporate executives, "would you feel comfortable about the standard-setting process if you knew that the FASB could be successfully lobbied? Some might, but I don't think most of you would. I think you would worry about what your competitors, legislators, regulators, and others were doing behind closed doors."[17]

Neutrality. Objectivity. Evenhandedness. Independence. Can it be that corporations' concern about standards being "too complex" and "too technical" reflects an intuitive sense that rules established on those principles, which are much admired by most thinking Americans, are at cross-purposes with the interests of Corporate America? If so, big-business bashing is likely to come back into vogue with a vengeance. That would be an unfortunate anomaly because despite the attention that has been given to the "downsizing" of large corporations compared with the growth and employment potentials of emerging businesses, the manifold capabilities of large, mature business organizations are just as essential to America's well-being as they have ever been.

And what of the once-vaunted independence of the public accounting profession, which for many decades put forth such qualities as neutrality, objectivity, and evenhandedness as being essential to its independent audit function?

In 1988, the managing partners of the (then) Big Eight firms lay down with the Business Roundtable's Accounting Principles Task Force and joined in elaborating on a list of "suggestions" (read complaints) regarding FASB operations, all of which had been heard before and are enumerated in Chapter 7. They also joined in supporting the supermajority voting requirement for the FASB and a "higher level of accountability" than the Foundation board of trustees—in other words, the Financial Accounting Standards Oversight Committee that John Reed was promoting. Two years later, however, in a joint letter to the FASB, heads of the surviving Big Six begged the Board to relieve the AICPA's Accounting Standards Executive Committee of a hot potato having to do with marketable securities on which the SEC was pressing for action but the firms' many banking clients were determined to resist. The FASB did have its uses in some circumstances after all, although three of the firms later declined to support the proposal it developed. A subsequent joint letter pleaded for the Board to give up its project on measuring the cost of stock options and adopt instead a simple package of disclosures (outside the financial statements themselves) proposed by an ad hoc group of important financial statement preparers and executives of large pension funds.

Reflecting on the interaction of major accounting firms with the Standards Board, Art Wyatt wrote in 1991: "Many attesters seem to have lost their ability and/or willingness to present their own views, leaving cynics to speculate that attesters are unwilling to incur potential disfavor with one or more of their clients by taking a position on controversial issues." In the past, large accounting firms had been the most consistent and significant sources of technical input on FASB projects. However, Wyatt said, "It has become commonplace for the Board to receive a letter from an accounting firm at or near the end of the exposure period [for a specific proposal] indicating its response will be delayed because the firm has not yet completed a survey of its clients."[18]

Walter Schuetze, onetime standard setter, longtime public accountant, and since 1992 chief accountant of the SEC, chided his former colleagues for what he sees as their wrongheaded, and therefore ineffectual, response to the mounting threat of class-action suits and other forms of litigation. With few exceptions, he said,

the profession is not doing anything about the underlying causes of litigation against itself. Why not? Well, that could involve being tough with a client. Maybe make the client angry. Maybe the client will go across the street to another auditing firm and that firm will agree to report on a balance sheet that has outdated or irrelevant representations in it.

Again with an exception or two, he went on, the firms

will not go to the Financial Accounting Standards Board and support realism in financial accounting and reporting. The profession will not reach tough, unpopular decisions. Is it because the profession has become so beholden to its clients that it will not speak to them about realism and relevance and credibility in financial accounting and reporting?

He concluded: "The profession has become a cheerleader for its clients," and he predicted that following this course will lead the firms to more lawsuits.[19]

It is not an environment in which self-regulation is likely to flourish. Nevertheless, until the issuers of financial statements finally succeed in seizing and consolidating effective control over the process, as they have been attempting to do since the mid-1980s, conscientious standard setters will continue to strive for rationalization of the financial reporting process as they grapple with difficult problems that are evident now and new ones that are certain to emerge. And controversy will continue to characterize the standard-setting process.

Problems that could not have been imagined by Paton and Littleton in 1940, or even Moonitz and Sprouse in 1964, occupied the standard setters in the 1970s and 1980s. Asked in 1990 to predict what problems would dominate the decade ahead, Denny Beresford identified continuing rapid proliferation of new kinds of financial instruments; the shift away from manufacturing toward service industries with a resulting diminution in the importance of "good old 'kick 'em and count 'em' hard assets" and more emphasis on so-called soft assets such as intellectual property; changes in the way businesses think about corporate size, structure, and ownership; rapidly increasing legal risks of conducting a business in an age of litigation; and perhaps most troubling in the United States, accounting for the costs of damage to the environment.

"While everyone prefers very general and simple solutions," he warned, "most of these developments don't lend themselves to general, simple solutions."

He said the greatest challenge for the standard setters would be to preserve their independence and neutrality.

We are seeing increased political pressure on business to work toward popular social goals without regard for economics. . . . We also are seeing some pressures to tilt our standards away from accounting rigor toward requirements that are perceived as being more favorable to Corporate America's international competitive position. As the world grows smaller, and international competition becomes more intense, it seems likely that such pressures will increase. Will these pressures bring about a consensus that supports harnessing accounting standards to the national interest? If so, we—and I mean all of us who are committed to free markets, and not just the FASB—are in for some heavy weather.

Financial statements, he concluded, "are not meant to be propaganda. They are intended to present the aggregated results of a company's transactions as they actually are—not as someone wishes them to be."[20]

NOTES

1. Bishop Joseph Butler, quoted from the seventh sermon in a series published under the title *Fifteen Sermons* (London, 1726).

2. Robert T. Sprouse, "Commentary," *Accounting Horizons*, March 1987, 87.

3. Oscar S. Gellein, "Neutrality Has Consequences" (address to the annual convention of the American Accounting Association, 1978); published in *Viewpoints*, September 29, 1978.

4. John C. Burton, quoted in "Blood Will Run in the Streets," *Financial World*, May 12, 1992, 16.

5. Dennis R. Beresford, remarks to the FEI conference on current financial reporting issues, November 6, 1989 (hereafter cited as Beresford, FEI Conference 1989).

6. Oscar S. Gellein, "The Conceptual Framework: Needs and Uses," paper delivered at a symposium sponsored by the FASB, June 24, 1980; published in *Viewpoints*, August 19, 1980.

7. Gellein, "Neutrality Has Consequences."

8. James J. Leisenring, comments at Board Member Forum, Norwalk, Conn., May 18, 1993.

9. Arthur R. Wyatt, "Standard Setting: Processes and Politics," *Viewpoints*, October 3, 1986.

10. Gellein, "Neutrality Has Consequences."

11. Donald J. Kirk, remarks at midyear meeting of the finance and accounting division, American Petroleum Institute, Houston, 1978.

12. Dennis R. Beresford, "The Economic and Social Consequences of Financial Accounting Standards," address to FEI conference on current financial reporting issues, November 1, 1988.

13. Eugene H. Flegm, quoted in *New York Times*, April 4, 1986.

14. James J. Leisenring, letter to Representative Fernand J. St. Germain, March 18, 1977.

15. "Who's in Charge Here?" *Forbes*, October 25, 1982.

16. Gellein, "Neutrality Has Consequences."

17. Beresford, remarks at FEI conference, 1989.

18. Arthur R. Wyatt, "Accounting Standard Setting at a Crossroads," *Accounting Horizons*, September 1991, 110.

19. Walter P. Schuetze, address at the annual convention of the American Accounting Association, August 1992.

20. Dennis R. Beresford, "Financial Reporting in the 1990s," address to the annual conference of the National Association of Accountants (now the Institute of Management Accountants), June 1990; published in *Management Accounting*, November 1990, 52.

Chapter Twelve

"The Public Interest"— or Public Intent?

> No great improvements in the lot of mankind are possible until a great change takes place in the fundamental constitution of their modes of thought.
>
> John Stuart Mill[1]

Although most of them don't seem to be fully accustomed to the fact, America's large corporations, though located in the private sector, have long been quasi-public institutions. The ramifications of their responsibilities to the general public only begin to become evident in their respective lists of tens, even hundreds, of thousands of shareholders. Pension funds and mutual funds hold their shares and debt instruments for the beneficial interest of many millions more.

The public accountability of corporations, however, extends far beyond their owners and the holders of their debt to a long list of nonowner, nonlender users of financial reports that includes more than a score of readily identifiable groups of people and classes of organizations having an interest in the performance of individual corporations and, in particular, their financial performance. Such a list is presented in Concepts Statement No. 1, and it includes the obvious categories of *potential* owners and lenders. This is just a snapshot at a point in time, however: It does not include interests that will develop in the future, probably the near future, in a rapidly changing (and splintering) political economy.

The public interest is one of the most loosely used shibboleths in the American lexicon. As indicated in the preceding paragraph, virtually the entire American public indeed does have an *interest* in its corporations. But, on analysis, the term *public interest*, with its pious, public-spirited ring, has little meaning as commonly used. There are many who claim to know but none who *can* know what the public interest really is in most matters—including the economic and social consequences of standards for financial accounting and reporting. That is because what is called the public interest is the elusive algebraic sum of all the particular contending interests that have a stake in any given issue. In common usage, *the public interest* is a favored and ubiquitous phrase in pleadings by special interests whose real concern for the public may range from casual to coldly indifferent—and this is not a recent development. In commenting on a political essay more than two centuries ago, Edmund Burke wrote, "It is a general popular error to imagine the loudest complainers for the public to be the most anxious for its welfare."[2]

Unfortunately, though it sometimes has been the refuge of rogues, *the public interest* also has been emblazoned on the banner of the FASB—with the best of intent, to be sure, but without a clear thinking-through.

In contrast, the public intent, or what Peter F. Drucker called "the general will," can be ascertained with a fair degree of accuracy if one makes a conscientious effort to observe and understand what goes on in the truly "real world," as distinct from the "real world" wistfully referred to by corporate chieftains and their minions. It becomes apparent over time through careful attention to election returns, the actions of political bodies, the public utterances of political personages, decisions by the federal courts, including the Supreme Court, public opinion polls, and various kinds of items appearing in the news media. A world is revealed in which the priorities of corporations do not take precedence over those of other groups in society, a world greatly changed in the four decades since a chairman of General Motors, Charles E. Wilson, told a Senate hearing on his nomination to be President Dwight D. Eisenhower's Secretary of Defense, "What's good for General Motors is good for America."

It also is a world in which, as far as financial reporting is concerned, the standard setters, though they are said by many to dwell in an "ivory tower," may just be closer to "reality" than anyone else by virtue of having to sort it out from all the conflicting claims that are presented.

In his 1980 book *Managing in Turbulent Times*, Drucker made the point that formerly special-purpose institutions such as corporations have become "carriers of social purpose, social values, social effectiveness. Therefore they have become politicized. They cannot justify themselves any longer in terms of their own contribution areas alone; all of them have to justify themselves now in terms of the impacts they have on society overall."[3]

Does this not suggest that the structure and process for developing financial reporting standards, as well as the standard setters themselves, should be politicized and made strictly accountable in terms of the economic and social consequences of standards? On the surface it might appear that what the accountants call "symmetry" thus would be achieved. However, as corporations increasingly are perceived as carriers of social purpose and social values, the public's very interest in them and expectations of them take on added dimensions, and the need for reliable, relevant, and comparable financial reporting becomes more urgent than if the economic and social consequences of their operations were *not* a consideration.

In their irritation with the constraints imposed by accounting and reporting standards, certain corporations and organizations like the Accounting Principles Task Force of the Business Roundtable and the Committee on Corporate Reporting of the Financial Executives Institute quickly lose sight of, or deliberately ignore, both the historical reasons for standard setting and the public consensus that supports it, beginning with the Securities Acts of 1933 and 1934 and continuing through a series of lesser legislative acts, repeated congressional investigations of financial reporting matters, and such indicators as the Harris surveys of 1980 and 1985. In so doing, it can be argued, a powerful segment of Corporate America denies—or ignores—the sovereignty of the people and the legitimacy of institutional arrangements through which the people make their intentions known.

On reading that last sentence, some will protest that "nobody elected the members of the Financial Accounting Standards Board," but such claims reflect a crude misreading of how the democratic process is intended to work. Democracy is a much more subtle and complicated system than is apparent in the popular voting for president, senator, and representative, or the voting within the Senate and House of Representatives. The institutional arrangements by which the public intent is transmitted through the tiresomely complex web of legislative bodies and their multitudinous committees, the executive departments, and the nominally independent regulatory agencies are difficult to understand and, even when understood, often are forgotten. The authority of the FASB, for example, derives originally from Congress in the Securities Acts of the early 1930s and comes down through the SEC, the sponsoring organizations, and the trustees of the Financial Accounting Foundation who are nominated by the sponsors and sanctioned by all those standing above them in the authorizing chain. Then, of course, at the operating level there is the array of contending interests that the standard setters somehow have to keep in harmony with both the objectives that originated in law six decades ago and the evolving needs of the financial community for reliable, relevant, and comparable financial information—along with the needs of the much broader public described above.

It was this delicate web that Denny Beresford had in mind when he told a national FEI conclave in 1989, "The Board's relationship with its constituents is a continuing test of the democratic process at a high level of sophistication and subtlety."[4]

Through their public relations staffs and counselors and their advertising agencies, corporations are fairly accomplished at measuring public reactions and preferences regarding products and services, but only to a limited extent regarding policy issues. That is probably because they do not lavish the same level of attention on such issues. Even when their research encompasses these areas, companies have shown little ability or inclination to adjust their actions to the public intent. It is not within the purview of this book to examine Corporate America's responses in other areas of concern to the public, but history shows a general resistance to the public intent for as long as possible on such matters as worker safety, product safety, protection of the environment, and so forth.

Clearly, the public intent is for there to be meaningful standards of financial accounting and reporting. For standards to be meaningful, they must have technical validity—and technical validity can be achieved only through a neutral process. If a standard is valid in those terms, it inevitably will gore somebody's ox because it will bring about the consequence that Oscar Gellein described a decade and a half ago: It will cause some competitors for capital to lose an unwarranted competitive edge in the capital markets.

Can the corporate community, particularly the great corporations, accept that? On the record to date, they seem only marginally able to do so.

Corporate America is a catalyst for more interests than it generally recognizes. There is no question but that large-scale corporations are needed to carry out functions too numerous to name on which our society depends for its well-being. And they should be given all reasonable encouragement to do so. But it is unreasonable to assume, despite all the earnest words in annual reports and other forms of corporate communication, that the leaders and managers of corporations give precedence to any mission other than their traditional one of creating wealth—and in its purest economic sense, that is not an unworthy mission.

In the classic capitalist model, wealth generated by an enterprise traditionally accrued to the owners in return for the risks they took in providing capital, but in the current model, the paid leaders and managers claim an increasing share of it. Regardless of the division of wealth between owners and managers, however, corporations also throw off wealth in the form of salaries and wages, taxes, and payments to suppliers. But since they perform their wealth-creating functions in generally intense competition with similarly motivated entities, it is extremely naive to assume that no corners are ever cut and that all the constituent publics of all corporations are treated fairly at all times. Human nature and the nature of competition being what they are, there is bound to be behavior in the marketplace that calls for some forms of restraint if the competitors are to meet on a level playing field—and if society at large is to enjoy optimum benefits from their competition. Standards for financial accounting and reporting are merely one of many forms of socially agreed-on restraint. Most of the others, however, are imposed by direct governmental authority.

The "consequences" view, if it were to be imposed on the standard setters, would have the effect of placing control of the process in the hands of the biggest preparers of financial reports as represented by the Business Roundtable and the Financial Executives Institute. The politics of it would favor a relative few—the big and strong—over all other entities and all other interests. Apart from ignoring the rest of our vast economic community, the flaw in such a scheme is the fact that "consequences" do not manifest themselves in the same way, or to the same degree, to all companies in all industries. Claims and counterclaims would continue to be pressed, but the arena for debate would be narrowed still further. Only the very biggest and strongest would be left holding high cards.

Worse than the political ramifications would be the inconsistency of standards that would afflict the preparers of financial information themselves. With the rules being set on a negotiated, case-by-case basis, they would not know how to anticipate the next rule making. The auditors and users of financial information would confront even greater confusion.

The chaos created by ad hoc standard setting in response to politicized views of possible consequences inevitably would lead to an ineffective, inconsistent body of standards, including internal contradictions, that would fail to meet the requirements of the SEC and the legislation that created it. Even if the Commission condoned such a situation temporarily, Congress could not accept it for long. It is alarming that Corporate America, with all its public relations and opinion research antennae, is unable to appreciate this simple political fact.

As we have seen, the standard setters never lack for suggestions, from critics and supporters alike, of ways to improve their operations. Perhaps in frustration, one academician, who confessed that he did not know how constituents should judge the Standards Board, suggested holding a conference of economists, political scientists, political economists, behavioral scientists, attorneys, regulators, accounting theorists, standard setters, and even constituents in hopes that "a conceptual framework for evaluating the entire operation of the FASB" might emerge. Such a conference has not yet been held.

In a kind of farewell address to members of the organization that has become customary for retiring Board members and others of similar stature, Paul Kolton chided the standard setters in the spring of 1992 by observing, "The world is demanding responsiveness, timeliness, and credibility. Eight or more years to complete a project is not credible." He suggested that the FASB needs to change its approach to addressing problems.

Kolton was alluding indirectly to an initiative being led by Tim Lucas, with Beresford's encouragement, to explore various avenues for doing just that. The purpose was to examine the Board's performance in light of its mission statement, as critics had been demanding for several years, and to identify ways in which standard setting might become, at the same time, both more effective in terms of serving its broad public and more understandable and acceptable to those required to apply the resulting rules. As all proposals must, those stemming from this exploration had a name: Selectivity, Simplicity, Speed. The main thrust of the effort would be to refine and tighten criteria for selecting the large issues to be added to the technical agenda and, probably more significantly, the smaller issues to be considered within projects already on the agenda or to be added to it in the future. The intent was to identify the 80 percent of issues whose resolution could be expected to bring about worthwhile improvements in financial reporting and to focus the Board's attention on those while at the same time imposing meaningful hurdles to be cleared before any of the remaining 20 percent might be considered. This paring down, it was believed, would result in standards that would be easier to understand and apply.

So far, it seemed that two of the major criticisms of the standard-setting process might be dealt with in ways that would be welcomed by the critics. The projected result of all this, however, was greater speed in standard setting and therefore a greater number of standards that might be issued in any period. That prospect was bound to arouse opposition, even though the Selectivity, Simplicity, Speed formula might be expected to result in standards that were easier to understand and apply.

Some heretical challenges to the Board's traditional ways of thinking also were presented, particularly with regard to broad versus detailed standards. One staff memorandum, for example, observed, "It is not clear that the current approach to detailed standards has reduced incidences of abuse," and went on to wonder whether in the long run it might "turn out that broader standards are more effective."

Lucas acknowledged that the ideas behind the Selectivity, Simplicity, Speed formulation are incomplete and that developing a program to combine them with elements of strategic planning and quality control would be "an evolutionary effort." He also stressed the difficulty of obtaining agreement within the Board on answers to questions the "3 S" approach poses, particularly what should and what should not be included in the 80 percent package of the most important issues. He cautioned further that "speed has to be weighed against due process, which is our greatest asset."

The standard setters might be forgiven if they reminded themselves, in a paraphrase, "You can please some of the people some of the time, but you can't please all of the people all of the time."

Another piece of advice Kolton left with the Board was even less likely to meet with the approval of conservative constituents. The standard setters should anticipate issues, he said, "and be on the cutting edge." He cited with approval their out-front positions on savings and loan accounting, mark to market, and stock compensation. Unfortunately, however, "cutting edges" are not greatly admired in the conservative world of financial reporting.

In a similar valedictory to the Board and staff at the end of 1990, Ray Lauver called the trustees of the Financial Accounting Foundation "the weak link" in the standard-setting structure. He pointed out that the overwhelming majority of them are placed on the FAF board of trustees by representational organizations—and are expected by their sponsors to represent the particular interests of specific segments of the constituency. None, he said, can have an overriding concern for *all* the interests concerned with financial reporting, let alone the public intent that there should be a level playing field for seekers of capital in competitive financial markets.

The consistent inability, or unwillingness, of the Foundation trustees in recent years to take a reasoned, principled stance in support of the stand-ard-setting structure and process, and their failure to recognize a clearly demonstrated public intent for the activity to continue along its originally charted course, or a course essentially similar to it, unfortunately presages the collapse of private sector standard setting before the end of the twenti-eth-century—unless the Foundation is radically restructured in the near future by its private sector sponsors. After two decades, a need has become urgently apparent to change not only the basis on which trustees are chosen but also the *kinds* of trustees to be charged with ensuring that standard setting will satisfy the public's intent. It no longer is sufficient that trustees represent the various interest groups: It has become clear that persons who have a commercial interest in the content of standards should not have responsibility for appointing the standard setters, funding their operations, approving their budgets, or exercising general oversight—even if the by-laws prohibiting the trustees from interfering directly in decisions on technical issues are rigorously observed.

Trustees of the Foundation need not be representatives (read advocates) of organizations that ostensibly are regulated in this otherwise sophisti-cated and public-spirited system of self-regulation. For example, in the late 1970s, AICPA perceived a need to impose tighter professional controls over the process by which financial statements of public companies are audited. It created an elaborate system of oversight through a new SEC Practice Section of the Institute, a new emphasis on "peer review" of one firm by another under Institute auspices, and a new high-level committee to in-quire into alleged audit failures. All of this activity would be carried out by accounting professionals, but to orchestrate and monitor the effort, a Public

Oversight Board (POB) was created, made up of nationally prominent personages who could have no self-interest in the outcomes of either the initial auditing process or reviews of it in specific problem situations because they were not active participants in the financial reporting process. In fact, with very few exceptions, they never have been and therefore have no prejudices. Over the years, their numbers have included former members of the president's cabinet, chairmen of his Council of Economic Advisers, commissioners of the SEC, and nationally prominent academicians. They are people who have no axes to grind.

The five-member POB, which is appropriately compensated, appoints its own members and staff. It meets at least twice as often as the FAF board of trustees and, in contrast to the FAF trustees, makes a point of having one or more of its members attend each meeting of the SEC Practice Section, which it is charged with overseeing.

There is not a direct analogy to the FAF trustees because the POB does not have administrative responsibilities comparable to those of the trustees, and it probably has fewer members than are necessary to administer the standard-setting structure, even when considerations of providing acceptable representation to constituent organizations are eliminated. Its self-perpetuating character also is inappropriate to the standard-setting milieu. Nevertheless, the POB's basic outlines suggest a model that could become meaningful for standard setting if the current custodians of the system can recognize in time the fatal flaws of the present arrangement.

All is not lost—yet.

Sobered by their mishandling of the 1991 Board member appointment process, the trustees approached the 1993 task of replacing Vic Brown, who was completing the two terms allowed by the bylaws, and Clarence Sampson, who opted for golf and gardening after one term, with circumspection. The appointments, decided on after a lengthy process, and generally applauded, were of Anthony T. Cope, senior vice president and director of fixed income research at Wellington Management Company, and John M. ("Neel") Foster, former vice president and treasurer of Compaq Computer Corporation. Cope had been active for many years on AIMR's financial accounting policy committee, and Foster was a member of FASAC.

With the votes of Brown and Sampson before they retired, the Board issued not only the proposed standard on stock compensation but an almost equally controversial final Statement on marketable securities, popularly known as "mark-to-market" accounting.

Also in 1993, organizations representing each of the three major segments of the standard setters' constituency—auditors, users, and preparers of financial reports—were working on ambitious projects to define the future of financial reporting from their own perspectives.

An AICPA Special Committee on Financial Reporting was exploring "the nature and extent of information that should be made available . . . by management, and the extent to which auditors should report on the various elements of that information." Significantly, the Committee was focusing on the information needs of users of financial reports.

The users themselves, through AIMR, issued a draft of a research report entitled "Financial Reporting in the 1990s and Beyond," which devoted considerable attention to "the shortcomings of, and need for change in, the accounting model."

Meanwhile, through its Financial Executives Research Foundation, the FEI was working on a project called "Economic Reality in Financial Reporting" whose objective was "to create a framework of financial and operating performance measurements and disclosures that should be the basic components of financial reports."

The FASB was providing staff assistance for the AICPA study, Denny Beresford was on the steering committee of the FEI project, and close liaison was being maintained between the standard setters and AIMR.

Although at first glance it might appear that these efforts impinged on the standard setters' turf, there was reason to hope, even expect, that their cumulative effect would be to enhance understanding of the multidimensional demands on financial reporting among all the major players and thus enhance the standard-setting process.

If there should be a final demonstration of inability on the part of the private sector to recognize the public intent that a neutral—and meaningful—standard-setting process must continue, one of several scenarios, all highly unattractive to Corporate America, would be almost certain to follow.

One would be establishment by Act of Congress of a wholly new agency—complete with political appointees—to develop standards for financial accounting and reporting. A second, and more likely, possibility would be for the task either to be taken over by the SEC or specifically assigned to it by Congress, with the attendant short-term political uncertainties and long-term bureaucratic rigidities.

The third, and most likely, possibility is creation of a congressionally mandated "self-regulatory organization" under control of the SEC along the lines of the Municipal Securities Rulemaking Board, whose rules covering municipal bond trading are subject to formal approval by the SEC and official review by the three federal bank regulatory agencies prior to becoming effective.

None of the alternatives outlined above would be pleasing to the corporate community, but continued acquiescence in the obstructionist policies of the Business Roundtable and Financial Executives Institute by the board of trustees responsible for maintaining the private-sector process surely will result in one or another of them. The permissive atmosphere of the 1980s and early 1990s could not endure for long, even in a nominally "conservative" national administration—and we no longer have that kind of administration.

Human nature being what it is, the trustees are not likely to yield their prerogatives voluntarily to a Public Oversight Board–type body. It probably would take a strong and insistent nudge from the SEC and/or Congress to make it happen. This would be seen by many in the private sector as unwarranted interference by Washington, but it would be the most constructive thing that could happen to preserve control over financial reporting standards in the private sector.

NOTES

1. John Stuart Mill, *Autobiography* (London, 1873), Chapter 7.

2. Edmund Burke, "Observations on a Late Publication," a response to a political tract, London, 1769.

3. Peter F. Drucker, *Managing in Turbulent Times* (New York: Harper & Row, 1980), 207.

4. Dennis R. Beresford, address to FEI current financial issues conference, New York, November 6, 1989.

Epilogue

Long before there were controversies over standards for financial accounting and reporting, the elderly and ailing Benjamin Franklin demonstrated an objective, philosophical approach to evaluating a work of much greater import about which there were severe differences of opinion and many compromises. On the final day of the Constitutional Convention in 1787, he offered these remarks in a motion for acceptance of the historic document that delegates had so painstakingly cobbled together over a long, hot Philadelphia summer:

Mr President:

I confess, that I do not entirely approve of this Constitution at present; but, sir, I am not sure I shall never approve it; for, having lived long, I have experienced many instances of being oblig'd by better information or fuller consideration, to change my opinions even on important subjects, which I once thought right, but found to be otherwise. . . . Thus I consent, sir, to this Constitution because I expect no better, and because I am not sure that it is not the best. The opinions I have had of its errors I sacrifice to the public good. . . . If every one of us, in returning to our constituents, were to report the objections he has had to it, and endeavour to gain partisans in support of them, we might prevent its being generally received, and thereby lose all the salutary effects and great advantages resulting naturally in our favour. . . . Much of the strength and efficiency of any government, in procuring and securing happiness to the people depends on *opinion*, on a general opinion of the goodness of that government, as well as of the wisdom and integrity of its governors. I hope, therefore, for our own sakes, as a part of the people, and for the sake of our posterity, that we shall act heartily and unanimously in recommending this Constitution, wherever our influence may extend, and turn our future thoughts and endeavours to the means of having it well administered.

On the whole, sir, I cannot help expressing a wish, that every member of the Convention who may still have objections to it, would join with me on this occasion, doubt a little of his own infallibility . . . and put his name to this instrument.[1]

Franklin's plea was heeded. Though the debate over ratification was vigorous, protracted, and narrowly decided, opponents of the document ultimately put aside their arguments and accepted the judgment of the Philadelphia convention and of the state legislatures that ratified the Constitution of the United States.

More than two centuries later, that instrument is revered, but still argued over, still subject to interpretation—and amendment.

NOTE

1. Thomas Fleming, *The Man Who Dared the Lightning* (New York: William Morrow, 1971), 485.

For Further Reading

Beaver, William H. *Financial Reporting: An Accounting Revolution*. Englewood Cliffs, N.J.: Prentice-Hall, 1981.

Carey, John L. *The Rise of the Accounting Profession from Technician to Professional 1896–1936*. New York: American Institute of Certified Public Accountants, 1969.

———. *The Rise of the Accounting Profession to Responsibility and Authority 1937–1969*. New York: American Institute of Certified Public Accountants, 1970.

Flegm, Eugene H. *Accounting: How to Meet the Challenges of Relevance and Regulation*. New York: John Wiley, 1984.

Griffin, Paul A. *Usefulness to Investors and Creditors of Information Provided by Financial Reporting*. 2d ed. Norwalk, Conn.: Financial Accounting Standards Board, 1987.

Kelly-Newton, Lauren. *Accounting Policy Formation: The Role of Corporate Management*. Reading, Mass.: Addison-Wesley, 1980.

Miller, Paul B. W., and Rodney J. Redding. *The FASB: The People, the Process, and the Politics*. 1st ed. Homewood, Ill.: Richard D. Irwin, 1986.

Paton, W. A., and A. C. Littleton, *An Introduction to Corporate Accounting Standards*. Sarasota, Fla.: American Accounting Association, 1940.

Previts, Gary John, ed. *Financial Reporting and Standard Setting*. New York: American Institute of Certified Public Accountants, 1990.

Stevens, Mark. *The Big Eight*. New York: Macmillan, 1981.

———. *The Accounting Wars*. New York: Macmillan, 1985.

———. *The Big Six: The Selling Out of America's Top Accounting Firms*. New York: Simon & Schuster, 1991.

Storey, Reed K. *The Search for Accounting Principles*. New York: American Institute of Certified Public Accountants, 1964.

Weinstein, Grace W. *The Bottom Line: Inside Accounting Today*. New York: New American Library, 1987.

Index

Accounting Principles Board (APB), 3, 7, 44, 56, 123, 154, 169

Accounting Principles Task Force (APTF). *See* Business Roundtable

Accounting Standards Executive Committee (AcSEC), 88, 92, 107–8, 133, 146, 154, 183

Ad Hoc Committee on Full Costing, 61, 63

Administrative Procedure Act of 1947, 86

Alleman, Raymond H., 167

Alexander, Michael O., 81, 85, 88, 107

Alper, Merlin L., 99

American Accounting Association (AAA), 14, 195

American Bankers Association (ABA), 41, 88

American Institute of Accountants (AIA), 3, 5, 7

American Institute of Certified Public Accountants (AICPA), 3, 7, 9, 14, 18, 27, 107–9

American Management Association (AMA), 5

American Stock Exchange, 17, 87

Anania, Joseph V., 168–69

Antonio, James F., 158

Armstrong, Marshall S.: actions as president of AICPA, 8–9; FASB's mission, 23, 33–34; organizational changes at FASB, 28, 34, 63, 85; public comment on issues, 29, 41, 49, 173; relations with SEC, 26–27; response to House subcommittee report, 44–45

Armstrong World Industries, 123

Arthur Andersen & Co., 47, 85, 121

Arthur Young & Company, 16

Association for Investment Management and Research (AIMR), 14, 22, 31, 98, 100–101, 109, 143–44, 152

Association of Bank Holding Companies, 88

Association of Reserve City Bankers, 88

Atomic Energy Commission, 141

Bache Halsey Stuart Shields, Inc., 86

Ball, J.T., 88, 105

Bank Administration Institute, 88

Barr, Andrew, 26

Bartlett, Senator Dewey, 63

Bear Stearns & Co., 143

Beresford, Dennis R.: activities prior to FASB appointment, 104, 106, 130, 133; conceptual framework,

77, 135; international harmoniza-
tion of standards, 134; neutrality of
standards vs. economic conse-
quences, 2, 24, 111, 170, 174–75,
178–79, 183, 185
Berkshire Hathaway, Inc., 154
Block, Frank E., 86, 91
Bloyd, Dean, 61
Bouros, Gary L., 154
Breeden, Richard C., 141, 145–46, 151,
164
Briloff, Abraham J., 44–45
Brock, Horace, 57, 64
Brown, Victor H., 33, 49, 91–92, 106,
194
Buffett, Warren, 154
Burke, Edmund, 188
Burns, Arthur F., 41
Burton, John C. ("Sandy"), 26, 50, 68,
130, 134, 174
Bush, President George W., 141
Business Council, 78
Business Roundtable, 93, 100; history,
118; initiatives by John S. Reed,
109, 136–39, 141–42, 147, 150, 152,
183; initiatives by Roger B. Smith,
97, 107, 114, 119, 122–24, 127–28
130–31

Caterpillar Tractor Co., 15, 49, 85
Chalsty, John S., 57
Champlin Petroleum Company, 58
Chase Manhattan Bank, 42
Chung, Seungwha, 130
Citibank, 42, 147
Citicorp, 42, 135, 137, 140
Civil Aeronautics Board, 141
Columbia University, 34, 68
Committee on Accounting Procedure
(CAP), 3, 7, 34, 44, 102
Committee on Corporate Reporting
(CCR), 143, 149, 165, 167–68. See
also Financial Executives Institute
Compaq Computer Corporation, 194
Comptroller General of the United
States, 17, 65
Comptroller of the Currency, 146

Conceptual framework, 19–22, 74–81,
135, 176
Conway, E. Virgil, 87
Cook, J. Michael, 153
Coopers & Lybrand, 34
Cope, Anthony T., 194
Cornell University, 164–65
Coulson, Edmund, 139
Cummins Engine Company, Inc., 167

Daimler-Benz A.G., 147
Dammerman, Dennis D., 153, 170
Defliese, Philip L., 34
Deloitte & Touche, 16, 48, 153
Department of Energy, 64, 66
Department of Justice, 64, 66
Dingell, Representative John D., 102,
138
Dole, Senator Bob, 174
Donaldson, William, 146
Dougherty, William H., Jr., 88, 123
Dover Corporation, 154
Dow Jones Industrial Average, 5
Drucker, Peter F., 188
Dukes, Roland E., 33
Dusendschon, David, 110
Dyckman, Thomas R., 64, 164

Economic and social consequences of
standards, 31, 56–57, 68–69, 110–
11, 121–22, 136, 176, 178; emer-
gence as broad-based argument, 2,
4, 10, 22–23, 25, 29; implications in
savings and loan crisis, 179–80,
182, 191; inability to measure or
predict, 52, 113; standard setting
as political activity, 188–89
E. I. du Pont de Nemours & Co., 160
Eisenhower, President Dwight D., 188
Ellis, R. Leslie, 123, 126, 129
Emerging Issues Task Force (EITF),
94, 107, 133, 144
Employee Retirement Income Security Act (ERISA), 28
Energy Policy and Conservation Act
(EPCA), 28–29, 55–56, 63, 65
Engebretsen, Arden B., 164
Ernst & Whinney. See Ernst & Young

Ernst & Young, 16, 77, 133
Evans, Thomas G., 33
Exxon Corporation, 17
Exxon U.S.A., 77

Federal Administrative Procedure
    Act, 47–48
Federal Deposit Insurance Corpora-
    tion (FDIC), 146
Federal Energy Regulatory Commis-
    sion, 139
Federal Home Loan Bank Board
    (FHLB), 139, 141, 149, 180
Federal Power Commission, 17
Federal Reserve Board (FRB), 4, 17,
    41, 146
Federal Trade Commission (FTC), 6,
    64
Financial Accounting Foundation
    (FAF): financing, 15, 88; function,
    9; make-up, 16, 129, 169; need for
    structural changes in, 193–94; over-
    sight of FASB, 46, 48, 100, 112, 123–
    26, 140, 153, 160
Financial Accounting Policy Commit-
    tee, 98, 143. See also Association for
    Investment Management and Re-
    search (AIMR)
Financial Accounting Standards Advi-
    sory Council (FASAC), 9, 49, 111,
    144, 154, 164; make-up, 17, 87, 99
Financial Accounting Standards
    Board (FASB): attempt at self-regu-
    lation, 3, 7–10, 14–19, 82–83, 86–89;
    basis in history, 2–10, 27, 189; basis
    in theory, 20–22, 30, 32, 75–82, 189;
    central issue, 2, 4, 22–25, 52, 173–
    83, 190–91; challenges to legiti-
    macy, 39, 43–48; resistance by the
    business community, 40–43, 57–67,
    98–100, 102–4, 109–14, 118–24, 126–
    30, 135–45, 147–54; weaknesses in
    governance, 157–64, 166–70, 188–
    89, 193–96
Financial Accounting Standards Over-
    sight Committee (proposed), 140,
    183

Financial Analysts Federation (FAF).
    See Association for Investment
    Management and Research (AIMR)
Financial Executives Institute (FEI): at-
    tempts to influence Board member
    selection, 124, 165–68; cooperation
    with Business Roundtable, 123,
    143; positions on issues, 22, 25, 31,
    100, 112, 145, 149; role in financing
    standards setting, 14, 166
Financial Executives Research Foun-
    dation (FERF), 94, 165, 195
Firestone Tire and Rubber Co., 92
Flegm, Eugene H., 102, 121, 123, 126–
    27, 130, 179
Folks, William R., Jr., 33
Ford, President Gerald, 28, 57
Foster, John M. ("Neel"), 194
Franklin, Benjamin, 197

Gellein, Oscar S., 34, 43, 59, 76, 86,
    174–76, 182
General Accounting Office (GAO), 45,
    90
General Crude Oil Company, 58, 63,
    70
General Electric (GE) Company, 10,
    63, 153, 170
General Motors (GM) Corporation, 8,
    15, 118, 128, 131, 188
Generally Accepted Accounting Prin-
    ciples (GAAP): differences be-
    tween U.S. rules and those of other
    nations, 147; fallacy of general ac-
    ceptance, 7, 160, 162–63
Geo. S. Olive & Co., 16
Gerboth, Dale L., 23
Gorton, Donald E., 69
Governmental Accounting Standards
    Board (GASB), 9, 15, 34, 90–91, 138,
    157–58
Groves, Ray J., 161

Harris, Louis. See Louis Harris and
    Associates
Haskell, Senator Floyd K., 63–65, 68
Haskell Amendment. See Haskell,
    Senator Floyd K.

Haskins & Sells, 16, 34, 76
Hawkins, David M., 23–24
Heath, Loyd C., 129
Hercules Incorporated, 164
Humphrey, Senator Hubert H., 31

Ihlandfelt, William J., 98
Institute of Management Acccoun-
    tants (IMA). *See* National Associa-
    tion of Accountants (NAA)
Intel Corporation, 165
Internal Revenue Service (IRS), 52
International Accounting Standards
    Committee (IASC), 133–34
International Business Machines Cor-
    poration (IBM), 165
International Paper Company (IPCo),
    58, 63, 70
Interstate Commerce Commission
    (ICC), 13, 141
ITT Corporation, 167

Jacobsen, John C., 98
Jilling, Michael, 33
Jones, Reginald H., 10, 171
Jones, Thomas E., 168
J. P. Morgan & Co., 158

Kapnick, Harvey E., 47–48, 121
Karmel, Roberta, 64
Kennedy, Joseph P., 6, 21
Kent, Ralph E., 16
Kirk, Donald J., 16, 50, 78–81, 105,
    120, 124, 174; concerns about
    GASB jurisdiction, 91, 158; corre-
    spondence with chief executives of
    GM, 118–19, 128; international har-
    monization of standards, 134; oil
    and gas controversy, 60, 63, 65–67,
    69–70; views of the nature of stand-
    ard setting, 7, 24, 30–31, 33, 43,
    144, 165–66, 177–78
Knutson, Peter, 112
Kolton, Paul, 17, 87, 99, 111, 182, 191,
    193
Kripke, Homer, 78

Larson, Rholan E., 125–26, 130, 137–
    39, 159–60
Lauver, Raymond C., 52, 74, 92, 106,
    112, 168, 193
LeGrange, Ulyesse J., 77
Leisenring, James J., 107, 109, 130,
    151, 175, 181
Levin, Senator Carl, 151, 153–54
Liedtke, J. Hugh, 60
Litke, Arthur L., 17, 85
Littleton, A. C., 16, 105, 184
Lochner, Philip R., Jr., 142–43, 145–46
Lockheed Corporation, 168
Loomis, Carol J., 140, 142, 149
Louis Harris and Associates, 78, 94,
    97, 117, 124, 126, 189
Lucas, Timothy S., 103, 110, 120, 127,
    192

McConnell, Patricia, 143, 152
McCracken, Paul, 51
McNiff, John F., 154
March, John W., 76, 85
Markey, Representative Edward J.,
    155
Mays, Robert E., 17, 85
Mead, Ronald H., 129
Mesa Petroleum Co., 59
Metcalf, Senator Lee, 45, 76, 102
Meyer, James M., 113
Mezias, Stephen J., 130
Miller, Paul B. W., 163
Minard, Lawrence, 121
Moonitz, Maurice, 17, 22, 134, 184
Morgan, Robert A., 49, 85, 91
Morgan Guaranty Trust Company,
    159
Morison, Samuel Eliot, 5
Morris, Earle E., Jr., 159
Moss, Representative John E., 44–45,
    55, 65, 102
Mosso, David, 52, 73, 85, 179
Motor Vehicle Manufacturers Asso-
    ciation, 127
Municipal Finance Officers Associa-
    tion, 90
Municipal Securities Rulemaking
    Board, 195

Murphy, Thomas A., 15, 118, 122
Myers, John H., 62

National Association of Accountants
    (NAA), 14, 124, 130
National Association of College and
    University Business Officers
    (NACUBO), 91, 159
National Council on Governmental
    Accounting (NCGA), 90–91
Neutrality in standard setting: discus-
    sions of concept, 4, 22–24, 67, 165–
    67; as guiding principle of FASB,
    174–76, 178–79, 181–83, 185, 190,
    195
New York Stock Exchange, 5, 146–47
Nixon, President Richard M., 16
Norr, David, 58, 62
Northcutt, Robert H., Jr., 168
Northrop, C. Arthur, 165–66
Nuclear Regulatory Commission, 141

O'Brien, Edward, 111
O'glove, Ted, 27
O'Malley, Shaun F., 166, 168
Orben, Robert A., 167

Pacioli, Luca, 2, 3
Pacter, Paul A., 101
Palmer, Russell E., 46
Paton, W. A., 16, 105, 184
Peat, Marwick, Mitchell & Co., 16
Pecora, Ferdinand, 5
Pennzoil Corporation, 60
Pickens, T. Boone, 59
Practice Fellow program, 34–35
Price Waterhouse, 16, 56, 92, 166, 168
Proxmire, Senator William, 64
Public Oversight Board (POB), 193

Queenan, John W., 16, 27, 34
Quindlen, John F., 160, 162–64

Redding, Rodney J., 163
Reed, John S., 135–37, 139–40
Regulatory accounting practices
    (RAP), 180

Research and Technical Activities Di-
    vision (RTA), 88
Reserve Recognition Accounting
    (RRA), 68, 70
Robert Morris Associates, 88
Rockefeller, David, 42
Rocky Mountain Energy Company, 58
Roderick, David, 51
Roosevelt, President Franklin D., 5, 6
Roubos, Gary L., 154
Roy, P. Norman, 143, 149, 166, 168
Ruder, David S., 138, 140
Ruffle, John F., 158–59, 163–64

Sampson, A. Clarence, 14, 133, 194
Savings and Loan Crisis: failure of
    economic consequences argument,
    175–76, 179, 181–82; FASB posi-
    tion, 180–81; legislative and regula-
    tory measures, 179–80; rejection of
    neutrality concept by S&L support-
    ers, 181
Schuetze, Walter P., 16, 43, 82, 99, 184
Screening Committee on Emerging
    Problems, 34, 105
Searle, Philip F., 164
Securities Act of 1933, 6, 169, 189
Securities and Exchange Commission
    (SEC): change in mission, 141, 143–
    44, 146; interface with FASB, 26–
    27, 138, 144, 163; oil and gas
    controversy, 68–70; oversight role,
    6, 43
Securities Exchange Act of 1934, 6,
    169, 189
Securities Industry Association (SIA),
    14, 53, 111
Seidler, Lee J., 18, 113–14, 117
Selectivity, Simplicity, Speed, 192
Self-regulation, 13; conditions neces-
    sary for success, 14, 18, 47, 117,
    155, 176; environment for, 11, 13–
    14, 18, 134; limitations, 83; pro-
    posed definition, 14; steps needed
    to preserve in standard setting,
    176, 184, 196
Shell Oil Company, 98, 106
Sims, Joe, 66

Small Business Advisory Group, 94
Smith, J. Stanford, 63
Smith, Roger B., 8, 74, 97, 114, 119,
    131, 135, 166
Solomons, David, 24–25, 184
Spacek, Leonard, 121
Sprouse, Robert T., 17, 34, 173, 184
Staats, Elmer B., 65
Staggers, Representative Harley, 76,
    102
Standard Oil Company of Indiana, 49
Stanford University, 17, 165
Staubus, George, 85
Steele, Charles G., 121
Sterling, Robert, 77
Strauss, Norman N., 109
Study on Establishment of Account-
    ing Principles. *See* Wheat Commit-
    tee
Sullivan & Cromwell, 65
Sunshine in Government Act of 1977,
    86
Swieringa, Robert J., 52, 165–66

Taylor, Humphrey, 126–27
Technical Bulletins, 23, 89, 106–7
Tesoro Petroleum Corporation, 61
Texaco, Inc., 60–61
Thompson, Robert C., 106
Thrift Forbearance and Supervisory
    Reform Act, 181
Touche Ross & Co., 8, 46, 61, 85, 92
Touche Ross International, 48
Trueblood Committee, 8, 20, 34, 78

Union Pacific Corporation (UPC), 58
United States House of Repre-
    sentatives, 35, 39; Banking Com-
    mittee, 181; Committee on Energy
    and Commerce, 43, 138; Commit-
    tee on Interstate and Foreign Com-
    merce, 43; Committee on Ways
    and Means, 48; Subcommittee on
    Oversight, 48; Subcommittee on

Oversight and Investigations, 43,
    138; Subcommittee on Telecommu-
    nications and Finance, 155
United States League of Savings Insti-
    tutions, 181
United States Senate, 35, 39; Commit-
    tee on Banking and Currency, 5,
    145; Committee on Government
    Operations, 45; Committee on La-
    bor and Human Resources, 122;
    Subcommittee on Oversight of
    Government Management, 151;
    Subcommittee on Reports, Ac-
    counting, and Management, 45
United States Steel Corporation, 34, 51
United States Supreme Court, 81, 188
University of Buffalo, 92
University of California at Berkeley,
    85
University of Pennsylvania, 92

Vanik, Representative Charles A., 48
Volcker, Paul A., 41

Walker, Wilbert A. ("Wib"), 34
Walters, Ralph E., 48, 80, 92, 111
Way, Alva O., 170–71
Wellington Management Company,
    194
Wharton Symposium, 98, 100, 109, 143
Wheat, Francis M., 8–9
Wheat Committee, 8–9, 24, 87, 117,
    119, 123, 125, 169
White, Gerald I., 98, 100, 109, 143
Whitehead, John C., 53
William M. Mercer-Meidinger, 179
Williams, Harold M., 51, 65, 69, 73
Williams, Senator Harrison, 90
Wilson, Charles E., 188
Wriston, Walter B., 42–43, 50, 135
Wyatt, Arthur R., 74, 80, 92, 130, 175,
    184

Zeff, Stephen A., 22, 145

About the Author

ROBERT VAN RIPER is a retired senior member of the staff at the Financial Accounting Standards Board, 1973–1991. Prior to that he was senior vice president of N. W. Ayer, Inc. He is the author of many articles in business and professional journals and two novels.

ISBN 0-89930-907-0

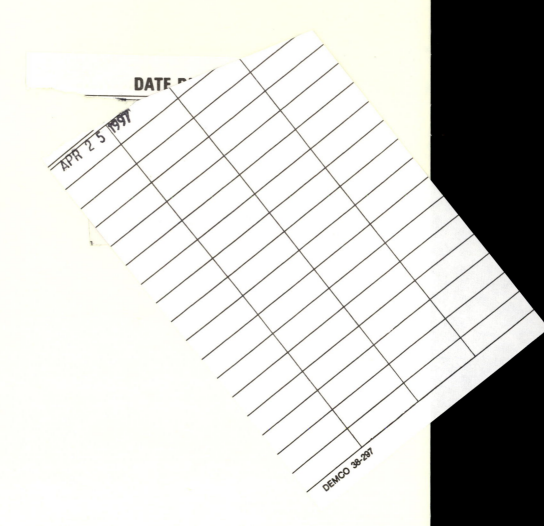